Louis Albert Banks

The Fisherman and His Friends

A Series of Revival Sermons

Louis Albert Banks

The Fisherman and His Friends
A Series of Revival Sermons

ISBN/EAN: 9783337116941

Printed in Europe, USA, Canada, Australia, Japan

Cover: Foto ©Lupo / pixelio.de

More available books at **www.hansebooks.com**

THE
Fisherman and His Friends

A SERIES OF REVIVAL SERMONS

BY

Rev. LOUIS ALBERT BANKS, D.D.

PASTOR OF HANSON PLACE M. E. CHURCH, BROOKLYN, N. Y.

AUTHOR OF

"The People's Christ," "White Slaves," "The Revival Quiver,"
"Common Folks' Religion," "The Honeycombs of Life,"
"The Heavenly Trade-Winds," "The Christ
Dream," "The Saloon-Keeper's Ledger,"
"Christ and His Friends," etc.

FUNK & WAGNALLS COMPANY.
NEW YORK AND LONDON.

COPYRIGHT, 1896, BY
FUNK AND WAGNALLS COMPANY.

[*Registered at Stationer's Hall, London, England.*]

[*Printed in the United States.*]

To

MY NEIGHBOR AND FRIEND,

REV. THEODORE L. CUYLER, D.D.,

THAT PRINCE OF GOSPEL FISHERMEN,

THIS VOLUME

IS AFFECTIONATELY DEDICATED

BY THE AUTHOR.

AUTHOR'S PREFACE.

THE sermons in this volume were delivered in Hanson Place Methodist Episcopal Church, Brooklyn, N. Y., during the month of January, 1896, in a series of revival meetings. The themes were selected long before, illustrations gathered as the months went by, more especial thought and attention given to plan and outline as the time drew near, but each sermon was finally constructed on the day of delivery. They are practically stenographic reports of the discourses as delivered from day to day. The blessing of God was upon them in their delivery, and a large number of men and women were persuaded by them to accept Christ as their Savior. The welcome given to "Christ and His Friends," both in this country and in England, has been so hearty and encouraging, that I send out this companion volume with the hope and prayer that in suggestion and illustrative material it may be still more valuable to earnest Christian workers, who, in the Bible-class of the Sunday-school or in the pulpit, are seeking to win souls to the Master. To every Gospel fisherman the wide world round into whose hand this book may come, I extend a brother's greeting.

LOUIS ALBERT BANKS.

BROOKLYN, *March 7th, 1896.*

CONTENTS.

	PAGE
CHRIST'S PRAYER FOR THE CHURCH,	1
PETER'S BLUNDERING SWORD,	14
THE CRISIS IN PETER'S LIFE,	29
THE FATE OF JUDAS ISCARIOT,	39
CHRIST BEFORE PILATE,	53
VOICES FROM THE CROSS,	65
THE THREE MARYS BESIDE THE CROSS,	76
JOSEPH AND NICODEMUS AT THE BURIAL OF JESUS,	87
THE POWER OF THE RISEN CHRIST,	97
THOMAS, THE DOUBTER, RECLAIMED,	111
SIMON PETER, THE FISHERMAN,	122
SWIMMING FOR CHRIST,	135
A BREAKFAST WITH JESUS,	146
THE GIFT OF POWER,	161
WITNESSES FOR CHRIST,	172
THE ASCENSION OF JESUS,	181
THE SYMBOLS OF THE SPIRIT,	195
PRICKED HEARTS AND THEIR CURE,	206

CONTENTS.

	PAGE
PETER, JOHN, AND A CRIPPLE,	217
TURNING OVER A NEW LEAF,	226
THE ONE SAVING NAME,	238
CHRISTIANITY, A RELIGION OF JOY,	249
PHILIP AND THE FIRST GOSPEL WAGON,	261
ÆNEAS, A MAN WHO WAS HEALED,	271
CORNELIUS, THE TRUTH SEEKER,	279
THE GOLD MINE OF HUMANITY,	289
THE CONVERSION OF A FAMILY,	304
HEROD, THE KING WHO WAS WORM-EATEN,	313
A LIGHT IN THE PRISON CELL,	324
THE LIVING HOPE,	335
THE DRIED-UP SPRINGS OF LIFE,	345
PETER'S CONFIDENCE IN OLD AGE,	354

THE FISHERMAN AND HIS FRIENDS.

CHRIST'S PRAYER FOR THE CHURCH.

"I pray not that thou shouldest take them from the world, but that thou shouldest keep them from the evil one. They are not of the world, even as I am not of the world. Sanctify them in the truth: thy word is truth. As thou didst send me into the world, even so sent I them into the world. And for their sakes I sanctify myself, that they themselves also may be sanctified in truth. Neither for these only do I pray, but for them also that believe on me through their word."—*John* xvii. 15–20 (*Revised Version*).

JESUS CHRIST believed in prayer. Throughout the record of his ministry we find frequent references to his separating himself from his disciples and spending sometimes an entire night alone on the mountain-side in prayer to God. He sometimes prayed in public when he was about to perform miracles. He taught his disciples to pray, and has left on record for us that sweet and simple petition, simple enough for a little child, but deep and comprehensive enough to voice the cry of the greatest man, which we call our Lord's Prayer.

This prayer for his disciples, just before his sacrifice of himself on the cross as a sin-offering for the world, is of wonderful significance and ought to be of the deepest interest to every human soul. The example of Christ in regard to prayer should be constantly emphasized in order to give ourselves a proper estimate of its supreme importance. A Christian life can not be lived without sincere and frequent prayer. And if there are those present who have grown cold and indifferent in their Christian life, and no longer enjoy, as they once did, the gladness of the assurance that they are the forgiven and accepted children of God, I doubt not they are admitting, as I speak, that their backsliding began by failing to keep up the frequency and earnestness of their prayers to God. I repeat it, that a Christian life is impossible without prayer. As James Montgomery, the sweet hymnist, sings,—

> "Prayer is the contrite sinner's voice,
>   Returning from his ways;
> While angels in their songs rejoice
>   And cry, 'Behold he prays!'
>
> "Prayer is the Christian's vital breath,
>   The Christian's native air,
> His watchword at the gates of death;
>   He enters heaven with prayer."

It is the gateway into the Christian armory, where we are clothed upon with power from on high.

E. P. Allen relates the story of a veteran missionary who, on returning to China after a long absence from the field, received, on the very day of his return, a visit from a former convert. The Chinese Christian brought with him six countrymen who had been led to Christ out of the horrible filth and degradation of the opium habit. "What remedy did you use?" asked the rejoicing missionary. The Chinaman's only answer was to point significantly *to his knees!* Ah! he had prayed for them; he had induced them to pray for themselves; and when one of these men came to him saying, in despairing tones, that he had prayed, but it had done him no good, this man of faith sent him back to his knees. "Pray again," he said. And when he came the second time he sent him back to his knees; and so when he came the third time, and many more times. And as a result, here these six men were, clean and sound in body and mind, the cruel chains broken, and the new songs of joy and praise to God upon their lips. Let us learn this great lesson at the beginning of our special campaign for the salvation of lost souls. Our greatest resource is that we are invited to come boldly to the Mercy Seat, and find strength to help in every time of need.

In the Scripture we are studying we find suggested the separating power of knowledge. The Savior says that because he has given the disciples his word, the result has been to separate them from the world and bring them into a new fellowship of their own. We have revealed here the absolute necessity of the Christian church, and that it is the part of wisdom for one entering upon the Christian life to unite himself as closely as possible in fellowship with others who love Christ. This is absolutely necessary in order to have a strong, growing life. Very often we are asked the question, "Can't I live a Christian out of the church?" The editor of *The Outlook* answers this very pertinently when he says that an individual may live a Christian outside the church "just as easily as you can make a fire with one stick." Anybody that has observed a good wood fire knows that it takes several sticks in order to have much heat. And though the sticks may be blazing splendidly, if you take them away from each other and lay them out singly on the ground the flames die down almost at once. They will smoke for a little while, but will soon be black and dead. I have known a good many people who have joined the church and have failed to live bright Christian lives; but I can testify to the faithfulness of the great majority of those who, after having found the Lord

Jesus, have come into the fellowship of the Christian church. On the other hand, I do not recall one out of all the men and women I have known who have been happily converted to Christ and for various reasons remained out of the church (and I have, in the course of the last twenty years of my ministry, known a large number of such persons), who through any prolonged period of time has continued to be a bright and shining light for Jesus Christ. God has made us to need congenial human fellowship, and we cannot disobey that law without suffering the penalty.

A touching little story is told of the child-queen of Holland, who is being brought up according to the strict etiquette of the court, which forbids her playing with other children. She is reported to have said to her wax doll one day, "If you are so naughty, I shall make you into a princess, and then you won't have any other little children to play with."

A New York newspaper man relates an incident similar to this in its pathetic suggestiveness: A little blind boy who had been rescued from the most wretched surroundings and placed in a wisely managed institution, was told by the manager that he was to have a vacation. "I don't want no vacation," said the poor little chap; "I ain't got no folks; I don't want to go away from here on no vacation; please let me stay here all the time!" When he was finally assured that he was not to be returned to the miserable place whence he had been taken, but was to have for a few weeks a pleasant home in the country, provided for by the good woman with the soft, beautiful voice, which had seemed to him that of a rsecuing angel, his foreboding changed to delight. The same boy greeted his good angel, on the occasion of her first visit to him in the institution, with the glad announcement, "I've found me mate"—the mate being a much larger boy, also blind, with whom he was walking. Their arms were around each other's necks in that boyish enthusiasm of affection which is more than brotherly, and that little neglected boy had, at last, gained a glimpse of the joy without which even those who have the boon of sight are poor indeed.

Our Christian lives are no exception to this great law, and if we are wise we will make much of the Christian fellowship of the church. Let us cultivate more and more within ourselves and in the hearts of our brethren a taste for conversation concerning spiritual things, and in that way we shall add fuel to the heavenly flame which shall make the church like "a city that is set upon a hill, that can not be hid."

In this prayer of Christ strong emphasis is

laid on the fact that Christ is our example, and that our mission is indissolubly bound up with his. We are each to be what Christ would be if he were in our place. As Dr. Greer of New York said to some young preachers not long since: "It is not enough that you preach Jesus Christ. You must be, each in his place and according to his ability, a Jesus Christ." And that is not applicable to preachers only, but to every one who has found in Jesus a divine Savior from his sins. Let us thank God we have so high and glorious an ideal. Let nobody say the ideal is too high. It is the very glory of our Christianity that it puts before us this sublime ideal and inspires poor human hearts, whose courage has been broken by sin, to struggle after it in brave and heroic effort.

The story is told that once during the War of the Rebellion, as a charge was being made, an officer shouted to a standard-bearer who was bravely pushing forward to plant his colors on the enemy's breastworks, "Bring back the flag to the men!" "No," he responded, "bring up the men to the flag!" That's what we are to do by the grace of God. We must bring the army of Christ up to the flag of our glorious Leader!

How splendid is this statement of Christ that for the sake of his disciples he sanctified himself. Wonderful statement! Rich, he became poor, that he might know how to sympathize with poor men; honored and worshiped, he became lowly, and was spit upon and treated with contempt, that he might know how to sympathize with those who are scorned; he hungered and thirsted, and was lonely, and had not where to lay his head, in order that he might know how to sympathize with the outcast; he was forsaken by his friends, and denied, that he might know how to sympathize with the broken-hearted; he died a cruel death on the cross and went down into the grave that he might know how to sympathize with those who are sick and dying. The old proverb says, "A fellow-feeling makes us wondrous kind." Christ put himself in our place, bore our sorrows, and was tempted in all points like as we are, that he might share with us in all the troubles of life.

He is our example in this. And we ought to learn by all the troubles and difficulties that come to us in our lives how to sympathize with others. It is wicked for us to brood selfishly over our sorrows. We ought so to trust God as to get divine comfort wherewith we ourselves have been comforted of God. Some poet sings:

"Because of one small, low-laid head, all crowned
    With golden hair,
Forevermore all fair young brows to me
    A halo wear;

I kiss them reverently.   Alas! I know
      The pain I bear.

"Because of dear but close-shut holy eyes
      Of heaven's own blue,
All little eyes do fill my own with tears—
      Whate'er their hue;
And motherly I gaze their innocent
      Clear depths into.

"Because of little pallid lips, which once
      My name did call,
No childish voice in vain appeal upon
      My ear doth fall;
I count it all my joy their joys to share,
      And sorrows small.

"Because of little dimpled hands
      Which folded lie,
All little hands henceforth to me do have
      A pleading cry;
I clasp them as they were small wandering birds
      Lured home to fly.

"Because of little death-cold feet, for earth's
      Rough roads unmeet,
I'd journey leagues to save from sin or harm
      Such little feet,
And count the lowliest service done for them
      So sacred—sweet."

God give us that tender spirit of fellowship and brotherhood!

I think one of the most pathetic incidents that

I have noted for a long time occurred when, a few weeks after the sinking of the *Elbe*, of the North German Lloyd line, the *Ems*, of the same line, was passing the spot where the wrecked steamer lay. On board the *Ems* was a passenger who lost his wife and three children when the *Elbe* went down. He had requested the captain of the *Ems* to pass slowly by the place where the *Elbe's* masts could be seen above the water. The order was given to move slowly, the whole crew was called to quarters, flags were hoisted at half-mast, officers and crew stood uncovered, and while a salute of nine guns was fired, the passenger, with tears streaming from his eyes (and indeed every eye on shipboard was wet in tearful sympathy with him), cast into the sea a flower-wreath, heavily weighted with lead. The waves closed over the flowers, and the *Ems* proceeded on her voyage.

There was something in that story that touched me very deeply. It seemed to me to be specially in harmony with the spirit of Christ that the great ship, with its commercial treasures and carrying hundreds of passengers desirous of rushing forward in the earnest race of life, should pause to show this sympathy and brotherhood to one so deeply smitten. Above all else the church of Christ must have that spirit. We are surrounded by multitudes who are having hard lives. They are tired and worn; they have sickness and pain; they have griefs and heart-breaks; and what we need above all else to win them to Christ is the spirit of him who with sympathetic face and tender word went about "doing good."

A man paused in front of the village doctor's house and asked of the small child playing on the door-step: "Is your father at home?"

"No," said the little boy, "he's away."

"Where do you think I could find him?"

"Well," he said, with a considering air, "you've got to look for some place where people are sick, or hurt, or something like that. I don't know where he is, but he's helping somewhere."

And so, my brother, if you want to enjoy the fellowship of Jesus Christ, if it is your desire to live this new year in the gladness of his constant presence, if you wish to walk with him and learn of him, to grow in his grace and favor—then you must go with him, seeking after the lost. Set yourself hard at work helping somewhere—to the lifting of somebody's burden, to the sharing of somebody's heavy load—and you will soon find that Christ is there in loving fellowship with you.

How tender and precious to each one of us is the message conveyed in the last verse of the Scripture we are studying: "Neither for these only do I pray, but for them also that believe on me through their word." That means you and me. It breaks my heart when I think of it—how in those last dark hours, when the Savior had so much upon his mind and thought (when the mob was already gathering to carry him before the high priest, and on, by way of Pilate and Herod, to the agony of the cross), even then his great heart thought about me, and about you, and about every one to whom we have the privilege of carrying this precious word, and prayed for us with infinite tenderness and love.

Oh, there is nothing so faithful in this world as sincere love! A young Englishman came to this country during the great gold excitement in California in 1849, and became very wealthy by his labor and good fortune in the mines. During his prosperity he sent a large nugget of gold to England to the woman he loved, and to whom he was engaged to be married. But, as often happened in the mines, in a few months, in an evil turn of fortune, he lost his wealth, and was reduced to direst poverty. He wrote to the lady informing her of his change of fortune and releasing her from all obligations. But what was his surprise and joy to receive, as soon as an answer could come to his letter, a gold ring, made of the nugget he had sent, engraved with these words: "Entreat me not to leave thee." He was not worthy of her if that was not worth more to him than all the fortune he had lost. But that, glorious as it was, is faint illustration of the faithfulness of love when compared with the supreme sacrifice of Jesus Christ who, for a race that did not love him, but was lost in sin and in defilement, put aside the glory of heaven and came down and took our poor human life at its worst, and suffered and died to ransom us from sin and from eternal night.

How faithful he has been to us since we have given our hearts to him! Not one of us can, for a moment, claim that he has ever deserted us. We may have been unfaithful to him. Possibly you have admitted into your heart such evil guests that he could no longer abide there; but he has never deserted you; and though he has been driven out of the guest-chamber of the soul he still lingers near, and knocks at the door of your heart. Poor backslider, if you will rise and open the door to-night, this last night of the old year, Christ will come in again, and the new year will dawn upon your soul with a flood of heavenly glory.

And you who have never known him, if you will open your heart to receive this word, what a glorious day-dawn it may be for you! Your condemnation shall pass away and the light of God's reconciled face shall give you peace.

PETER'S BLUNDERING SWORD.

"Simon Peter therefore having a sword drew it."—*John* xviii. 10 (*Revised Version*).

THE picture suggested by the text is very dramatic. It is in the darkness of the midnight, and Judas has just led his band of men and officers with their lanterns and torches and weapons into the Garden of Gethsemane, seeking his Master whom he has betrayed. When they come to where Jesus is, he, standing there in composure, inquires, "Whom seek ye?" They answer him, "Jesus of Nazareth." The Lord quietly answers, "I am he." They are at first startled and alarmed, and fall backward in terror before the majesty of the man after whom they have been seeking. Then, as they gather courage and draw near to arrest Jesus, Simon Peter draws his sword and, leaping before his Master, thrusts at the first enemy that comes in his way; but Jesus rebukes him and says: "Put up the sword into the sheath: the cup which the Father hath given me, shall I not drink it?"

It was a generous deed on the part of Peter, a

deed born of his love and devotion to his Master, and it is impossible not to admire it. However unwise it may be, however futile it may be in its results, an exhibition of sincere human love taking all risks and all hazards in the expression of its devotion is always interesting and impressive. It is impossible to think of poor Rispah watching her sons who were hanged on that faraway hill-top so long ago, as all through the long summer time she keeps the birds off their poor bodies by day, and in her mad and reckless devotion frightens away the wild beasts by night, so that until the rain came in the autumn neither by day nor by night is the precious clay disturbed, without admiration and reverence for the motherlove expressed in the deed. Who can listen unmoved to David's cry over his dead son Absalom, even though he have the greatest contempt for that traitorous and wicked young man? There is something sublime in David's forgetfulness of all Absalom's sins against him, and our hearts are heavy with him as we hear him cry, "O my son Absalom! my son, my son Absalom! Would God I had died for thee, O Absalom, my son, my son!" We know that his grief is useless and that his love is like water poured upon the ground, but it stirs our hearts, nevertheless.

And so in this case of Peter and his blundering

sword, we can not help but admire him and think better of him for the deed, the while our reason tells us that the cause of Jesus Christ can never be advanced by the weapons of worldly warfare. All will admit to-day that this is true of attempts by a sword like Peter's; but we need to have the emphasis put upon the fact that efforts to push forward Christianity by means of wealth, or culture, or social position, or political influence, taken by themselves, are as blundering and useless and as certain to be futile as the sword of Simon Peter. The cause of true Christianity is often really retarded because the church is burdened down by material and worldly things which might be excellent as helps but are certain to be deadly weights when they are depended upon as masters or as essential motive power.

Somebody has recently written a fable telling how once, in a jungle in India, there was a great elephant which was out walking one day, when a little fly accosted him. "Kind elephant," said the fly, "I am little, and you are very big. Will you not give me a ride?" "With pleasure," said the elephant, and strode on, with the fly upon his back. He had not gone much further until he came upon a mouse. "Kind elephant," begged the mouse, "I am not much bigger than that fly. Won't you give me a ride too?" "With pleasure," answered the obliging elephant, and he let the mouse climb upon his back. A short distance further the elephant met a turtle, who politely said, "Kind elephant, I am sure you will be glad to lend your strength to one so small as I, who gets over the ground by himself so slowly." "With pleasure," the elephant started to say, but changed the sentence to, "You are very welcome." In the same way, by one pretext or another, the great beast gave riding-room to a boa-constrictor, a wolf, and a bear. Thus burdened, the elephant was greeted by a tiger, who, leaping from a thicket, preferred the same request the other animals had set forth. "Kind elephant, you are big, and I am so much smaller. Surely you will give me a lift." "Unfortunately," replied the elephant, "I already have more than I ought to carry, and can scarcely stir a step further." "In that case," answered the tiger, "this is precisely the moment I have long been waiting for." Whereupon he sprang upon the great animal, who, weighted down by the beasts upon his back, could do nothing in his own defense, and was quickly destroyed.

Many a church could well learn a lesson from this simple fable. Wealth at the disposal of Christlike spirit may help on the cause of Christianity; but wealth upon the back of the church, dictating its policy from a worldly standpoint, will betray it to the devil as surely as Judas sold his Master for thirty pieces of silver. Intellectual culture and social position, if they are sincerely consecrated to Jesus Christ, may be, and are, great and valuable talents for use in the Lord's cause; but in many a church such influences, not being so consecrated, serve only to freeze the spiritual life to death. Every little while we see the account of some vessel that is destroyed by running afoul of an iceberg. Such a ship has a better chance, however, than a church which undertakes to carry an iceberg on board. Some poet aptly sings:

"Ill fares the church, to hastening ills a prey,
  Where wealth accumulates and men decay;
  Bishops and priests may flourish or may fade,—
  A breath can make them as a breath has made,—
  But a working laity, the church's hope and pride,
  When once destroyed, can never be supplied.

"As some fair female, unadorned and plain,
  Secure to please while youth confirms her reign,
  Slights every charm that dress supplies,
  Nor shares with art the triumph of her eyes;
  But when those charms are passed—for charms are frail—
  When time advances and when lovers fail,
  She still shines forth, solicitous to bless,
  In all the glaring impotence of dress,—

> "Thus fares the church by luxury betrayed;
> In heaven's simplest charms at first arrayed;
> But verging to decline, its splendors rise,
> Its steeples strike, its palaces surprise;
> While, scourged by famine, from the smiling land
> The mournful member leaves his former band;
> And while he sinks without one arm to save,
> His church becomes a garden and a grave."

Numbers are equally as impotent as wealth or culture or position. The story of Gideon illustrates the fact that a cowardly or a selfish horde is not so effective as a picked few whose eyes are single and hearts true in loyal devotion.

What, then, are some of the forces which the church may depend upon with confidence in its attempt to make conquest of the world for Jesus Christ? The answers to this question are very simple and plain. Our first great weapon is the Bible. This is true both for our individual experience and as a weapon of warfare in seeking to capture others for Christ. A recent writer in one of our religious journals relates that once upon a time he commenced to backslide. He still had something of the love and fear of God in his heart, and desired to do his duty; but he felt that his spiritual strength was gradually slipping away. He no longer took delight in the service of God. His private devotions became a burden. He became depressed in spirit. Morbid fancies assailed his mind. Evil thoughts disturbed his peace. He became dead to his duties to others and thought only of self. People who had once spoken of him as an earnest Christian began to call him a hypocrite. Yet, in spite of all this, he felt the inward promptings of the Holy Spirit, and desired to do better. One day while arranging his study table he came upon the cause of his troubles. *His Bible was covered with dust.* Like a flash it came upon him that the reason of his deadness was that he had been depriving his soul of its proper nourishment, and that his lethargy was the result of slow starvation. And as he went back to the Bible with a new zest and enthusiasm, his hungry soul fed upon the bread of life, and he was soon strong again in Christian effort. Perhaps there are some that hear me at this time who—like one looking into a mirror—see their own features in this story of another. If so, I pray that your interest in God's Word may be renewed. If the keen edge of your interest in the spiritual services of the church is wearing off, look and see if there be not dust on your Bible. If I were sure that every member of this church would read, every day this month, one or two chapters of God's Word, earnestly seeking out the heart-searching and spiritual portions, prayerfully trying to seek out God's will, and desiring to have their souls fed with the bread from heaven, all doubts in my mind of a great spiritual revival would be dissipated in a moment. The Bible is the one book which must be in constant use in any great religious awakening. It alone contains the words of eternal life. Men are dying in their sins all about us for the lack of having emphasized in their thought and affections the message which is given so simply and so tenderly in the Bible.

Du Chaillu tells a pathetic story of a poor girl, Okondaga, in Central Africa, who was compelled to drink poison because she was accused of having bewitched a person who had recently died. As she was borne along by her furious accusers, the cry rang in the traveler's ears, "Chally, Chally! Do not let me die!" But he was powerless and could only shed bitter tears. With two other women she was taken in a canoe upon one of their beautiful rivers, and the fatal cup was placed to their lips. Soon they reeled and fell, when they were instantly hewn in pieces and were thrown into the water. At night the brother of Okondaga stole to the traveler's house in his distress. He had been forced to join in the curses that were heaped upon his sister. He was compelled to conceal his grief. Du Chaillu tried to give him comfort, and spoke to him of God. The poor man cried, "O Chally! When you go back to your far country, America, let them send men to us poor people to teach us from that which you call God's mouth."

We must not fail to send the message from "God's mouth" to the poor people in Africa, neither must we fail to give the people the message in the city of Brooklyn. Scarcely a day passes in these great cities but some man or woman—and on some days two or three—poor souls weighed down by their sins, held in a bondage unbearable and from which they know no way of escape, haunted by an accusing conscience, take their own lives and die the death of the suicide. Oh, the sins and sorrows of this great city! We must carry the people the message that is in this blessed Book, that God so loved the world that he gave his only begotten Son to die upon the Cross, that whosoever believeth on him might not perish, but have everlasting life. Thank God, the Bible presents to men a divine Savior who is able to do for the poor sinner what no mere man can do!

Another sure dependence for the Christian church is prayer. And this is always within our reach. It is within the reach of the humblest and poorest as surely as those who are rich and powerful. It is within the reach of those who are full of business cares, who, as they go about their work, can breathe out their heart's petition to God in the midst of the noise and bustle of the city, unheard by any ear save the compassionate ear of God. There are no times and no places where we can not pray to God. Nehemiah, standing in the presence of the king in the palace, found a way to send his petition to heaven asking for access to the heart of the monarch, and his prayer was graciously answered. I have heard of a young man whose custom it was to pray for every member of his family and the members of his Sunday-school class by name while riding to town in a public omnibus; and a trolley-car can be turned for the moment into a church, and become a heavenly place in Christ Jesus, as you lift up your heart to God. Do you never look up at the telegraph and telephone wires along the streets and highways and wonder how many messages unknown to you are passing along them; so countless messages may be wafted to the throne of God as we go about our daily work.

Another great force upon which we can depend is personal Christian experience. On the human side this is the mightiest power in convincing men of the reality of the Christian religion. A frontier examining committee was once examining a young man for admission into the Methodist ministry. He was a big, broad-shouldered fellow, lacking a good deal in educational qualifications but with a heart in proportion to his body. One asked him the question, "How do you know that Christ is divine?" The young giant looked at the examiner for a moment in silence, and then, as his eyes filled with tears, he exclaimed: "Why, bless you, sir, he saved my soul!" It was another way of saying: "I know whom I have believed, and am persuaded that he is able to keep that which I have committed unto him until that day."

The historic Christ which you preach men may doubt and argue about; but the "Christ in you, the hope of glory;" the Christ that strengthens a man against temptations to strong drink and that keeps him sober; the Christ that makes profane lips prayerful; the Christ that makes the selfish man generous and self-denying; the Christ that turns anger into love, and supplants greed with generosity—the living Christ, incarnate now in our human nature, that is the Christ who can break down all opposition.

The great French savant and skeptic, Littre, when his daughter was born, said to his wife: "My dear, you are a good Christian, bring up your daughter in the ways of religion and piety which you have always followed; but I must exact one condition, and that is that when she is fifteen years of age you will bring her to me. I will then explain my views to her and she can choose for herself." The mother accepted the condition. Years rolled on, the fifteenth birthday of the child soon came, and the mother entered her husband's study. "You remember what you said to me, and what I promised," she said. "Your daughter is fifteen years old to-day. She is now ready to listen to you with all the respect and confidence due to the best of fathers. Shall I bring her in?" "Why, certainly," replied Littre. "But for what special reason? To explain to her my views? Oh, no, my dear; no, no! You have made of her a good, affectionate, simple, straightforward, bright, and happy creature. Happy? Yes; that is the word which, in a pure being, describes every virtue. And you fancy that I would cover all that happiness and purity with my ideas? Pshaw! my ideas are good enough for me; who can say that they would be good for her? Who can say that they would not destroy, or at least damage, your work? Bring her in so that I can bless you in her presence for all that you have done for her, and so that she may love you more than ever."

There is something so divine about a Christianity incarnated into a human life that it can not be denied or gainsaid.

And, finally, it is the Holy Spirit vitalizing the

Bible, quickening and intensifying our prayers, glorifying our fellowship with Jesus Christ, wooing the hearts of those whom we try to win, that is to make effective all the agencies which we use to bring men from sin to righteousness. If we do our work faithfully and well, God will oftentimes give it victory where for the moment we see only defeat. One raw December night in 1856 there had been announced a missionary meeting in London. A Londoner said to the man who was to speak: "The night is so black and the rain is coming down in such torrents that it is impossible to have a respectable audience. Is it worth while to hold the meeting to-night, do you think?" "Perhaps not," answered the other, doubtfully; "but I do not like to shirk my work, and as it was announced, some one might come." "Come on, then," said the first speaker; "I suppose we can stand it." The meeting was held in a brightly lighted chapel in Covent Garden. A business man passing by took refuge from the storm, and made up half the audience that listened to an earnest plea for the importance of giving the Gospel to the North American Indians in British Columbia. "Work thrown away," grumbled the Londoner, as they made their way back to Regent Square. "Who knows?" replied the man who had spoken. "It was God's word, and we are told that it shall not fall to the ground unheeded." I have always noticed that it is the man that has not been doing anything himself who is skeptical about results of other people's labors. If we were to go through this church we would find that it is the people who never win anybody to Christ themselves who are entertaining the strongest doubts about the conversion of sinners during these meetings. What was the result of that missionary meeting with its two listeners? The passer-by who stepped in by accident tossed on his couch all night, thinking of the horrors of heathenism of which he had heard that night for the first time. And in a month he had sold out his business and was on his way to his mission work among the British Columbian Indians, where he has had great success, and has won hundreds of benighted souls to the Light of the world.

May God inspire the hearts of every one of us with courage for the great battle that is now before us! Our forces are invincible if we shall go forward humbly in the strength of God. The same God who saved your soul is able to save the souls of the sinners who need him so much to-day. "The Lord's hand is not shortened, that it can not save; neither his ear heavy, that it can not hear." When David wanted to go and fight Goliath, the big Saul looked down on him with pity and said:

"Thou art not able to go against this Philistine to fight with him: for thou art but a youth, and he a man of war from his youth." Then I see the flush of embarrassment glow on the cheek of David for a moment, but it dies down to live again in a quickened flash in his eye as he exclaims: "Thy servant kept his father's sheep, and there came a lion, and a bear, and took a lamb out of the flock; and I went out after him, and smote him, and delivered it out of his mouth; and when he arose against me, I caught him by his beard, and smote him, and slew him. Thy servant slew both the lion and the bear: and this uncircumcised Philistine shall be as one of them, seeing he hath defied the army of the living God. The Lord that delivered me out of the paw of the lion, and out of the paw of the bear, he will deliver me out of the hand of this Philistine."

We have the same almighty arm on which to rely. "If God be for us, who can be against us?"

THE CRISIS IN PETER'S LIFE.

"Peter remembered the words which Jesus had said, Before the cock crow, thou shalt deny me thrice. And he went out, and wept bitterly."—*Matt.* **xxvi.** 75 (*Revised Version*).

THIS story of Peter's denial of Christ ought to humble every one of us before God. It shows the weakness of even the strongest of men when relying on his own strength. When, a little while before, Peter had said to Christ, "Tho all men shall be offended because of thee, yet will I never be offended;" "Tho I should die with thee, yet will I not deny thee;" "Lord, why can not I follow thee now? I will lay down my life for thy sake"— when Peter uttered these strong sentences we can not doubt that he meant them in all sincerity. Insincerity was not one of Peter's faults. He was a blunt, plain man, impetuous, impulsive, who might do a rash thing under provocation; but no man would ever suspect him of being a hypocrite. And only a few hours before the scene which we are now studying, at the betrayal of Christ into the hand of his enemies through the treachery of

Judas, we have seen Peter's sword drawn in generous and brave defense of his Master. Yet when the Master submits to the arrest he seems to have forsaken Christ with the others and fled. But a little later he grows bolder, and goes into the palace of the high priest and crowds up to the fire. Suddenly charged with being a disciple of Jesus, he denies thrice, and the last time with an oath, that he ever knew him. What a strange glimpse we have here of the fearful possibilities of weakness in our human nature. Here is a man who only a few hours ago could face a whole company of armed men with his single sword, undaunted; but now his cheeks are blanched and his lips soiled with profanity and lies at the accusation of a servant-girl. "Let him that thinketh he standeth take heed lest he fall." No man is safe who depends upon his past record or upon his present consciousness of fidelity as an assurance that he will not fall into grievous sin in the future. Our safety can only come from constant reliance upon God. The greatest saint in the world as well as the greatest sinner, may appropriately sing,—

> "Rock of Ages, cleft for me,
> Let me hide myself in thee."

It is well for us to consider the solemn and earnest truth suggested by this Scripture, that no man or woman who is trying to live a godly life will escape temptation. Those who are congratulating themselves upon their freedom in the past from dangerous temptation may be already entering the shadow of a struggle that will test their souls to their profoundest depths. Ian Maclaren, who has been writing for us those sweet Scotch stories so profitable for their spiritual insight, well says that one of our most amazing mistakes about life is when we divide people into the tempted and the untempted, supposing that while many are constantly exposed to severe trials, others are secluded from danger; but the fact is that our temptations come to us from our own peculiar circumstances, and no one of us is able to estimate accurately his neighbor's situation. The difference between the best man and the worst is not that one is tempted and the other is not, but that one is given victory by the grace of God and the other meets defeat by neglect of divine aid which would be as freely given to him as to the other. Sometimes young men look on some gray-haired man—whose face is the mirror of his holiness—and they imagine that he lives somehow on a mountain height where the poisonous breath of the low swamps of evil never reaches him or troubles him. But all such ideas are mistaken. The noblest and purest men in the world are often tempted by evil thoughts and troubled by perplexing doubts. Temptation in this world is human discipline. Read over the lives of the Bible heroes, and any other honest biographies that you can find, and you will find that the best men that ever lived have been beset by temptation and trials all their lives long, and have had use for all their armor and need for the Sword of the Spirit and the help of God to the very last. Jesus Christ is the only perfectly good man whose life is portrayed to us in history, and he was the most fiercely tempted man that ever lived. All the artillery of the bottomless pit played about his head. It is in this furnace of temptation that men are tried and come to be strong soldiers for Jesus Christ. When you see a man who holds himself in hand as a good driver controls a pair of thoroughbred Kentucky horses, then you may know that he has paid for that self-mastery by many a struggle which only he and God know about.

The fierce temptation of Jesus came as a preparation to his public work. There is no disgrace in temptation. The shame and condemnation come when we yield to the temptation and it becomes sin. If when one is tempted to evil he shuts the door of his heart against it and says, "I will not," the shaft of the enemy glances from his shield; but if he cherishes the thought, and con siders how pleasant it would be to yield, and half wishes he might yield, then the poisoned arrow touches his blood. "When a man defends his castle unto blood, it matters nothing that the walls show bullet-marks; if he creeps down and opens a postern-door, he is a traitor to himself. When the will weds temptation, the result is sin, and the end death."

The tenderness and long-suffering kindness of Jesus Christ are nowhere more clearly illustrated than in his dealings with Peter. That tender, disappointed, beseeching, heart-broken look that he gave Peter is one of the strongest incidents of the whole story of his human life. Elizabeth Barrett Browning sings with spiritual appreciation:

> "Two sayings of the Holy Scriptures beat
> Like pulses in the church's brow and breast;
> And by them we find rest in our unrest,
> And heart-deep in salt tears, do yet entreat
> God's fellowship, as if on heavenly seat.
> The first is, 'Jesus wept,'—wherein is prest
> Full many a sobbing face that drops its best
> And sweetest waters on the record sweet.
> And one is, where the Christ, denied and scorned,
> Looked upon Peter. Oh, to render plain,
> By help of having loved a little and mourned,
> That look of sovran love and sovran pain
> Which he, who could not sin yet suffered, turned
> On him who could reject but not sustain

"'The Savior looked on Peter.' Ay, no word,
No gesture of reproach! The heavens serene,
Tho heavy with armed justice, did not lean
Their thunders that way. The forsaken Lord
Looked, only, on the traitor. None record
What that look was; none guess: for those who have seen
Wronged lovers loving through a death-pang keen,
Or pale-cheeked martyrs smiling on a sword,
Have missed Jehovah at the judgment-call.
And Peter, from the height of blasphemy,—
'I never knew this man'—did quail and fall,
As knowing straight *that God*, and turned free
And went out speechless from the face of all,
And filled the silence, weeping bitterly.

"I think that look of Christ's might seem to say—
'Thou, Peter! art thou then a common stone
Which I at last must break my heart upon,
For all God's charge to his high angels may
Guard my foot better? Did I yesterday
Wash *thy* feet, my beloved, that they should run
Quick to deny me 'neath the morning sun?
And do thy kisses, like the rest, betray?
The cock crows coldly,—go, and manifest
A late contrition, but no bootless fear;
For when thy final need is dreariest,
Thou shalt not be denied, as I am here—
My voice, to God and angels, shall attest,
Because I *know* this man, let him be clear.'"

The crisis moment of Peter's life was when he encountered that tender, appealing look of Jesus. If he had hardened his heart against that he would have been a doomed man. In his quick yielding to that was his salvation. Let us learn from this picture that the first step toward salvation, when we have fallen into sin, is repentance. No salvation is possible without repentance. You might as well ask a man to swim a wide and swiftly running stream with a hundred-pound weight about his neck, as to tell a man to believe on Christ and be saved so long as he clings to some sinful and wicked habit. The first step toward salvation is in that repentance of our sins which not only gives us sorrow of heart because of sin, but causes us to turn from it and begin to do with earnest heart what God requires of us. If there are any here this evening who have been tempted into denying the Lord Jesus, and you feel to-night condemned that you have not been more faithful to him, I pray God that the Holy Spirit may reveal to you that tender and appealing look which Christ gave Peter, and that it may break down the hardness and indifference of your heart; and that, like Peter, it shall cause you to weep bitterly because of your sins; and that, like him, also, you may go forth to be more perfectly than ever a witness to the divine power of Jesus Christ to save the soul.

Dr. Cuyler tells the story of a presumptuous Alpine climber who, anxious to find a shorter path over the glaciers, quits his guide and sallies off to be a guide unto himself. He shouts back gaily to his companions, and laughs at their fears, while they are shuddering at his folly. A snow-drift lies across his path, soft as eider-down, and with headlong haste he plunges into it. In an instant he disappears from view, and the ring of the icicles in the depths of the crevasse is the last sound that strikes upon his ears as he plunges, mangled and senseless, into the ice-cavern that yawns to receive him. When consciousness returns he is barely alive, and that is all. It is impossible to climb up the perpendicular wall of the crevasse. If he remains where he is he will soon freeze to death in this awful sepulcher. As he listens for some sound, he faintly hears the musical tinkle of dripping water, and as he creeps slowly toward it he hears a running stream. It is pitch dark; but he gropes his way through the channel of the stream until he discovers a slight gleam of light on the ice walls of the aperture before him. He hails it as the dawn of hope. It tells him there is a possibility of salvation. Onward he struggles, until at last he emerges at the base of the glacier into sunshine and safety! Altho terribly bruised, he is a saved man; and is so saved as to be able to save others from the presumptuous sins that came so near being his destruction. How ready he is to warn others from that treacherous crevasse; and perhaps he puts up a finger-board of caution to warn other climbers who might be as reckless as himself. And when he again climbs such dangerous heights, how careful he is to have a trusty guide! Saved himself from the jaws of death, he tries to save others from a course as rash and reckless as that which has cost him so dearly.

Such was the issue of Peter's salvation. After his bitter repentance and gracious recovery through the mercy of Jesus, he went forth to proclaim salvation faithfully as long as he lived. If you find yourself to-night a sinner against God, follow the example of Peter; do not wait for an hour, but immediately forsake your sins and seek for forgiveness.

> "Manlike is it to fall into sin;
> Fiendlike is it to dwell therein;
> Saintlike is it for sin to grieve;
> Christlike is it all sin to leave."

It is the joy of my heart that I may preach to you the same divine Savior who so graciously saved Peter, and who is as strong and as willing to save now as then. He has not lost either his power or his love. He is "the same yesterday, to-day, and forever." You can not find me a single case in all the Scriptures of God's tenderness and forgiveness toward a repenting sinner, or toward any humble, prayerful soul, that he can not and will not repeat now, in your case, if you will come to him in humility and penitence and faith. Tho your backsliding may be as black as David's; though your life may be as scarred and impure as the poor woman who bathed the Master's feet with her tears; yet if you will come to God as they did, your sins shall be blotted out and the perfume of your salvation shall rise to heaven. We read sometimes that in cases of shipwreck the life-boats are insufficient, and passengers are so crazed with a sense of danger that they forget everything but their fear of death and their desire to live, and fight for places in the life-boat; but I bless God that in the life-boat which Jesus Christ has launched to save sinners there is room for all! "He is able to save unto the uttermost all that come unto God by him."

THE FATE OF JUDAS ISCARIOT.

"Judas fell away, that he might go to his own place."—
Acts i. 25 (*Revised Version*).

IN studying this history, I have been very much interested in noticing the care and earnest purpose of Christ in trying to save Judas from his besetting sin. If you have never looked over with this thought in mind the conversations and sermons of Jesus as recorded in the four Gospels, I am sure you will find it an exceedingly interesting thing to do. When you remember that Judas was present to hear them, light is thrown on a good many things which Christ said, showing that he knew Judas' great danger of making shipwreck of his soul, and was tenderly seeking to save him. Take, for instance, the Sermon on the Mount. I can imagine that, deep down in his heart, Judas must have felt that the Lord meant him when he said, "Lay not up for yourselves treasures upon earth, where moth and rust doth corrupt, and where thieves break through and steal: but lay up for yourselves treasures in heaven. . . . For where your treasure is, there will your heart be also."

And still further on in the same sermon the Savior was evidently trying to give Judas his meat in due season when he said, "No man can serve two masters: for either he will hate the one, and love the other; or else he will hold to the one, and despise the other. Ye can not serve God and mammon." That was exactly what Judas was trying to do. And Christ was speaking to the man's conscience as plainly as if he had singled him out and said, "Judas, you can not serve two masters; if you are going to serve me, and enter into my spirit, you must put your feet on this idolatrous love you have for money. If you do not, in the end you will hate me and sell your soul for greed."

Or take the parable of the Sower. See how earnest was his warning to Judas as he speaks of the seed which fell among the thorns, and, altho it sprang up and began to grow, it was choked out with the cares, and riches, and pleasures of this life, and brought no fruit to perfection.

Or notice again his parable of the rich farmer who as he grew richer increased still more in covetousness, and, tho all his crops depended on the sunshine and showers which God could alone bestow, gave God no thanks; but when he went out in the springtime and saw the prosperity of his crops he said to himself, "What shall I do, because I have no room where to bestow my fruits?

And he said, This will I do: I will pull down my barns, and build greater; and there will I bestow all my fruits and my goods. And I will say to my soul, Soul, thou hast much goods laid up for many years; take thine ease, eat, drink, and be merry. But God said unto him, Thou fool, this night thy soul shall be required of thee: then whose shall those things be, which thou hast provided? So is he that layeth up treasure for himself, and is not rich toward God." Judas heard all this. And on many other occasions Christ evidently had Judas' particular temptation in mind. Christ was as faithful to Judas as he was to Peter, or John, or any of the rest of his friends; but Judas resisted the good spirit and went on clinging to the bad and giving his soul up to greed. It grew upon him until in the end he flaunted it in the very face of Jesus.

Take that case just before he goes to sell Christ to his enemies. It is in the house of Simon the leper. You remember the story: A woman came in having an alabaster box of ointment of spikenard, very precious; and she broke the box and poured the ointment on Jesus' head; and Judas was so angry that he grumbled loudly about it right there at the table, and asked in hypocritical sanctimoniousness, "Why was this waste of the ointment made? for it might have been sold for three hundred pence, and given to the poor." Little cared Judas about the poor! John, whose judgment of people was likely to be tender enough, certainly in his old age, when he wrote his Gospel, tells us: "This he said, not that he cared for the poor; but because he was a thief, and had the bag, and bare what was put therein." But Jesus only looked at Judas in tender reproach and said, "Ye have the poor with you always, and whensoever ye will ye may do them good: but me ye have not always." It is significant that immediately after this occurrence it is recorded, "Judas Iscariot, one of the twelve, went unto the chief priests, to betray him unto them. And when they heard it, they were glad, and promised to give him money."

What a wonderful lesson we have here in regard to our own personal responsibility! Here is a man who for three years associated intimately with Jesus Christ. He had as good a chance to become a good man and live a noble life, one that would be a benediction to all who came in contact with him, and find heaven at last in eternal fellowship with his Lord, as any one of the friends of Jesus. He was a bright man, evidently as clear-headed at least as the majority of them, and he had the same opportunities to know Christ that the rest had. And yet what mellowed them and made them tender and gentle and loving, seemed to make his heart the harder. He stood by when Jesus wept over the fate of Jerusalem, but it aroused no kindred feeling in his heart. The trouble was that Judas was a selfish man, and while surrounded with men of generous feelings whose hearts were drawn out in love for Christ, selfishness banished love from the heart of Judas. I wish to urge this awful example upon any hearers who may have been thinking that because they have been reared in Christian homes and have grown up in association with Christian people, there can be no great danger that it shall not turn out all right with them in the end. Alas! history and observation show us that many who have been thus blest from childhood up, by their carelessness and indifference drift farther and farther away from God until they resist the Holy Spirit to the last and are lost forever.

We have also here a suggestive lesson of the danger of entering upon a course of wrong-doing. The reading of explorations and travels in new lands has always had great fascination for me. In these stories of adventure I have marked with interest the many cases of lives lost by drowning in the waterfalls and cataracts and rapids of streams upon which the unfortunate voyagers have trusted themselves for the sake of exploration and easy travel. The explorer, when he launches his canoe or raft upon waters that are new and unknown to him, takes every possible precaution to guard against the probable dangers of his voyage; yet in spite of all this, many a hardy and trained traveler loses his life because of unforeseen perils. But those who launch their boat upon the stream of sin and wrong-doing know beforehand that it is a river fraught with ever-increasing danger. Its current is strong and treacherous; there is an undertow which is forever sucking beneath the surface multitudes of those who float upon its bosom; there are rapids, and along the shore are ever bleaching the skeletons of victims beaten to death upon the cruel rocks. The whole story of mankind, the warnings of Scripture, the record of every-day observation—all bear testimony that whoever launches his boat upon the stream of sin does so in the face of ten thousand warnings that, tho it may seem safe, "the end of that way is death."

We may take warning of the danger of setting our affections on the things of this world and making ourselves believe that the treasures of greatest value are worldly possessions. In Judas the greed for wealth grew day by day, until at last he sold his Master for thirty pieces of silver. A physician told me the other day that one of the most terrible things he ever saw was a man afflicted with paresis, in whom the predominant faculty came into supreme control. This man would sit for hours and hours at a big table, counting off with his fingers imaginary bills, ever and anon announcing to himself the number of thousands or millions of dollars which in his mind's eye he saw piled up in heaps on the table before him. Once the doctor came in unexpectedly. The man glanced up, but went on counting until he had finished nine hundred thousand dollars. Then he turned with flashing, excited eyes, and said: "My ship has just come in this morning! Splendid cargo! A great fortune aboard her!"

Mr. Moody tells a similar story of a man in one of our insane asylums who walked up and down in the mad-house constantly, and his cry was, "If I only had!" That was his cry from morning till night in all his wakeful hours. His story was this: He was employed by a railroad company to take care of a swing-bridge, and he received a despatch from the superintendent that an extra train would pass over the road, and that he must not turn the bridge until the train had passed. One after another came and tried to have him open the swing-bridge, and he refused to do it. At last a friend came and over-persuaded him, and he opened the bridge. He had no more than done so, when he heard the train coming. There was not time to close the bridge, and he saw the train leap, with all its living freight, into the abyss of death. His reason reeled and tottered upon its throne, and the man went mad. His cry was: "If I only had! If I only had!" Ah, that was the terror of poor Judas. Memory and remorse awoke within him and would give him no peace.

This suggests to us a very solemn truth which is illustrated in the Scripture we are studying — that all the promises of the devil are lies. The devil made Judas believe that Christ's mission was going to fail anyhow, and that it was a shrewd stroke of policy for him to make some money out of the transaction and light on his feet in the new order of things. But poor Judas soon found that he had sold his soul for naught. He had left God out of the account; he had left his own conscience out of the account; but he soon realized that he must deal with them. His conscience awoke within him and would not let him sleep. He had no peace day nor night. As Longfellow, in his "Divine Comedy," makes him say,—

"Lost, lost, forever lost. I have betrayed
The innocent blood. . . .

. . . .

Too late. Too late, I shall not see him more
Among the living. That sweet, patient face
Will nevermore rebuke me, nor those lips
Repeat the words: One of you shall betray me."

Oh, the terrors of an aroused conscience! The fearful reckoning that comes when sin is illuminated by the search-light of an awakened memory! As Dr. Thwing says, "Sin before the moment of commission is often like that image used in the Inquisition, which at a step's distance seems glorious and joy-giving. Sin after commission is like the same image which, once touched, draws the victim into its crushing embrace, piercing eye and heart and limb." At last poor Judas is so aroused and awakened that even his greed palls on his palate. He had sold his soul for silver, and now he despises it. In his remorse and his horror at himself he goes back to the chief priests, his fellow-plotters, and says to them, "I have betrayed innocent blood." They disdain him, and scoff at him, and coldly say, "What is that to us? See thou to that." That is the way the devil treats his victim always. I have seen a saloon-keeper do it over and over again. I have seen him flatter a young man—one with strong health, a good salary, and a pocketful of money. I have looked on while he fascinated the unwary youth and enticed him to become a visitor at his saloon. I have watched until the young man traded his health, and his salary, and his pocketful of money, and his good reputation—yes, and his own manhood—for strong drink. Then these eyes have seen him kick the same young man like a drunken dog into the street, and leave him there to die. That is a sample of what the devil does.

When the priests mocked him, poor Judas knew not what to do. He could not endure to have the silver about him. It burned his pockets. It burned his fingers. It burned his conscience. And he flung the pieces down on the temple's pavement, and turned to flee. Ah, whither can he go? Oh, there was one place he might have gone even yet! If he had gone to Pilate's judgment-hall, even at that late hour, and crowded his way through the mob that were shouting, "Crucify him! Crucify him!" If he had fallen on his knees at the feet of Jesus, and let his poor heart break there at the feet of the Savior, he who forgave Peter, who prayed for his enemies, and who pardoned the dying thief on the cross, would have forgiven Judas. But, alas! he rushed out into the outer darkness, and died the death of the suicide.

We must not to fail to pause for a moment before the significant lesson so apparent in the words of our text—"That he might go to his own place." The two worlds are joined together. Life is a school-time of preparation. We are in this world's school, fitting ourselves for immortal destiny. It does not require any special edict of God to make happy in the world to come a good man who has loved Christ and his people and his cause while here on earth. He has already come to breathe the heavenly spirit; it is his natural atmosphere. He loves the people of God, he delights in prayer, in meditation on the Word of God, and in communion with those who love his Savior. Like the angels in heaven, he gets his greatest joy in beholding sinners in repentance at the Mercy Seat. Having entered into the spirit of heaven, when death shall set him free from the circumstances of earth he shall go to "his own place." Neither does it require any special edict of God to make the sinning soul miserable and full of remorse in the world to come. Having lived in rebellion against God, refusing to be governed by the spirit of Christ, careless about the salvation of lost souls, given over to his own selfish ways—when made free from the circumstances of earth he, too, in the very nature of things, will go to "his own place."

Do not shut your heart against this message because you imagine Judas to be so terrible a sinner that it is not fair to compare you with him. Do not be self-deceived. There is no evidence that Judas was a greater sinner than others who follow their own selfishness, harden their hearts against the love of Christ, and refuse to yield to him their loyalty and devotion. Alas! all sin is akin. The only safety is in forsaking your sin and finding forgiveness in the mercy of Jesus Christ. I trust the fatal mistake of Judas may not be yours, but that now, having been convicted by the Holy Spirit of your sin, you will not grieve him away, but will permit the tenderness of Jesus and the sympathy of those who love him to win you from your sin to the cleansing fountain.

The story is told of a gentleman who was standing, one morning, on the platform of the Grand Central Railroad Station, in New York city, holding the hand of his little girl, only seven years old. There was some slight detention about opening the car in which they wished to sit, and the child stood looking quietly about her, interested in all she saw, when the sound of the measured tramp of a dozen heavy feet made her turn and look behind her. There she saw a sight such as her young eyes had never looked on before—a short procession of six policemen, two of whom marched first, followed by two others between whom (chained to the wrist of each) walked a fierce-looking man, and these were followed by two more, who came close behind the dangerous prisoner. The man was one of the worst ruffians in the city. He had committed a terrible crime, and was on his way to the State prison, to be locked up there for the rest of his life. The little girl had heard of him, and she knew who it must be, for only that morning her father had said he would have to be sent up strongly guarded, for it had been suspected that some of his comrades would try to rescue him from the officers. The little company halted quite near her. Her father, who was talking with a friend, did not notice them. The child stood and watched the man with a strange, choking feeling in her throat, and a pitiful look in her eyes. It seemed so very, very sad to think that after this one ride in the sunshine by the banks of the river, the poor man, all his life, would be shut up in a gloomy prison, no matter how long he might live. Even if he should become an old, old man, he could never walk in the bright sunlight a free man again. All at once the prisoner looked at her, and then turned suddenly away. But in another moment he glanced back, as if he could not resist the sweet pity of that childish face. He watched it for an instant, his own features working curiously the while, and then turned his head with an impatient motion that told the little girl that she had annoyed him. Her tender little heart was sorry in a moment, and, starting forward, she went up close to the dangerous man, and said, earnestly: "I didn't mean to plague you, poor man; only I'm sorry for you; and Jesus is sorry for you, too." One of the policemen caught her up quickly, and gave her to her father, who had already sprung forward to stop her. No one had caught the quick words she had uttered save the man to whom they were spoken. But he had heard them, and their echo, with the picture of that tender, grieved child's face, went with him through all that long ride, and passed beside him into his dreary cell. The keeper wondered greatly that his dreaded prisoner made no trouble, and that as time passed on he grew gentler and more kindly every day. But the wonder was explained when, some months after, the chaplain asked him how it was that he had turned out such a different man from what they had expected. "It is a simple story," said the man. "A child was sorry for me, and she told me that Jesus was sorry for me, too, and her pity and his broke my heart."

How much more should you—who have been surrounded all your life by the tender mercies of God, and have, perhaps, many praying for you, whose hearts would be gladdened at your salvation—be melted down to repentance by the tenderness of Jesus! But however lonely or friendless you may be, you may be sure that Jesus is sorry for you, and watches you with sympathy, and even now holds out his arms to you in entreaty, offering you fellowship, and rest unto your soul.

CHRIST BEFORE PILATE.

"Jesus stood before the governor."—*Matt.* xxvii. 11 (*Revised Version*).

"Pilate saith unto them, What then shall I do unto Jesus which is called Christ?"—*Matt.* xxvii. 22 (*Revised Version*).

MANY of you have seen and studied that famous painting of Munkacsy's entitled, "Christ before Pilate," and perhaps all who have not seen the original have seen a copy of it. The artist has done a great deal to place the scene we are studying before the eye of the multitudes of mankind. The picture is very impressive: Jesus stands before Pilate to receive the sentence of death. Caiaphas, the high priest, in official robes, with all the bitterness of cruel prejudice, is the accuser; while all around the brutal mob cry out for the crucifixion of Jesus. The central figure is the Christ. The portrait of Jesus is the personification of spirituality, dignity, and majesty. He stands alone. His hands are tied together with stout cords. The position of the crossed hands and the poise of the body indicate not the despair of a prisoner, but the composure of one who is conscious that at any moment he could summon to his aid "twelve legions of angels." You instinctively feel that Christ is the real judge and Pilate the prisoner of indecision and cowardice. Jesus is so ideal, yet so real; his carriage so manly, yet so submissive; as another has said, the Man of Sorrows and the heroic soul are so closely joined in the person of Jesus that you do not know where one begins and the other ends. There confronts you on the canvas the raging, wicked mob; and in their midst the glorious Christ stands radiant with the nobility of a great soul. His eyes are so calm and spiritual, his face so full of peace and love, that we would not be astonished to hear him tenderly say, "Father, forgive them, for they know not what they do." The whole appearance of the Christ reveals the mighty Savior that he is. Carrying on his shoulders the fate of nations, he can calmly pass unheeded the scorn and hate of his enemies.

We turn from the Christ, with his pure, heroic soul shining in his face, to Pilate. He is arrayed in the white robe of a Roman senator, around which runs a border of purple. He sits on the judgment seat. He has the large, round head, the short hair, smooth face, and haughty bearing of the typical Roman under the Cæsars. With his deep-set eyes he surveys the multitude, trying to discover what would be popular. Outwardly he is a calm politician; but his uneasy, restless eye and the nervous twitching of his fingers betray a deeply perplexed soul. Caiaphas, the high priest, a large man with full white beard, dressed in ecclesiastical robes, his outstretched hand pointing defiantly at Christ, stands in front of Pilate, a little to the right. Prejudice, deep and malignant, shows in his cruel face. Between Christ and Caiaphas sits a rich Pharisee who gazes at Christ with insolent indifference. His air is that of proud satisfaction, as if he thanked God that he was holier than the prisoner before Pilate. The vicious, howling mob is painted with intense realism. A Roman soldier of fine proportions and imposing figure pushes back the surging crowd with his extended spear. To the left of the soldier there stands a rude fellow of gigantic stature, a perfect type of the ruffian in all ages, who with uplifted hands shouts: "Crucify him! Crucify him!"

Next to Christ, the most attractive figure in the great picture is a beautiful young mother, holding a little child in her arms. Her face charms you, and lingers in your memory. All that is tender, sympathetic, and lovely in woman's nature the artist has personified in this Madonna. Her loving face looking into Christ's with a sweet, holy trust, speaks volumes. These wicked, prejudiced men hate him. She loves him as her friend. You see it in her eyes. You behold her heart in her beautiful, sympathetic face. It was a true stroke of genius in Munkacsy to symbolize Christianity by a young mother. She accepts the rising faith for herself and her child.

As we look on the picture we can almost hear the uneasy, crafty Pilate as he asks the question of our text, "What then shall I do unto Jesus which is called Christ?" But this question is not Pilate's alone; it is as truly our question, and as seriously, and awfully, our question as Pilate's. Think for a moment of the credentials of him who stands there before Pilate. There never was any other individual in human history certified to by so many witnesses as Christ. Back yonder at the beginning, coming as a ray of hope in the midst of the desolation wrought by the first sin, God had promised that the seed of the woman should bruise the serpent's head. To Abraham in the desert God had renewed that promise in the declaration that in his seed all the nations of the earth should be blessed. And along down the line of history for thousands of years every prophet who walked with God and to whom God revealed the future beheld in the distance the coming of the Messiah, the Christ who was to be the Savior of the world. Isaiah's poetic and glowing pages are filled with the story of the One who was to come to preach good tidings unto the meek, to bind up the broken-hearted, to proclaim liberty to the captives, and the opening of the prison to those that were bound. One whose pleasure it should be to proclaim the acceptable year of the Lord, to comfort sorrowing hearts, to give unto them beauty for ashes, the oil of joy for mourning, and the garment of praise for the spirit of heaviness. And when, at last, the infant Christ was born, Simeon, who had lingered beyond his time, took the little babe in his arms and exclaimed: "Lord, now lettest thou thy servant depart in peace, according to thy word: for mine eyes have seen thy salvation."

Angels gave their testimony to Christ. When Gabriel made the announcement to Mary, he said, "He shall be great, and shall be called the Son of the Highest." When the angels came to the shepherds on that first Christmas night they said, "Unto you is born this day, in the city of David, a Savior, which is Christ the Lord." And on the first Easter morning, when the women came to the empty tomb, it was an angel who bore witness, "He is not here, for he is risen."

God, the Father, bore witness also to the mission of his Son. At the baptism of Christ the

Holy Spirit descended in the form of a dove upon the Savior, and a voice out of the heavens above declared, "This is my beloved Son, in whom I am well pleased."

The friends of Jesus, both true and false, bore testimony that he was what he claimed to be. Peter, speaking for his true friends, exclaims on one occasion: "Thou art the Christ, the Son of the living God." And on another occasion he declares: "Neither is there any other name under heaven, that is given among men, wherein we must be saved." And Judas, speaking for his false friends, bears this testimony: "I have sinned in that I have betrayed innocent blood."

Even the devils bore testimony to Jesus Christ. In the synagogue at Capernaum one cried out to him: "I know thee who thou art, the Holy One of God." And the demons that possessed that poor man over in the land of the swineherds, at Gadara, remonstrated: "What have we to do with thee, Jesus, thou Son of God?"

Neither Pilate nor Herod could find anything wrong with him. After the most earnest attempt to find some excuse for yielding to the Jews, and for the crucifixion of Jesus, Pilate is compelled to say: "I find no fault in this man." Ah, but all the witnesses are not there! If we could bring up the poor widow whose son he brought back from the grave; the lepers whom he cleansed; the deaf whose ears he unstopped; the blind whose eyes he opened; the palsied whose nerves he quieted; the sick whose fever he cooled; the poor, sinful, despairing souls to whom he gave freedom and purity and hope; what loving testimony they would bring! And, thank God, we do not have to go back to the past for it. All along down the centuries the cloud of witnesses has been growing. Wherever his precious name has been proclaimed, numberless thousands have found in him the divine power that could forgive their sins, illuminate their darkness, and save their souls. I could call up around me to-night, in this church, witnesses who, if they were to tell but the simple story of their personal salvation, it would be as marvelous as anything recorded in the New Testament, were it not that we are so accustomed to such incidents. Every day that the sun rises in the east and hastens to his setting in the west, there are thousands of men and women among the multiplied tribes of humanity who bow at the Mercy Seat and find that he is still able to separate their sins from them "as far as the east is from the west."

Let us bring this question home to our own hearts. What are we personally going to do with this Christ? You, Christians, what are you going to say about him?—not only by your words, but by the practical answer of your daily lives. Many incidents have been related of tests to which professed Christians have been submitted by curious and skeptical worldlings to see if their religion was genuine. The story is told of a merchant who professed to become a Christian. Some of the men with whom he dealt in business placed before him for decision a question of conduct. Would he sell a package of adulterated goods, marked and guaranteed as genuine? A converted lawyer was sought after almost immediately to take charge of an unrighteous case, to touch which would be sin. A large retainer was offered him to test his principles. Bets have, on many occasions, been exchanged upon the probability of a minister of the Gospel swerving from his plain duty for the sake of gain. Many times young Christians are solicited to enter into questionable amusements on purpose to test the honesty of their Christian profession; but while these things occasionally occur, the real testing is going on all the time, and I pray God that the Holy Spirit may make this question very heart-searching to every Christian in this presence: "What am I doing as a Christian unto Jesus; is my daily conduct such that the people who have dealings with me, those who associate with me most, and know the details of my life best, are sure that I am faithful to Jesus Christ and that he is exercising a purifying and holy influence upon my heart and life?" If you can not answer this question in the affirmative, then the question comes to you as straight as to Pilate or to the Jews of his day, and with equal responsibility and importance—"What then shall I do unto Jesus which is called the Christ?"

The question comes to any here who have been Christ's disciples, have once borne glad testimony to his saving power, but have fallen from that first love and whose Christianity to-day is only nominal. Whatever others may think about it, or know about it, you know, and God knows, that you are backslidden in heart. To you the question comes—"What shall I do unto Jesus? This Jesus who gave his life upon the cross for me; who sought me out when I was a poor, lost sinner; who gave me unspeakable joy in the forgiveness of my sins; and now that I have wandered away from him, and crucified him afresh, and put his cause to an open shame by my coldness of heart and my carelessness of life, still follows after me with patient love, saying unto my wayward heart, 'I am married unto the backslider,'—what shall I do unto Jesus?" I commend unto all such the words which David Livingstone wrote in his record on his last birthday. He was in the heart of

Central Africa, alone in the midst of the darkness of barbarism, but there he wrote: "March 19, 1872—Birthday. My Jesus, my King, my Life, my All; I again dedicate my whole self to thee. Accept me. . . . In Jesus' name I ask it. Amen. So let it be." Oh, that every backslidden heart here might behold Jesus again as King, Life, All, and dedicate your whole selves anew to him!

The question comes to every burdened and weary soul here. I am sure there must be such— those whose burdens are too heavy for them to carry, who are weighed down by the cares of life, whose hearts often cry out for some resting-place. What are you going to do unto this Jesus who comes pleading with infinite tenderness, "Come unto me, all ye that labor and are heavy laden, and I will give you rest."

The question comes to you whose time and attention are taken up with the world, who say you are too busy to give thought to spiritual things. What are you going to do unto Jesus who says to you, "Seek ye first the kingdom of God, and his righteousness; and all these things shall be added unto you?"

At Aix-la-Chapelle is the tomb of the great Emperor Charlemagne. He was buried in the central space beneath the dome; but the manner of his burial is one of the most impressive sermons ever preached. In the death-chamber beneath the floor he sat on a marble chair—the chair on which kings had been crowned—and, wrapped in his imperial robes, a book of the Gospel lay open in his lap; and as he sat there, silent, cold, motionless, the finger of the dead man's hand pointed to the words of Jesus, "What shall it profit a man if he gain the world and lose his own soul?"

How the question must ring in the ear of every one here who is conscious that there is resting upon his soul the guilt of unforgiven sin! What are you going to do unto Jesus, "The Lamb of God, which taketh away the sin of the world?" What are you going to do unto Jesus, who offers to be your sacrifice for sin? It is one of the fearful possibilities of the freedom of your will that you may reject him, that you may refuse his offer, that you may harden your heart against his pleading, and count the blood of the covenant an unholy thing, and make even his deathless love upon the cross in vain, so far as you are concerned. Some people did this when he was here on earth, and he said about them with tear-choked voice, "Ye will not come unto me that ye might have life." O brothers and sisters, conscious of your sins, having no other escape for them, what are you going to do unto this Jesus who comes offering to be your Savior, your Redeemer? I beg of you to accept him and crown him Lord over all in your hearts. He rightly asks of you an open discipleship. He says to you, "If any man will confess me before men, him will I confess before my Father and his holy angels." Don't refuse him to-night, but give him the brave and open confession of your penitence and love.

VOICES FROM THE CROSS.

"They crucified him, and with him two others, on either side one, and Jesus in the midst."—*John* xix. 18 (*Revised Version*).

WHEN I try to preach to men about the cross of Jesus and the exhibition of his deathless love in that one supreme sacrifice in the story of mankind, I envy the missionaries who have a chance to tell the story for the first time to ears that never have heard it before. If I could bring it to you as a fresh story to-day, it could but melt your hearts and bring sinners to repentance. But you have heard it so often, you have looked at it from every side, it has come to be a matter of course to you, until I fear that many hear it without appreciating its profound significance. I would I had the power with simple but skilful words to put before your imagination that excited and bloodthirsty crowd that poured out of Pilate's judgment hall after the order had been given for the crucifixion of Jesus. See them for a moment! See the fierce hate and the cruel expectation expressed in their eyes and faces as they glare with mocking, sneering ferocity at the Christ bending beneath the weight of the cross upon which he is to die. About him there is a little group of soldiers who, while they protect him from the rabble, goad him on toward Golgotha. Remember he is wearing your flesh and mine; he has a human brain and tender, sensitive, human flesh; nerves delicate and susceptible to ache and pain. Think of what he has already endured. He has been led from Pilate to Herod, and from Herod back to Pilate again. His brow has been pierced with that cruel crown of thorns. His shoulders have been made bare for the smiters. He has been beaten until the blood has run down over his body, and now he goes out tremblingly, bending beneath the weight of that huge cross. At the foot of the hill he staggers, and stumbles, and falls. The mob shout derisively, but the soldiers see that something must be done. Perhaps they fear he will die on the road and the cruel sport will be spoiled; and so they press a stranger — Simon the Cyrenian — into service, doubtless because he is big and strong; probably a black man from Africa. Poor black man, he has had to bear many a cross in the progress of civilization! But never was man, black or white, forced into a more honorable place than Simon the Cyrenian who carried the cross for Jesus up the rugged slope of Golgotha.

And now they are come to the place. Two thieves are there to be crucified also. The horrible work of preparation begins. The holes in which the bases of the crosses are to rest have been already dug, perhaps. The victims are stretched upon their instruments of torture. The cruel nails are driven through the hands and feet. A low moan of agony comes from the sufferers. The pain is too awful, the agony too deep and terrible, for outbreaking screams. Men scream when they are hurt a little; when the iron enters their souls they only moan. Then great strong arms and massive shoulders are thrust beneath the crosses, and they are lifted into the air with their bleeding victims. With a dull, heavy thud the center pieces fall into their places. There they hang before the cruel and pitiless multitude! There are three crosses—on either hand a thief, "and Jesus in the midst." Below is the pitiless mob and the no less cruel soldiery. Some of the more bold of the crowd come up close to the Christ to taunt him in his agony, and they cry out at him, "Ah, you're the man that was giong to destroy the temple and build it again in three days! You saved others, but now you cannot save yourself!"

But as we look up into the face of the Christ we see no answering flush of hatred or revenge. We see only pity and tenderness and imploring love on that white, drawn face. The eyes are turned toward heaven; the lips move as in prayer. We lean forward to catch the words that may fall from those piteous lips; even the mob is hushed for a minute with curiosity to hear what he will say in reply, but he is not replying to them. It is the voice of pleading that falls on our hushed ears, and the plea is to the heart of God, "Father, forgive them; they know not what they do." Oh, was there ever love and pity like that!

> "When I survey the wondrous cross
>   On which the Prince of glory died,
> My richest gain I count but loss,.
>   And pour contempt on all my pride.
>
> "See, from his head, his hands, his feet,
>   Sorrow and love flow mingled down;
> Did e'er such love and sorrow meet,
>   Or thorns compose so rich a crown?
>
> "Were the whole realm of nature mine,
>   That were a present far too small;
> Love so amazing, so divine,
>   Demands my soul, my life, my all."

In spite of their agony, the two men who are dying on either side of Jesus can but have their attention drawn to the great interest aroused in the multitude by the figure on the central cross. One of these malefactors was evidently a very hardened man, and though he was himself at the close of a wicked and terrible life, he joins with the mob in scoffing at Jesus, and rails on him, saying, "If thou be Christ, save thyself and us." But the man on the other side seems to have gotten a little glimpse of the divine meaning of the death of Jesus. Perhaps the tender, loving prayer of Christ to which he had just listened had been a revelation to him, and so he rebukes the other, saying, "Dost not thou fear God, seeing thou art in the same condemnation? And we indeed justly; for we receive the due reward of our deeds; but this man hath done nothing amiss." And then with a look of infinite longing he turns his eyes on Christ and says, "Lord, remember me when thou comest into thy kingdom." It was the prayer of penitent faith and the Savior answered it at once. How tender must have been his look, sending a divine glow of hope to the poor dying sinner's heart, as he exclaimed, "Verily I say unto thee, To-day shalt thou be with me in Paradise." There are some here this morning who, above all other needs that they have, for this world or the next, need to behold that look of the Lord Jesus, about which the poet sings:

> "I saw one hanging on a tree,
>   In agonies and blood,
> Who fixed his languid eyes on me,
>   As near his cross I stood.

> "Sure never till my latest breath
>   Can I forget that look:
> It seemed to charge me with his death,
>   Though not a word he spoke.
>
> "A second look he gave, which said,
>   'I freely all forgive;
> This blood is for thy ransom paid;
>   I die that thou mayst live.'"

Thank God, Jesus is able to save unto the uttermost every one who will come unto God by him! One of the saddest things they ever do in a hospital is to send away a patient who has come to them a few weeks, or a few months, before, in great hope that the skill of the physicians would be able to heal his disease and make him a well man, with the sad message that they can keep him no longer because they have found him incurable. There are no incurable cases to the Great Physician except those who refuse his treatment. David told Saul about one lamb of his flock that he rescued out of the very jaws of the lion, and one other that he plucked from the paws of a bear; but Jesus has multitudes that he has seized as "brands from the burning," and he is as able to save now as he was when that poor dying thief lost all his sins at one word from his gracious lips. The other thief who was crucified with Jesus might have been saved as well if he had not hardened his heart against the Savior's love. Christ never has to do as men sometimes are compelled to do—choose between those whom they would save in times of danger and peril.

I think one of the saddest stories I ever heard was of a man who was in a shipwreck. They were not far from the shore. He was a strong swimmer, but his wife was clinging to one arm and their only child to the other. So encumbered, he felt that his strength was giving way, and that to save both was impossible. Which one should he leave behind?—for it was that, or all three must die together. It was a heartrending alternative! But it was do or die, and with a breaking heart and almost frenzied brain he shook off his child and swam away with its mother from its dying cries. Oh, I bless God that Jesus never has to make such a choice as that! He did not carry one of these poor men up to heaven alone because he was not strong enough to take both with him, but because the other hardened his heart against the Savior and refused his tender love. And so I say to any who are listening to me, if your mother, or your wife, or your child, is saved at last while you are lost, it is not because Jesus is not willing to save you, for he is seeking after you most tenderly. His word is full of gracious invitations. Listen to some of them. If you never heard them before, listen to them now: "Him that cometh to me I will in no wise cast out;" "I am the door; by me if any man enter in, he shall be saved, and shall go in and out, and find pasture;" "I am the resurrection and the life: he that believeth in me, tho he were dead, yet shall he live: and whosoever liveth and believeth in me shall never die;" "If ye abide in me, and my words abide in you, ye shall ask what ye will, and it shall be done unto you;" "And the Spirit and the bride say, Come. And let him that heareth say, Come. And let him that is athirst come. And whosoever will, let him take the water of life freely." "He that hath ears to hear, let him hear."

Pilate wrote over the cross of Jesus, "Jesus of Nazareth, King of the Jews." The priests tried to get him to change it, but he would not do it. O Christian men and women, if you want to sweeten the crosses you bear, put the name of Jesus on your cross also. Do not forget to put the word "King," in remembrance that your Savior is "King of kings, and Lord of lords." I call you to the way of the cross. It is the only way of safety. In the heart of Switzerland, in the high Alps, where the roads and paths climb up into the domain of perpetual winter and ice, and where the way is often cut out of the face of the precipice of rock where a single false step would mean a horrible death to the unfortunate traveler, they set at the most dangerous places huge crosses to tell where the path lies; and in the winter time, when that mountain track is covered over with the deep snow-drifts that hide the yawning gorge and the dangerous crag, the traveler's only safety is to keep in line with the great crosses that rise above the drifted snow. So I call you at this hour to the only path of human safety, the path of the cross.

It is only those who come by way of the cross, and who have entered into fellowship with the Savior in self-denying service, who are welcomed at the gate of heaven, where Jesus reigns supreme. Laura Ormiston Chant sings this truth very clearly in her song of "The Calvary Road:"

"Once there came a soul to the doorway of heaven
Calling to the angels, 'Open the door!
I am one of the great
Of the earth, and my state
And my splendor were such men have striven
To catch sight of the print of my feet where I trod;
I have come to be welcomed and honored of God.'

"Spake the angels low as they paused in their singing:
'Hast thou served thy brethren there on the earth?
Hast thou righted the wrong—
Saved the weak from the strong—
Hast thou humbled thyself for love, flinging

Thy soul to the dark and the sinning of men—
Hast thou suffered, loved, saved to the best of thy ken?'

"But the soul was angry—left the doorway, crying,
  'These are not the words they should say to such as I!
      They must have heard my name
      For the trump of my fame
  Must have blown to the sky, when my dying
  Put the town into mourning a month at the least,
  And stopped all the music, the dance and the feast.'

"Sang a little angel to her bright harp golden,
  Carols sweet and high of a poor man's love;
      Whom the rich knew not
      And the great one forgot
  In the centuries time-blurred and olden;
  But who blessed little ones, a life that should save them.

"So the ages passed, and the angels still waited
  Singing and watching to open the door,
      When one night in the rain
      Of earth's winter, the pain
  Of a soul asking help, and belated,
  Came into the light, where the angels in white
  Were all gazing on God and aglow with the sight.

"Then there came a sound as of knocking and praying—
  'Open, angels, open! Let the outcast in.
      For the Lord's dear sake
      Whose heart had to break
  To teach men pity, know no delaying.
  Here's a hurt soul I bring to the mercy of your King,
  She is 'shamed and sorry, angels, O let her hear you
      sing!'

"How the angels of time flew to the gold door of heaven—
Welcomed the two souls, saying, 'Evermore
　　　Be thou the greatest
　　　Who servest and waitest,
Thou who gavest service art forgiven;
Thou hast lost self in love, and the Christ-path hath trod;
'Twas the Calvary road to the homestead of God.'"

THE THREE MARYS BESIDE THE CROSS.

"There were standing by the cross of Jesus his mother, and his mother's sister, Mary the wife of Clopas, and Mary Magdalene."—*John* xi. 25 (*Revised Version*).

IN the group that stood about the cross of Jesus on that awful day of crucifixion all the faces were not bitter and full of hate. Among those there who were friendly were three women who were loyal and faithful to Christ to the end. The first one to be named is his mother, Mary. How natural it seems, and how true to our knowledge of human nature, that his mother should have been faithful when so many others forsook him and fled. A mother's love is proverbial for its tenderness and constancy. It will stand more testing, and go through a hotter furnace, coming out like pure gold, than any other love save that of Jesus Christ. A man may wander from the path of honor, he may bring disgrace on the name of his ancestors; the father's heart may get hard against him and refuse to forgive the family shame; even the brothers and sisters that played with him about the fireside may turn coldly from him; but so long as the wanderer lives he knows there is one spot that is true to him—his mother's heart. Mary, the mother of Jesus, is by no means the only mother who has followed her son to the cross.

I have been very much interested in an article in one of our religious journals by Rev. Gerald Stanley Lee on "Being a Madonna." The writer calls attention to that wonderful painting of the Sistine Madonna by Raphael, in the Dresden Gallery. It is a wonderful, innocent face, filled with a child's wonder at her own child, worshipful with worshiping. Her whole being seems to so shine with the consciousness of him that you see him not only beautiful in her arms, but again and more beautiful in her eyes. Yet Mary was not a perfect mother. You remember the time when they had been up at Jerusalem and she forgot Jesus. She was not the Sistine Madonna always. The Sistine Madonna was what she wanted to be; but there were occasions when she did not realize it. It is impossible that she could have had that Sistine Madonna look in her face when, taken up with the sight-seeing, or the interesting conversation of the other women, she forgot her Son, and lost him in the great city. She looked then as Marys often look now. She did not have that Sistine Madonna look when, with anxious heart and quivering lips and tearful eyes, she hastened about through the company from one to another crying, "Have you seen my Son? Have you seen my Son?" It ought to be a comfort to the mothers to remember that even the mother of Christ had her weaknesses and her faults. But the crown of Mary was her humility. Her sweet, confessing, wondering unfitness chose her to be the mother of the King. Henceforth, forever, the highest token of motherhood is the beautiful awe of the child. Every child, through Mary's child, is henceforth a mine of unsearchable riches, with the tiny seeds of divine possibilities nestling in its little heart. The shepherds still sing to waiting mothers. There is a vision over every cradle, and the wise men bring their gifts to every beginning life. "Glory to God in the highest!" seemed to sing in the air above her boy's head—to his mother. All the mighty prophet voices that reverberate through the history of her people followed him, as she watched him in the door-yard and playing among the shavings of his father's carpenter shop. She remembers the prophecy, "A little one shall become a thousand, and a small one a great nation," and sings, and, like all mothers, whatever the words, as she goes about the house, all her songs are of her child. As she rocks him to sleep and softly lays him down and gives the mother kiss that seals his sleep with sweetness, she smooths the covering and stands over him dreaming; and she listens to the peaceful breathing and wonders in her innocent soul what Isaiah could have meant to say of him: "He is despised and rejected of men," "He was bruised for our iniquities;" and she bends over and looks again, and the pure lines of the child Savior's face seem to say, "Peace, peace," and she wonders, and she steals away. "With his stripes we are healed, and the chastisement of our peace was upon him," rings through all her household cares, with the dim shadow of a dark cross coming and going, and the haunting of a far-away cry. She can not bear it, and leaving all she creeps back and bends over him once more. "It was not easy to be a 'Madonna.' From the beginning to the end Mary was anxious, as are other mothers. To and fro, over the beautiful awe, swept the great sorrow shadow. Jesus was crucified on the cross. Mary was crucified at the foot of it. Mothers know." What a glorious consciousness it must have been to Mary on that awful day of separation to remember that she had never thwarted the will of God, and though beset by weaknesses like other mothers, she had, from the day that she brought him a little babe to Simeon in the temple, sought to point his feet in the way of righteousness and truth. There had been much about his mission she could not understand, but that she did not stand in the way of it we know by her utterance at that first miracle, at the wedding feast in Cana, when she spoke to the wondering servants and said, "Whatsoever he saith unto you, do it."

O mothers who hear me, are you seeking with all your heart to bring your children to God?—to turn their feet to the paths of righteousness and truth? The best gift you can ever give them is the gift of a sweet and simple piety in their very childhood. Do not wait until they are grown up and gone out to be the hot-bed of evil seeds sown by worldly hands; but now, while they are young, while their love for you is simple and unaffected, while your influence upon them is almost all-powerful, bend all your energies to win their heart's love to God. Then for you, as for Mary, the time may come when you shall have to go with them to the cross, see them pass through many sorrows and severe trials, but you will never need to blush for them if their hearts are pure and their lives "hid with Christ in God."

It is certainly a very interesting and suggestive fact that the sister of Mary should be with her, sharing the terrible danger and the tender devotion of this trying hour. She has no doubt been led to this supreme fidelity to Christ through her love for her sister—showing us the magical power of human influence in winning people to Christ. How speedily the world would be won to Christ if every Christian now living appreciated in its full measure the power of influence! Every one of us is so situated in little narrow circles that there are some one or two relatives or friends so close to us in sympathetic fellowship that if we were to set our hearts upon it, as the one thing we desired above everything else, we could soon win them to the Lord. Oh, for a devotion to Jesus that will make us ashamed to go month after month empty-handed of those who might be rescued from sin through our sympathy and friendship!

Dr. Conwell tells of a visit to the Hospice of St. Bernard, where are kept the wonderful St. Bernard dogs, of whose work in rescuing perishing travelers overtaken by the Alpine storms so many tales are familiar to all. Dr. Conwell says that one morning after a storm one of these great, honest creatures came struggling through the snow, hampered greatly in his exhausted condition by the little barrel of brandy that hung on his collar. The doctor waded deep in the drifts, following the floundering old fellow around the Hospice to the kennel, which was a room of considerable size. When the door opened to the wanderer, the other dogs within set up a chorus of barks and whines, and fell over one another as they crowded about him and eagerly followed him around with wags of their tails and inquisitive looks in their eyes, which were just as intelligent questionings as so many interrogation points. But the crestfallen beast held his head and tail to the floor, and sneaked about from corner to corner, and finally lay down, panting, in a dark niche of the stone basement. He lay there with his eyes glancing out at the corners in a most shamefaced way. The young monk who had charge of the animals called the weary dog by name, and when the beast would not leave his shadowy retreat, he tried to induce him to come forth by showing him a dish containing scraps of meat. But, hungry as he was, he merely opened his eyes a little wider, rapped the floor once or twice lightly as he gave a feeble wag to his tail, and then shrank back and seemed not to hear or see the invitation. The impatient keeper turned away with an angry gesture, and said that the dog would get over his sulks very soon, and that the creature was ashamed that he "had not found any one." The thoughtless remark shot into Dr. Conwell's soul with a thrill. The noble old dog seemed to have felt so sorry, so ashamed, or so guilty, because he had returned without saving any one, that he would not eat. It was not his fault that no benighted wanderer had been out benumbed and dying on the mountain-road that awful night. He had grandly done his duty, but he was just dog enough not to reason so far, and just human enough to feel that it was his imperative duty to save some one. Grand old dog! How he ought to put to shame many a human soul who knows there are travelers going down in the biting cold, and freezing to death in the cruel storms that sweep over life's mountainous highways, and yet never lose a night's sleep because they have never yet saved a lost man from death.

What we need is a passion for soul-saving; one that will make us feel that above everything else that is the supreme mission of our lives. Let us see to it that we turn to account every friendship we have, every bit of sympathy and gratitude that is owing to us in the heart of every man and woman we know, that it may aid in winning them away from their sins to our Savior and our Lord.

There is another Mary at the foot of the cross—Mary Magdalene. When we think about it we are not astonished to find her there also. When she first became acquainted with Jesus she was a poor, wicked, demon-possessed woman. Christ was kind to her. He dispossessed her soul of the evil spirits, and in her great gratitude and love she became his devoted and loyal friend forevermore. Peter might deny the Master if he would, others might forsake him and flee, but she owed all she was to him and it never occurred to her that it was possible for her to desert him in the hour of his trial. How many there are of us who have the same reason for loyalty that Mary Magdalene had! We, too, were poor, lost sinners. The devils of anger, and selfishness, and appetite, and passion, possessed our poor hearts, and were leading us, bound hand and foot, to be the slaves of evil. Then Christ came to us and inspired our hearts with the hope that there was for us something infinitely better; the hope that he was able to set us free from the bondage of sin and death. And when at last our faith was aroused, and we besought him, he came into our hearts, drove out the evil spirits, and gave us the gladness of his peaceful presence. He taught us to sing:

> "Oh, happy day that fixed my choice
> On thee, my Savior and my God!
> Well may this glowing heart rejoice,
> And tell its raptures all abroad.
>
> "'Tis done, the great transaction's done;
> I am my Lord's, and he is mine;
> He drew me, and I followed on,
> Charmed to confess the voice divine."

He did all that for us. What have we done for him? He is still being crucified among men.

Are we showing forth everywhere our gratitude to him? He asks us that we shall wear his name; that we shall tell men what great things the Lord has done for us; that we shall so testify to him that others, hearing of his goodness to us, shall forsake their sins and accept him. There is no greater sin than ingratitude. I put it home to your heart, I pray that the Holy Spirit may put it to your conscience, whether you are showing forth in your daily conduct and conversation the gratitude which is due from you to the Lord Jesus Christ.

And you who are not Christians, I urge upon you this blessed truth that the same Christ who cast out from the heart of Mary Magdalene seven devils, and gave her this great cause for thanksgiving, is able to save you from every sin which haunts you and masters you. Some of you are mastered by evil habits that have been growing for a long time. They seemed insignificant at first, and you dallied with them. You thought you could break them off when you pleased, but you are coming to understand that you are not your own master; that when you determine to do good, the devil who possesses you and to whom you have yielded the fortress of your heart makes you do evil. Perhaps you are discouraged and disheartened, as Mary Magdalene was until she met Jesus; but when she met him the devils were cast out, her poor heart was cleansed, and her life dawned anew. O my brothers and sisters who are conscious of overmastering sins and wicked habits, I pray that you may meet Jesus Christ to-night! He is here now. He is in his Word. He is in the hearts of his people. He is even closer to you than that—he is knocking at the door of your heart and saying to you, "Open the door and let me in, and I will sup with you and you with me." Heed, I pray you, that tender appeal!

JOSEPH AND NICODEMUS AT THE BURIAL OF JESUS.

"Joseph of Arimathæa, being a disciple of Jesus, but secretly for fear of the Jews, asked of Pilate that he might take away the body of Jesus: and Pilate gave him leave. He came therefore, and took away his body. And there came also Nicodemus, he who at the first came to him by night, bringing a mixture of myrrh and aloes, about a hundred pound weight. So they took the body of Jesus, and bound it in linen cloths with the spices. . . . In the place where he was crucified there was a garden; and in the garden a new tomb wherein was never man yet laid. There . . . . they laid Jesus."—*John* xix. 38-42 (*Revised Version*).

THE great sacrifice was complete. Having perfected his gift of himself as "the Lamb of God," offered for "the sins of the world," Jesus had cried, "It is finished!" As if rebelling against the ingratitude of mankind, the veil of the temple and the sky overhead and the rocks beneath burst forth in expressive sympathy at the stupendous sacrifice. There is an old story of a dumb son who had followed his father to battle. In the midst of the fight, seeing his father had been struck down and was lying on the ground with a sword pointed at his breast, under a sudden impulse of love and fear for his father's life he burst the impediment that had tied his tongue from his birth and cried aloud in exclamations of terror. So at the crucifixion of Christ, when our ungrateful race was silent, the rocks and skies, hitherto dumb, uttered cries of anguish.

This last testimony to the divine mission of the Son of God seems to have had the effect of bringing two distinguished men from their cowardly concealment of faith in Jesus, and causing them to risk everything in showing for him their reverence and their love. One of these men, Joseph of Arimathæa, had been a disciple, we are told, but secretly, for fear of the Jews. He was a member of the national legislature, or Sanhedrin; a rich man, and belonged to the highest and ruling social class; he was also a man of excellent reputation. We are not told how he came to know about Jesus in such a way as to believe on him and love him, while the other public men rejected him; but he seems to have been a man whose mind and heart were open to receive the truth, and from what he had heard and seen of Christ he believed that he was the true Messiah. When the vote was taken in the Sanhedrin, he cast his vote against the condemnation of Jesus; but until after the crucifixion he did not have courage to come out boldly and avow his faith in Christ's divine mission and declare his own love for him. How much he might have done to have won the men of his own station by such avowal we can not tell, but there can be no doubt that his influence, while it would not have saved Christ from crucifixion, would have been a powerful weight in favor of Jesus among the younger men of his own circle. What luster it would have added to his name, what glory to his character, throughout all time if he had thrown his wealth and position generously and bravely into the scale in a courageous effort to win the Jews to Christ! There have been deeds like that. There is a story of a noble sacrifice which was once made to save the life of a king. The tide of battle was against him; he had become separated from his guard and was threatened with immediate death; he was surrounded by his enemies — their swords ringing on his helmet, every one eager to obtain the honor and reward of his capture or death. In that crisis-moment a brave man who loved his king, seeing his danger, spurred his horse into the thick of his enemies, shouting, as he waved his bloody battle-ax above his head, "I am the king!" and thus caught in his own bosom the sharp blades that in a moment would have been buried in his master's flesh. Alas! Joseph missed his greatest opportunity.

The other conspicuous figure at the funeral of Jesus was Nicodemus. He was a man of the same situation in life as Joseph and also a member of the Sanhedrin. He had become very much interested in Christ and in his teachings during the early part of his public ministry. Once his interest had been so deep that he had come to Christ at night and had had a most heart-searching personal conversation with him about the great realities of the spiritual life. He, too, had voted with Joseph against the condemnation of Christ; but, like his rich neighbor, had not had the courage to publicly show his interest in the Savior. Perhaps, as Bishop Walker suggests, he was afraid of the sneers of his fellow-Pharisees, and thought the new religion was not yet reputable enough for the august senators of Judæa to accept. It was well enough for fishermen, "but have any of the scribes or Pharisees believed in his name?" was their query. It is plain from the conversation of the night when Jesus told him "Ye must be born again," that he believed the Savior to be a teacher sent from God. He was no doubt in earnest in seeking for light. Had Christ's religion been popular among the people with whom he associated, he would gladly have become his open disciple; but he could not get the consent of his pride to wait on the teachings of a carpenter from Nazareth, and take his place with common sinners, despised tax-gatherers, and poor fishermen. And so after his night talk with Christ he went away with a sigh. When the Sanhedrin were seeking some excuse to murder Jesus he tried to do something to help the Lord without committing himself as his disciple. He raises a legal question: "Doth our law judge any man before it hear him and know what he doeth?" He did not have the courage to stand up before those bigoted men and say frankly: "I was troubled and ill at ease in my own conscience, and wondered what I ought to do in order to be at peace with God, and I went one night to see this Jesus, and had a frank talk with him; and I tell you, my friends, I have never seen any other man yet who impressed me as he did. He searched my conscience to its very depths. I never shall forget the impression he made upon me when, looking me in the eye with that heart-piercing look of his, he said to me, with the authority of a prophet, 'Except a man be born again, he can not see the kingdom of God.' And I confess to you, brothers, I came away from him that night with the profound conviction that he is a teacher sent from God." What a bombshell that would have been in the midst of their wicked plotting! But poor Nicodemus had not the courage to rise to such heroism, and when some sneering plotter called out to him, in reply to his meek question about the law, "Art thou also of Galilee?" he slunk back into his seat and did not dare utter another word. "That silence is guilt, for it was submission to the act of murder by which the Son of the great God was slain. The want of resolution, the poor amiability which could not thunder its protests against that wrong in the senate chamber of Israel, is as colossal a wickedness in the eyes of high heaven as their voices were who on the day of the Calvary tragedy cried, 'Crucify him! Crucify him!' The voice that was not brave enough to be heard when by decision it might have averted a crime, was doubly guilty, because it omitted to help when it might save."

But how many there are to-day who are represented by this cowardice of Joseph and Nicodemus —men and women who have been born in a Christian land, have been reared in Christian communities, know well the gracious influence of Christian civilization, have been blessed by the influences of the Christian church all their lives, and yet have never given any open expression of their gratitude to Christ. They are by no means unbelievers; if you ask them, they tell you they wish the church well, they would not put a straw in its way; and yet in this mighty struggle which Jesus Christ and his friends are making to capture the world for righteousness and liberate lost souls from the tyranny of sin, they refuse to give their open friendship and loyal service to the Christ whom they believe to be their only hope of salvation. There are many members of the church who stand practically in this ungrateful position. Their names are on the church roll and they are counted in its statistics; yet whenever the church is marshaled for battle against the world and the flesh and the devil, they are conspicuous by their absence. If it is a gala occasion, they will be there; but in great emergencies, when the pastor and earnest souls are seeking to hurl the latent Christian power of the church as a battering-ram against evil, or to send it forth seeking after the wandering and the lost, winning them to God and salvation, they can not be counted upon. God help us, that we may not belong to that class! An outspoken, daring friendship for Jesus Christ on the part of its members is what, above all else, the church needs and must have to give it the full measure of its divine power.

But when on that awful day of crucifixion the rocks were rent, the sun veiled its face, the very graves were opened and the dead came forth, and dumb nature groaned in agony at the death of Jesus—then the lethargy of Joseph and Nicodemus was broken, and with one accord, throwing prudence to the winds and daring everything, they came to do what they could to show, even at this late hour, their love for Christ, the expression of which they had denied him during his life. We can not tell whether they had talked it over together or not. It seemed to be just the overflowing of their broken hearts. Chaplain McCabe tells about a superannuated Methodist preacher, who was an officer thirty years ago and more at Missionary Ridge, who amid the rain of bullets and bursting of shell shouted to his soldiers, "Come on! Come on!" and they followed him in a glorious charge up the mountain. General Grant, who was present and looking on, said to General Sheridan: "Did you order that charge?" "No," said Sheridan; "they are doing it themselves." In that awful hour after the Savior's death the repressed, but now irrepressible, admiration and love of Joseph and Nicodemus for the Savior burst forth, and they came to do what they could for their Lord. Joseph went and begged of Pilate the body. He had to hurry or it would have been thrown to the ravens and the jackals. I can imagine I hear him saying to himself, as with an aching heart and a lump in his throat he hurries through the city to see Pilate: "It is the only thing left for me to do. Oh, that he was only alive again that I might put my arms around his neck, if only for once, and look in those dear eyes and say, 'Jesus, I love thee!' It is too late for that now, but perhaps I can save his poor body from indignity." And so he hurries on and gets permission to take the precious casket from which the loving spirit had flown. In the mean time Nicodemus, broken-hearted, too, at his ingratitude in the past, is searching the shops for the finest linen and the most precious myrrh and aloes, that he may assist Joseph in the last loving tribute they can pay the Lord. They meet at the cross, and with John the beloved disciple and the Marys they tenderly take down the poor wounded body of Jesus. They wash away the dust and blood, anoint the body with the fragrant spices, wrap it in clean linen, and then that little funeral procession wends its way into the garden to Joseph's new tomb, which, after the fashion of the rich, he had prepared to receive his own body when death should have wrought its work upon it. Ah, now that these men have broken the seal of their secrecy, and given their hearts' love unreservedly to the Savior, there is nothing too good for Jesus. The finest linen, the most precious spices, the new tomb built for the rich—everything that is best is at the disposal of the Lord when once the broken and contrite heart has crowned him Lord over all.

Let me plead with you who, like Joseph and Nicodemus, have been delaying your open espousal of the Savior. Let me assure you that every day you stay away from Christ, refusing him your open friendship and your outspoken love, you are laying up for yourselves reasons for regret. I have heard many thousands of people testify concerning their Christian experience. I have never yet heard one testify that he was sorry he had given his heart to Christ when young. But, on the other hand, I have heard multitudes deeply regret that they had hardened their hearts against him so long. I have never met a man or a woman that came to Christ in childhood who did not rejoice over it in later life and regard it as the wisest possible step that could have been taken. This universal testimony ought certainly to be of weight with you, and I urge you that you do not delay longer. "To-day is the day of salvation!"

THE POWER OF THE RISEN CHRIST.

"He is not here; for he is risen, even as he said. Come, see the place where the Lord lay."—*Matt.* xxviii. 6 (*Revised Version*).

THAT was a "Black Friday" indeed to those mourning friends of Jesus when, late in the afternoon, they laid his wounded and broken body in Joseph's new tomb. Black Friday has been changed to Good Friday because of the halo of glory thrown around it by after events. But to the disciples that afternoon was dark and hopeless. A dear friend whom they had loved with all the tenderness of their hearts, and whom they had hoped would be the Redeemer of their suffering land, had been slain. Altho Jesus had again and again sought to give them the idea of the resurrection, and the promise that he would break asunder the bonds of death, they had not been able to grasp the great significance of his words. They mourned him as one dead and lost to them. How long that Saturday or Sabbath must have seemed to their sore and weary hearts! But at last it drags itself by, and as the first flush of dawn comes over the hills and across the city, the women who so loyally and faithfully kept their vigil by the cross, and followed with Joseph and Nicodemus and John to the burial of their master, brought with them precious spices and came again to the tomb, to pay a farther tribute of love to the body of Jesus.

But great things have been transpiring about that tomb since last they saw it. Spurgeon says that when the sacrifice of Christ was finished, and he had paid the ransom price to redeem us from under the law, that price was presented before the Father's judgment seat. He looked at it and was content. But as it was a solemn matter, it was not hurried over. Three days were taken, that the ransom price might be counted out and its value fully estimated. The angels looked and admired. The "spirits of the just" came and examined it, and wondered, and were delighted. The very devils in hell could not say one word against the sacrifice of Christ. The three days passed away, the atonement was accepted. Then the angel came from heaven; swift as the lightning-flash he descended from the spheres of the blessed into this lower earth, and he came into the prison-house in which the Savior's body slept—lying there as a hostage for his people. The angel came and spoke to the keeper of the prison, one called Grim Death, and said to him, "Let that Captive go free." Death was sitting on his throne of skulls, with a huge iron key at his girdle of iron; and he laughed, and said, "Aha! thousands and thousands of the race of Adam have passed the portals of this prison-house, but none of them have ever been delivered. That key has been once turned in its wards of destiny, and no mortal power can ever turn it back again, and draw the bolts from their resting-places." Then the angel showed to him heaven's own warrant, and Death turned pale. The angel grasped the key, unlocked the prison door, and stepped in. There slept the royal Captive—the divine Hostage. And the angel cried, "Arise, thou Sleeper. Put off thy garments of death. Shake thyself from the dust and put on thy beautiful garments." The Master arose. He unwound the napkin, and laid it by itself. He took off his grave-clothes and laid them by themselves, to show he was in no hurry, that all was done legally and therefore orderly. So was the Master set at liberty—by heaven's own officer, who came down from heaven to give him just liberty—God's proof that the atonement was complete.

And so when these mourning women came toward the tomb that morning, wondering among themselves who should roll away the stone for them, they did not know that it was an empty grave to which they were coming. And how astonished they were, when they drew near, to see the stone rolled back from the door of the sepulcher and on it the angel of the Lord. But the angel comforts them by saying: "Fear not ye: for I know that ye seek Jesus, which hath been crucified. He is not here; for he is risen, even as he said. Come, see the place where the Lord lay. And go quickly, and tell his disciples, he is risen from the dead; and lo, he goeth before you into Galilee; there shall ye see him; lo, I have told you." "And they departed quickly from the tomb with fear and great joy, and ran to bring his disciples word. And behold, Jesus met them, saying, All hail. And they came and took hold of his feet, and worshiped him. Then saith Jesus unto them, Fear not; go tell my brethren that they depart into Galilee, and there shall they see me."

There is no fact in human history more thoroughly established by credible testimony than the resurrection of Jesus. Paul, who was learned in the law and who had the legal temperament very strongly marked, summed up the evidence in the most careful manner and calls attention to the fact that Christ appeared to Mary Magdalene, to Cephas, to the eleven, to five hundred brethren at one time, to James, again to the eleven, and, last of all, to Paul himself. Such a variety of appearances, such a diversity of revelations of himself, the fact that he ate and drank with them, on some occasions carried on long conversations with them, and all this extending through forty days, leaves no ground for reasonable doubt. It is absurd to say that these men were deceived. They knew the Lord Jesus by constant intimate association with him for years. Was the mother that bore him likely to be deceived? Was Thomas the kind of man that was likely to be duped? And yet before the nail-prints in his hands, and the wound in his side, he doubted no more and cried aloud, "My Lord and my God!" Five hundred people at one time were not likely to be deceived, and Paul, one of the hard-headed men of his time, throughout his life made the resurrection of Jesus Christ the foundation-stone of his ministry. And every one of this inner circle of the disciples of Jesus not only continued to preach the fact of the resurrection while they lived, but they endured all manner of persecution because of it, and they suffered martyr deaths with joy because of this glorious faith.

It is doubtful if any of us fully appreciate how much light and glory has been thrown upon human living by the diffusion of the knowledge of the resurrection of Jesus and the consequent promise of blissful immortality to all that believe in him among the minds and hearts of the race. Dr. Kane, the Arctic traveler, tells us that when the six months of darkness in which he and his men had been held in the far north had at last begun to pass, and every day for a little longer time the sun began to look above the horizon, to stand in that gracious light was like bathing in perfumed waters. A darkness worse than that, brought about by sin and the consequent fear of death, had been hanging like an Arctic midnight over the race of mankind. But Jesus came and went down into the grave, and burst asunder the bands of death, and came up out of the grave, the Sun of Righteousness, rising on our poor benighted world with healing in his beams.

To all of us who love Christ how much this precious faith means when we are called from time to time to earthly separation from our loved ones! For it is the resurrection of Christ that has discovered to the eyes of our faith that summer-land of immortality where we hope to meet those who have fallen asleep in Jesus. In "The Ministry of Bereavement" a recent writer has given us a most touching fable, illustrating divine truth: A little boy was heart-broken because his sweet young sister was dying. The child had heard that if one could secure but a single leaf from the tree of life that grew in the garden of God, every illness could be healed. No one had dared to attempt the quest, however, for the way was very hard and a great angel guarded the gate of the garden against mortals. The child loved his suffering sister so well that he resolved to find the garden and plead with the angel for the healing leaf. So over rock and moor and hill he went, until in the golden sunset the beautiful gate appeared, and he tearfully made his request to the angelic sentinel. "None can enter this garden," replied the angel, "but those children for whom the King has sent, and he has not called for you." "But one leaf," pleaded the child, "one little leaf to heal my sister. The King will not be angry. He can not wish that my sister should suffer so and die and leave me all alone. Have pity, great angel, and hear my prayer." The angel looked down on the little suppliant with deep love and pity, and said: "The King has sent my brother, the Angel of Death, to bring your sister to himself. If you are allowed to keep her, will you promise me to see that she shall never again lie tossing on a sick-bed in pain?" "How can I?" said the wondering child. "Not even the wisest physicians can keep us from sickness always." "Then will you promise me that she shall never be unhappy, nor do wrong, nor suffer sorrows, nor be spoken to or treated harshly?" asked the angel. "Not if I can help it," answered the child, bravely; "but perhaps even I could not always make her happy." "Then," replied the angel, tenderly, "the world where you would keep her must be a sad place. Now I will open the gate just a little, and you may look into the garden for a moment, and then, if you still wish it, I will ask the King for a leaf from the tree of life, to heal your sister." And the astonished child looked in where grew the living tree, and where flowed the crystal river, and where stood the bright mansions, and where walked and talked immortal children under a light more beautiful than that of the sun, and with friends more loving than those of earth, and where love and blessing reigned forever. He looked until his eyes widened in surprise and glowed with joy, and, turning to the angel, he said, softly: "I will not ask for the leaf now. There is no place so beautiful as this; there is no friend so kind as the Angel of Death." So the child turned back under the stars that shone now like celestial eyes upon him. And as he went a ray of holy light fell upon his path, and wonderful music, such as he never before heard, filled his ears, and he knew that the golden gate had opened to receive his sister. And it was so that when he saw her silent form upon her little bed at home, he was comforted.

How many of us have been comforted in like manner! And if I now speak to any whose present life is robbed of much of its joy and beauty because of the horrible fear of death that hangs over you, I preach you the glorious Gospel of Him who brought life and immortality to light. "The sting of death is sin." I preach you a Savior who has been victorious over both sin and death. Jesus Christ came to destroy the works of the devil, and he is able to blot sin out of your heart, to forgive the sins of your life, to give you victory over sin, and thus by removing the cause to drive away the fear of death and fill your heart with the radiant sunshine of an immortal hope.

The Christ who has been victorious over the mightiest enemy of the human race is the conquering Christ in whose strength we may be more powerful than all that can be against us. By his divine aid we may get victory over every sin that has held us in bondage. One of the sisters connected with the West End Mission in London, two years ago this winter had the following remarkable experience: It was a dark, cold, foggy night in December. A message had come from one of the slums in the West End, "Please come and see me at once." The good woman found her way with great difficulty to the address given. An untidy landlady answered her knock, carrying in her hand two inches of tallow candle.

"Does Mrs. T. live here?"

"Yes," she replied, ungraciously.

"Could I see her?"

"Umph! you'll be silly enough if you do, I sha'n't go with you."

"But she has sent for me, and I should like to see her."

"Well, as I said before, if you're silly enough; but you'll go by yourself. I've seen too much of her already; I left her dead drunk an hour or two ago."

"Come," said the sister, as cheerfully as she could, "you can't leave me to go up-stairs alone, a stranger; just show me the room, and then you can leave me."

"I've said I wouldn't," replied the woman, obstinately, "and I don't want to."

"Never mind, go along," and pushing her gently, the sister got her up the stairs. The landlady opened the door, lifted up her candle, and found another, which she lighted.

It was a terrible place which was revealed by the dim candle-light. Every piece of furniture in the room was broken; on the unsteady table stood a few unwashed pots, and in one corner an un-

THE POWER OF THE RISEN CHRIST. 107

tidy bed, upon which lay a young woman not twenty-five years of age, half dressed, with long black hair hanging over her shoulders, her voice hoarse and thick, her mind dazed by drink.

"There," said the landlady, "that's a pretty sight; a young woman with as good a husband as ever lived, who has forgiven her over and over again; but it's come to the end now, he'll have no more of it, and out she goes to-morrow. I'll leave you to her." She banged the door, and the sister thought she was gone. Putting her head in again she said, "Oh, sister, I'll just tell you her last trick: she's pawned nearly everything in the place, and lately she's gone out tidily dressed and come back without frock or bonnet or boots—all has gone for drink."

After delivering that information with great vehemence, she went away and left them alone. For a few moments there was silence, in which the Christian woman lifted up her heart to God for help; then a thin, unwashed hand was slipped into hers, and an unsteady, thick voice said:

"Schister! schister! Give me some gin; gin, gin, I want; give me some gin!"

"It is gin that has brought you to this."

"Yes, but I can't live without it."

"Then you had better die."

She had brought three bottles of gin in with

her. The sister made her tell her where they were. She put them out of the room, and as the woman began to grow sober she sat down and listened to her story. The wretched woman had married four years before; she had been accustomed to a busy, active life, and having little to do had become dull and at times depressed. She found a glass of wine a great enlivener, and quite unconsciously became a slave to it, until, step by step, she had sunk to this awful depth of degradation. Her husband had forgiven and endured for four years; he had done all that love could devise, and that day was the last he would live with her.

When she reached this point, she put out her arms pleadingly, and cried with heartrending agony: "Save me, sister, save me! I long to be free; I long to give it up. I have tried hundreds and hundreds of times. Sister, save me; there is no one else in the world to help me. Save me!"

"I can't save you," said the sister; "but there is One who can. Jesus Christ came into this world on purpose to save you. He is stronger than any sin; yes, stronger than drink. He will save you if you will let him."

> "There is a time, we know not when,
>   A point, we know not where,
> That marks the destiny of men,
>   To glory or despair."

That point had come in this life. This devoted Christian woman felt that if this wretched creature was ever to be saved it must be accomplished that night.

"How can I let him save me?" said the now thoroughly aroused woman.

"By never touching drink again as long as you live."

"But I wish I could give it up. I can't."

"You can't; but when Christ is in you—when Christ is part of you—you can."

A gleam of hope was beginning to dawn in her sin-marked face, and very tenderly she asked, "Sister, will you ask him to help me?"

Then that earnest Christian woman prayed as seldom before. And the poor woman prayed for herself; beginning timidly at first, but as she prayed, gathering hope and faith; and there, in that desolate place, where sin has wrought such riot and havoc, the resurrected and conquering Christ broke the snare of the devil.

And tho there was many a temptation and struggle afterward, for two years that woman has come off more than conqueror through Him that loved her and gave himself for her. Her husband's heart is glad, her home is happy, and she is greatly blessed of God in rescuing others who are lost as she was until Jesus found her.

I urge upon you all that there is no case too hard for the Christ, who has won the victory over sin and the grave. He is the mighty conqueror forever.

THOMAS, THE DOUBTER, RECLAIMED.

"Then saith he to Thomas, Reach hither thy finger, and see my hands; and reach hither thy hand, and put it into my side: and be not faithless, but believing. Thomas answered and said unto him, My Lord and my God. Jesus saith unto him, Because thou hast seen me, thou hast believed: blessed are they that have not seen, and yet have believed."—*John* xx. 27-29 (*Revised Version*).

WE do not know why Thomas was absent from the meeting of the disciples on the first occasion of Christ's appearance to them after his resurrection. It is quite probable, however, that he was not with them because he had fallen into a state of religious despondency. His faith that they were to see anything more of the Lord was not very strong, and therefore he stayed away from the meetings. I have heard that excuse given in all seriousness by some good people during this very series of meetings. If Thomas had expected that the Lord was going to meet with them, nothing could have kept him away. The reason he is with them at this time is, no doubt, because he has been so influenced by the testimony of the disciples that Jesus had appeared unto them and broken bread with them on the former occasion, that he has determined not to miss another chance. He would not receive their testimony, and declared unequivocally to them that unless he should put his finger in the nail-prints in the Savior's hands, and touch the wound in his side, he would never believe in the resurrection. Yet, notwithstanding all these statements, no doubt honestly made, the joyous enthusiasm of the other disciples had its effect on Thomas, and while he thought they were deluded, and had only seen an unsubstantial vision, he could not help but feel that they were a good deal happier than he was, and that something very remarkable must have happened to lift the terrible load of gloom off their hearts and fill them with such joyous assurance that their Master had triumphed over death and was at that very moment a living personage. Whatever may have been the working of Thomas' mind, he had evidently come to the conclusion that in the future he would stick close to the rest of the friends of Jesus, and if anything good did happen to them he would be on hand for a share in it. Thomas never came to a wiser conclusion than that.

In this conduct of Thomas and the reason for his changing his action there is suggested a valuable lesson for us all. If the Lord appears to you in the house of God, and blesses you with a consciousness of his presence and love, tell it abroad wherever you go, sound the good news to everybody you see. No other advertisement will draw to the church so many people who need to find the Lord as the testimony of glad hearts that have seen him and been blessed by him.

In this respect Christianity differs from anything else in the world. In worldly affairs, if a man finds a chance to make a large sum of money by a certain investment he is as silent as the grave about it until he has everything completed. Over in Colorado or Idaho, or up in Alaska, where prospectors are always out among the mountains seeking after veins of gold-bearing quartz, if the lucky miner comes upon a rich find he does not go talking about it to every other prospector he meets; but as far as possible he hides every indication of his good fortune and turns other prospectors off on another trail until he has made sure of his title to the newly discovered mine. That is the selfish standard of the world, but thank God it need not be so and is not so in the higher realm of spiritual treasure. The other disciples were none the less glad because they let Thomas know about the joyous fact of the Savior's triumphant conquest over the grave. Indeed, their gladness was largely increased by this generosity. Thomas, the doubter, the man in the blues, the grouty pessimist, was very poor company, and his gloomy face threw a shadow over all their joy and faith. But when they had stirred Thomas up enough to make him come to the meetings again, and the Lord had appeared to them a second time, Thomas, having seen him himself and having had all his doubts dispelled, found his face shortened by half and the gloom all gone. Joy and peace beamed from his strong countenance and the joy of all the others was multiplied. So it is that the conversion of any man in the community adds to the heavenliness of that spiritual climate which is constantly making the world a sweeter and brighter place to live in. If you want to add to your own spiritual joy there is no way you can so surely accomplish it as to bring some one else into the enjoyment of Christ.

In this picture we are studying there is another suggestion that is exceedingly comforting to our hearts—the gentleness and patient condescension of Jesus in specially singling out Thomas and lovingly meeting his doubts and using every method possible to dissipate them forever. The whole history of God's dealings with the world is in harmony with the divine gentleness illustrated in Christ's loving-kindness toward Thomas. Jesus Christ manifests to us the heart of God. As Dr. George W. Cooke has recently said, Jesus helps us to see that God is so like man that his heart may go out to us in every temptation, sorrow, and sin, and with a perfection which brings the strength of God to our help in any time of weakness or infirmity. He enables us to sing, with all confidence,

> "When other helpers fail, and comforts flee,
> Help of the helpless, O abide with me!"

When all other hopes have been dashed to the ground God remains to the open heart with his peace, benediction, and love. When the need is great and despair rises within us, as it did in the mind and heart of poor Thomas, God does not go away, but remains near and precious to the broken and contrite spirit. Even when we have tried to go our own way and failed, God does not reproach us or cast us off; but by tender revelations of himself, by gentle promise and the inspiration of hope, he quiets our restless spirits, and heals them with a deepened trust. We all need some heart to lean upon in which there is both strength and tenderness. Jesus Christ is, to every one that will open his heart to receive him, such a heart, that will never fail us, that never scorns us, that deals with us as gently as a mother with her child, that stoops to our own level, and in stooping lifts us up into a life more beautiful and precious than anything we could have ever known without his tender love and sympathy. Christ has made God real to us. He has been to us the face of God shining upon us in tenderness and peace.

But Jesus has not only revealed to us the heart of God, a heart that is equal to all our needs for sympathy and love; he has also revealed to us God's justice, truth, and holiness in such a way that we are able to understand them and rejoice in them. It was of little value that men should have thought of God as beautiful like Apollo, or possessed of huge strength like Titan. But Christ, coming into the midst of our human life, living the God-life before our eyes, has helped us to a larger conception that brings together loveliness and power in a being as gentle as he is majestic. Since we have seen Jesus walking the streets of our common life, going about doing good, it is possible for us to think of God as perfect holiness, without stain of impurity or defect, and yet capable of walking with sinners and laying his hands upon them with a gentleness which wins away all their love for that which is evil.

Since Christ has lived in the world and become the most vital character in all human history, revealing to us "God manifest in the flesh," God is no longer to the believing soul mere will, intellect, or holiness; he is not force, power, or law; he is a living, loving, saving personality, a friend we can lean upon, a Master who teaches us the word of life, a loving heart that trusts us and is trusted by us. He turns not from us when we forget him, but seeks to win us back again with loving patience. Though we forget him and revile him, and harden our hearts against his love, he grows even more anxious for our good, if that be possible, and tenderly continues to knock at the locked doors of our hearts.

It has never been very difficult for thoughtful people to conceive of God as masterful, powerful, sublime, and omnipotent. It has been more difficult to realize him as being holy and perfect and yet close enough to us to be a real helper and guide. No other ideal than that of the perfect love incarnate in Jesus Christ could ever satisfy these opposite needs. But love as we see it in the Man of Nazareth tenderly conversing with Thomas the doubter, is at once strong and tender, full of compassion and nobility. The highest ideal possible to the human mind is revealed to us in Jesus Christ, who in giving himself for us, as our ransom, finds in the very gift of himself his highest satisfaction. Oliver Wendell Holmes beautifully sings of the love divine,

> "That stoops to share
> Our sharpest pang, our bitterest tear."

It is this "love divine" which we find in Jesus Christ. In him we see revealed the God who will give himself for the world, who will suffer, who will love and forgive when reviled, and who did not stop short even at the cruel cross to ransom us from condemnation and make it possible for poor sinful men to be brought back to purity and heaven.

The story is told of a heathen who was translating for one of the missionaries a little book on the way of salvation, and when it came to the place where it was told that Christ's disciples are allowed to call God "Father," he was filled with the greatest wonder. It was almost impossible for him to believe it. Could it be true that the terrible Being whom he had often thought of as a horrible monster having a thousand hands, and in every hand a knife stained with human blood, was indeed a tender, loving father? Filled with joy at this new revelation, he begged of the missionary, "Let me write 'They will be permitted to kiss the feet of God.'"

My dear friends, I preach to you this tender, pleading, sympathetic Christ who does not desire that any should perish, but whose heart is seeking after you with the highest love the world has ever seen. Do not, I pray you, harden your hearts against his sympathy and his tender seeking. Is he not just the friend you need? So yield your hearts to him this very hour that afterward you shall be able to say, as David did so long ago (and no doubt Thomas has been joining with him in it for more than eighteen centuries around the throne of God), "Thy gentleness hath made me great."

Dr. Dickinson, of Orange, preaching on this grateful saying of David the other day, well says that there are two things we ought to thank God for as Christians as we look back. One is that he did not let our sins go unpunished, and the other that he revealed his pardoning grace, and held before our tearful vision the hope of high achievement still. You remember Nathan's words to David, when by his faithful preaching he had convicted him of dreadful sin. He exclaimed, "Thou art the man." But the tenderness of God is revealed in Nathan's words immediately after, when, seeing the penitent's tears, he said, "The Lord also hath put away thy sin." Before Peter's downfall Christ revealed to him his coming shame and disgrace, but immediately after told him that he would rise again, and a great work be committed to him. It is this divine Savior, strong in almighty power, but equally as strong in infinite tenderness and sympathy, that I beg you to accept as your Savior. The character of an eminent English lord was well summed up a few years ago at a London club, by a well-known writer, who, on the nobleman's leaving somewhat early, remarked to a friend: "I have many friends who would be kind to me in distress, but only one who would be equally kind to me in disgrace, and he has just left the room." Such friends are rare, but Jesus Christ is a friend like that. He is worthy to be, in your heart of hearts, this very hour, crowned Lord over all.

Do you ask me how you shall do this? My reply is, just take him at his word. Sandy Bates, a little Fresh Air boy, from his slum life of friendlessness was sent out into the country for a short breathing spell, and his first Sunday there was one glad song of delight. He was in a Sunday-school class that day, and the teacher told the simple story of redeeming love. Eagerly the poor boy listened to the oft-told tale of the Babe cradled in the manger, of the sorrowful life and cruel death and the glorious resurrection of the Christ. The old, old story was wonderfully new to the boy, and the passage of Scripture which he read and memorized that day made it plain to him. The week that followed was the brightest Sandy had ever known. The next time the Sunday-school teacher saw him, Sandy bubbled over with the fact that he now belonged to Jesus. "Are you sure?" asked the teacher, fearful that the child did not understand what he was saying. "Just as sure as that my name is Sandy Bates," was the instant response. "How do you know that he has accepted you?" urged the teacher. "Why, I just took him at his word; for when he told me to come unto him, I knew he meant it, and I am sure he will not go back on his word," replied Sandy, with glistening eyes.

Oh, my friend, throw your pride to the winds, and with the simplicity of a little child find in Jesus Christ forgiveness for your sins and peace for your weary heart!

SIMON PETER, THE FISHERMAN.

"Simon Peter saith unto them, I go a fishing."—John xxi. 3 (*Revised Version*).

PETER had been a fisherman from his youth up. His father was a fisherman before him. He was down by the sea engaged, with his brothers, mending their nets when Christ first called him to be his disciple. The Savior came along and stopped to look on the vigorous young men for a moment, though he had undoubtedly had some acquaintance with them before, and said to them, "Come, follow me, and I will make you fishers of men." They had been following Jesus, learning the art of service from the Great Teacher. But the marvelous transactions of the past few weeks had left them in a wondering state of uncertainty. The arrest and trial of Jesus, his cruel death on the cross, and his triumphant resurrection from the dead, with his after-appearances, had led them through a series of emotions that had stirred their hearts to their profoundest depths. While these later days were in a sense glad days, because they were now assured of the triumph of their Master over the grave, they were yet days of bewilderment. One afternoon, as the evening came on, Simon Peter started up and said to the rest of the little company, "I go a fishing." And several of the others declared their intention of going with him. It was not that they had the slightest idea of turning from their discipleship to Christ, but that for the moment they did not know what to do, and Peter solved the problem of occupying their minds and relaxing the strained tension on their nerves by going back for the night to their old calling. Whenever Christ should have need of them, they were ready at his call. They fished all night and had poor luck, for through all its hours they caught nothing. When the morning came Jesus stood on the shore, and called out to them, inquiring as to their fortune in the fishing, and if they had yet any meat, and they answered him, "No." Then the Lord directs where they shall cast the net, and on their obeying his word it is filled with fish.

This is not the first time Jesus had given them directions in regard to the fishing. On another occasion Christ borrowed Peter's boat for a pulpit, when the people thronged about him in great multitudes. In order to get a better chance to speak to them he had Peter pull out a little from land, and there he preached to them the word of life.

When the sermon was over the Savior asked Peter to go out into deep water and let down the nets for a draught. It so happened that it was a morning just after another such a night's bad fishing, and Peter said to the Lord that they had been out all night and had not taken anything, "But," he added, "nevertheless, at thy word I will let down the nets." Dr. McKenzie says that Christ was testing Peter's heart at this time to see whether he was ready to obey his Master. If this be so, Peter stood the test well. He was ready to take the risk of being called a fool by the people and his fisher friends, who watched his strange proceedings from the shore. And the only reason which he can give to himself or Jesus is, "At thy word."

This is the appropriate motto for every Christian life. People who have not come to know Jesus Christ can not understand this attitude of the Christian. But every one who has become acquainted with Jesus finds that a simple, childlike obedience to him marvelously simplifies life. There is nothing more certain in Christian experience than that the habit of obeying Christ makes life wondrously calm and clear. The habit of disobedience to the known will of Jesus makes men deaf and blind, and it is not long before that will is unheard and unseen. The very first characteristic of the successful Christian fisherman must be simple and genuine obedience to Christ. The fact that we are ourselves true to the core to the Christ whom we proclaim to others, makes our teaching tell; it gives an accent of sincerity, of certainty, in dealing with others which that person whose exhortations are haunted and made hollow by memories of disobedience can never have. If we are going to be "fishers of men" we must make "At thy word" the working motto of our lives.

A great many professed Christian people find it impossible to bring others into the kingdom because they are not really in the kingdom themselves. There is a vast difference between an intellectual assent to the great doctrines of Christianity, and an amiable admiration of the person and character of Jesus Christ, and the new birth which Jesus declares to be the condition of entrance into the kingdom of God. This is too serious a matter to be deceived about. Do not let the fact that you have been reared in a Christian family, that you have grown up in the Sunday-school, or that your name is on the church record, deceive you for a moment as to your real condition before God. Ask yourself, I entreat you, heart-searching questions. Are you conscious that your sins are forgiven through faith in the Lord Jesus Christ? Are you living a prayerful life, having fellowship and communion with Jesus Christ? Are you seeking above all things that your life shall be pleasing to him? Are you burdened for the souls of others? If not, do not let any false pride keep you from the Mercy Seat; but by sincere penitence and faith seek the Lord with your whole heart. Then, as Christ said to Peter, when you are yourself converted you will be able to be of help to your brethren.

Rev. Arthur Finlayson tells an interesting story of a soldier during the War of the Rebellion. He was a strong young man and was ordered on ambulance duty. He had to carry the wounded from the field of battle. At Chancellorsville the ground was strewn with all sorts of things which the men flung away so as not to be cumbered in the fight. While the soldier was helping to carry away the wounded, he picked up a little book from the trampled road. He put it in his pocket, as he had no time to see what it was. Soon after he came to a wounded man, and was about to carry him off the field to the hospital, but the surgeon said it was useless, as the man was dying. Presently the dying soldier turned his eyes on the healthy man, and as he did so he gasped, "Pray for me; I am dying; pray for me!" The soldier in attendance was a brave young fellow and very anxious to help his dying comrade, but he could only with shame stammer out: "I can not; I don't pray for myself!" "But," pleaded the other in a low moan, "you must pray for me; I am dying." The young soldier was in deep distress. For the first time for years he wanted to pray. What could he do? In his trouble he thought of the book he had picked up. What was it? He drew it from his pocket. It was a copy of "The Soldier's Prayer-Book," put out by some ministers in Philadelphia. In his despair the young man opened it, and found, to his joy, on the first torn and muddy page, a *prayer for a dying soldier*. The strong, healthy fellow uncovered his head, and with solemn feelings reverently read the prayer for his dying comrade. The Holy Spirit seemed to bless the words to the man's comfort and soon after he peacefully breathed his last. The young soldier was speedily called to attend to other wounded comrades, but he never forgot that death-scene. He felt so ashamed that, tho his duty was to attend the sick and wounded, he could be of no use to a dying soldier. He learned the great value of prayer, and became convinced that a man who can not pray is powerless in the battle of life. He was afterward taken captive and carried to a prison in Richmond. Away from the excitement of the battle-field, the Spirit of God visited him. He saw that his past life had been full of sin; he had lived without prayer. He was filled with distress, and in the solitude of the prison he raised his heart and voice to God. He found the value and the power of prayer. He became a changed man, and could pray with his fellow-soldiers and lead them to Jesus. The news was speedily sent home to his praying wife, and great was her joy to find that her husband had become a praying Christian. But though rejoicing in the light of the Gospel, he never forgot the day when he was obliged to say with shame to a dying comrade, "I can not pray!"

Put the question to yourself. What could you do in a case like that? If you were calling on some of your acquaintances and you were to find them in great distress about their soul's salvation, and they were to ask you to pray for them then and there, are you so living a life of prayer that it would come natural and easy for you to do it? Or would you have to sit there shamed and humbled before them and say, "I can not pray!"

There is another point that is equally important to the Christian who is called to be a fisherman for Jesus Christ (and that is a call which comes to every Christian in the world). It is that we shall live such lives that the people who know us would in times of trouble or in times of anxiety about their salvation have so much faith in the genuineness of our religion that they would naturally seek us out and ask us to pray for and with them. That is a question of infinite seriousness which it would be well for every one of us to put to our inmost soul: "Am I living such a life that the people who know me and are acquainted with my business relations, with my conduct in society, with my sorrows and my pleasures, with the tone of my conversation and the things which interest me most, can not help but believe that I am so personally acquainted with Jesus Christ, and have the welfare of his kingdom so on my heart, that in any time of great emergency when they wanted the sympathy of a sincere Christian and such an one to pray for them they would naturally come to me?" That is a question that will go to the very core of your being. If, after serious thought and prayerful, heart-searching meditation, you can humbly and gratefully answer it in the affirmative, then there is no person on earth or in heaven who has a greater right or a greater cause to be thankful and glad than yourself. But if, on the other hand, the question shames you and you stand abashed before it, and you are conscious that your life has been so indifferent and careless of the claims of Jesus, that it has been so prayerless, so given up to earthly things, that people who would ask your advice about many other things would never dream of coming to you to ask you to pray for them in the agony of repentance or the awful emergency of the dying hour, then I beg you to humble yourself before the truth of God.

I fear that many people make very light excuses for themselves for not giving more self-denying effort to save the unconverted who are about them. They average themselves alongside of other professed Christians who do not do any better than they. What folly is that! As if anybody else's failure could make our own the less terrible! Our obligation is to do our very best, without reference to what others may do or not do.

I have just been reading a wonderful story of how Edward Spencer, the brother of Dr. Spencer of the Methodist Church Extension Society, saved seventeen lives in the awful wreck of the *Lady Elgin* on Lake Michigan in 1860. It was a terrible wreck. Out of four hundred passengers, only thirty came through the breakers alive; and of these young Spencer saved seventeen. He was never a very strong young man, but he had been brought up on the banks of the Mississippi River, and was so skilful a swimmer that he was almost as much at home in the water as on the land. With a rope tied around his waist in order that his body might be recovered in case he should be killed by the floating wreckage, for six hours he went backward and forward saving human lives. It was a wonderful day's work. The last person saved that day was a man who was coming ashore in a difficult part of the surf, where the bank was high and precipitous. Any one reaching the shore there would be pounded to death on the steep bank. Those who came to this part of the surf were absolutely lost, as it seemed more than a man's life was worth to save them. Young Spencer saw this man, with one arm clinging to a piece of wreck, and in the other arm what was supposed to contain silver plate, or a bag of gold, or some other precious thing wrapped up in a bit of clothing. A sudden lift of the waves brought the man and the bit of wreckage to which he clung into full view, and there streamed out from the bundle the tresses of a woman's hair. Then Spencer knew that the man was attempting to save his wife, and, although already greatly worn, he said to those about him: "Cost what it may, I will save that man or die in the attempt." He ran down the beach, following the retreating wave, knelt down as closely as possible to the sand, and let the return wave pound him. When next seen he was far out in the water. He swam to the piece of raft to which the two were clinging. When within six or eight feet of them, the man cried out: "Save my wife! Save my wife!"

The brave young swimmer said: "Yes, I will save your wife and you, too." Fastening his hands in their clothing at the back of their necks, he said: "I can sustain you in the water, but you must swim for your lives and mine. We must push up northward to get beyond this dangerous surf if we are to be saved at all." To the joy of the on-looking spectators he came safely to shore with both the unfortunates for whom he had so bravely imperiled his life. The daily papers were full of his praises. The illustrated papers of New York and London contained his picture; but when he was alone with his brother in their own room, he fastened his great hungry eyes on him and said: "Tell me the truth, Will; everybody praises me. Tell me the truth. Did I fail to do my best?" He did not ask, "Did I do as well as somebody else?" That went without asking. He did not ask, "Did I do as well as two hundred others?" He did better than that. He did not ask, "Did I do as well as any man on earth?" No, no. He remembered the haggard faces of those who were lost, whom he was not able to save! The question that ran through him like a poisoned dagger as he remembered the three hundred and more who lost their lives in sight of land was, "Did I do my best?"

Dear friends, that is the question that you and

I must put to ourselves at the close of every day. There are so many that are being swept from their moorings by temptation and sin, so many whose vessels are being dashed to pieces, and they float about us within sight of our churches, clinging piteously to their little pieces of broken wreckage, soon to go down in darkness and despair unless somebody is brave enough and big-hearted enough to save them. Let us not be satisfied with measuring ourselves by anybody else, but let the supreme question that rings in our ears in the midst of these priceless opportunities be, "Did I do my best?" Nothing less than that will satisfy us in the dying hour; nothing less than that wil lsatisfy us when we stand before the judgment seat at last.

There is no joy so sweet on earth or in heaven as the joy of bringing home those who have been lost. Our Savior has told us that there is great joy in heaven over one sinner that repents. The story is told of an Arctic traveler who was hunting after beaver while the ice was breaking up. He was far away from human habitations and had no reason to believe that there was a human being within a hundred miles of him. But hearing the ice crack he looked up and suddenly beheld a lost man who had gone mad through hunger and cold and was wading in the icy water. The explorer persuaded the poor man to get into his canoe and made as rapidly as he could for the nearest land. As he drew near to the shore he saw to his astonishment that a great many people were gathered as if waiting for him. All the islanders had been looking for the lost man, and on seeing him approach in the canoe all the bells were rung and the guns were fired, and there was great rejoicing. And the hunter who had brought him back shared in it all, and they showered gifts and thanks upon him and could not do enough for him to express their thanksgiving. If you want to make happiness on earth and in heaven, and lay up treasures that shall endure forever, seek after the wanderer and bring him home to God.

SWIMMING FOR CHRIST.

"That disciple therefore whom Jesus loved saith unto Peter, It is the Lord. So when Simon Peter heard that it was the Lord, he girt his coat about him . . . . and cast himself into the sea."—*John* xxi. 7, 8 (*Revised Version*).

SOME years since Mr. J. K. Nutting painted this picture in a little poem, the very simplicity of which ought to impress the scene most effectively on our minds and hearts:—

Simon Stone, he spied a boat.
   "Oh, here is a boat!" cried Simon Stone.
"I've a mind to try if this boat will float;
   I'll fish a spell, if I go alone."

"Oh, no!" said the rest. "We are going, too."
   "Then jump aboard," said Simon Stone.
They sprang to the boat, a happy crew.
   Wouldn't you like to have counted one?

They rowed and they rowed, they sailed and they sailed;
   "Small luck, small luck," said Simon Stone.
They tried and tried, and they failed and failed,
   Till they ached in every muscle and bone.

They dipped and dipped, and they hauled and hauled;
  "Not a fin for our pains," said Simon Stone.
"Hark!" cried one, for somebody called,
  "Who can be out on the shore alone?"

"Never mind who, pull away, pull away!"
  "Let's give it up," said Simon Stone;
"We have fished all night, we have fished all day.
  Let's quit; I'm going ashore for one."

Then the strange voice called from the shore again.
  "Listen! listen!" said Simon Stone.
And now in the dawn they see him, plain,
  Walking along the shore alone.

"Boys, have you anything there to eat?"
  "Not a fin nor a scale," said Simon Stone;
"Not a crumb of bread, not a morsel of meat,
  Not a thing to offer a hungry one."

"Throw the net to starboard, and then you'll find,"
  Cried the voice. "Let's do it," said Simon Stone.
So they dropped the net with willing mind.
  "Heave, ho! There's a haul," cried every one.

They tugged and they hauled, but they hauled in vain.
  "Let's drag it ashore," said Simon Stone.
So they dragged and dragged with might and main.
  "It's the Lord," spoke softly Cousin John.

"What!" "What!" "What!" cried the rest in the boat.
  "What's that you're saying?" quoth Simon Stone.
"The Lord! Why, here, then, give me my coat."
  In a trice he had it, and had it on.

"Why, what in the world are you going to do?"
"I'm going ashore," said Simon Stone,
As he sprang, without any more ado,
Overboard into the sea alone.

Then the rest, they looked and said with a smile,
"What a man, to be sure, is Simon Stone!
He's up to some queer thing all the while."
"How he loves the Lord!" said Cousin John.

Oh! he swam for life, and he swam for love,
Till he stood on the shore with the Lord alone.
Who knows, but he and the Lord above,
How the Lord spake sweet to Simon Stone?

. . . .

Then tell me if ever you loved like him,
If ever you felt like Simon Stone:
"Whether I run or fly or swim,
I must have a word with the Lord alone."

I think it is very suggestive that John was the first one to know that it was the Lord. We have no reason to believe that John was as quick-minded as Peter, or that he was as learned a man as Nathanael; but he loved the Lord better than any of them. It was the intuition of love that made him know at once, when they had cast the net and found it immediately filled with fishes, that they were acting under the direction of the kindness and love of Jesus. Love makes us quick to hear the voice or to detect the form of one whom we love. As Dr. MacLaren says, in a sermon on this paragraph concerning John's detection of Christ, in religious matters love is the foundation of knowledge. A man can not argue his way into knowing Christ. Man's natural capacity within its own limits is strong and good; but in the region of acquaintance with God and Christ, the wisdom of this world is foolishness. "He that loveth not, knoweth not God, for God is love." Love will trace him everywhere, as dear friends detect each other in little marks which are meaningless to others. Love's quick eye pierces through disguises impenetrable to a colder scrutiny. Love has in it a longing for his presence which makes us eager and quick to mark the slightest sign that he is near; as the footstep of some dear one is heard by the sharp ear of affection long before any sound breaks the silence to others. Love leads to likeness to the Lord, and that likeness makes the clearer vision of the Lord possible. This is the secret of John's first knowledge of the presence of Christ on the shore. John had the most tender and intimate friendship with Christ. Their fellowship was evidently closer than any of the others in that little group. It was John who leaned his head upon the Savior's breast at the last supper, and when Peter desired to ask a question of Christ on that occasion he confided it to John and asked him to inquire of the Lord. It was to John that Jesus entrusted the care of his mother in the midst of his agony on the cross. When we reflect on all this, we are not astonished that John's sensitive heart was the first to know the presence of Christ. Much blessed knowledge came to John through this same higher sense of love. It is John who declares to us in his epistles, "We know that we have passed from death unto life, because we love the brethren." "We know that when he shall appear we shall be like him."

Again he declares, "We know that he abideth in us." Oh, that the divine love may possess our hearts, and our affection for Jesus be so simple and pure that we shall be sensitive to his presence. Well the poet sings,—

> "Nothing is true but love, or aught of worth;
> Love is the incense which doth sweeten earth.
> O merchant, at heaven's mart for heavenly ware,
> Love is the only coin which passes there.
> The wine of love can be obtained of none
> Save him who trod the wine-press all alone."

But the great lesson of our theme, the one which I wish to impress upon your hearts with all the simplicity and power God shall give me, is the complete self-surrender of Peter in leaving the boat, his companions, and the net full of fishes, and casting himself overboard into the sea, swimming for Christ as the one great goal of his life. That is the way of salvation. If you are a poor sinner against God, and you are anxious to know how you may find the way out of your sins into the kingdom of God, my advice is that you follow Peter's example. Jump overboard and swim for Christ! Christ has said, "Whosoever will" may come. It is all then in your will. Frances Willard says, "Will is the king-bolt of the faculties." The necessary thing for you to do to make sure of your salvation is to say from the depths of your heart, "By the help of God *I will* cut loose from everything that stands in the way and take Jesus Christ to be my Savior. It will seem easy enough when once you have jumped overboard, leaving worldly things behind, and begun to swim toward Christ and the safe shore-line of a Christian life.

Mr. B. Fay Mills tells the story of a young lady who was deeply concerned about her spiritual interest, and after a severe struggle started to visit her pastor to ask him to show her the way of life. As she entered the horse-car, in carrying out her purpose, she saw seated there several of her friends, who asked where she was going. The tempter immediately said: "Don't tell them where you are going, but answer them in some evasive way." At the same time the Spirit whispered to her: "Be brave and conscientious about this. Tell them of your purpose, and ask them to go with you." She obeyed the voice of God. Her friends declined to accompany her, and she went on alone. When she came to the minister's house he came to the door to meet her. She paused from embarrassment for an instant, and then said: "Doctor, I started to come to see you to ask you to lead me to Christ; but now that I am here I have come to tell you I have found Christ." It was with her as with some whom Jesus healed during his ministry on earth—"As they went they were cleansed." It may be so with you to-night if you will arise to come home to God.

I have recently reread the story of how Judson, the great missionary, was converted from infidelity to Christ. He was a brilliant young man and had been reared in a Christian home; but in college he came under the influence of a young man as brilliant as himself who destroyed his Christian faith. His father and mother were broken-hearted when he came home with the announcement of his infidel sentiments. He broke the sorrowful news to them just before starting on a long pleasure-trip thorugh New England and New York. He never forgot the grief-burdened utterances of his father and the silent tears of his mother at the family altar on the morning of his departure. In the course of his journey he stopped one night at a country hotel. As the landlord showed him to his room he apologized for placing him next to a sick man who might be dying. Judson assured him it would make no difference. He put out his light and got into bed, but the sounds from the sick-room fastened upon his ear and suggested the most agitating reflections. Was the dying man prepared for the change that awaited him? He blushed as he felt the faith of his childhood again creeping over him. Prepared! What preparation was needed for an eternal sleep? But still the question would return: into what scenes is his spirit to pass? The landlord had spoken of him as a young man. Was he a Christian or, like himself, a skeptic, the source of unutterable sorrow to pious parents? What were the feelings of the dying youth in this testing hour? What would be his own in like situation? Suppose he were now stretched on the bed of death, could he look with philosophic calmness toward the final moment, sure that the next instant his soul with all its capacities for joy and sorrow would have gone out like an extinguished candle? Ah! there was a shuddering in his soul which prophesied of a future either of conscious bliss and love or of just retribution. He tried to rouse himself from these fears by recalling the arguments which once had seemed so convincing. But they would not work there in the dark with the tragedy of death being enacted a few feet away. He thought of his infidel friends and asked what they would think of such weakness, especially the witty and brilliant friend who had been the chief agent in leading him to throw over the faith of his father and mother. The poor youth cowered in his bed as he imagined the pitying smile and the keen shafts of ridicule with which that firm mind would meet such nursery superstitions. But all would not do, and through the whole night his spirit was tossed upon a restless sea of disquietude and doubt. But when the morning came he sprang up relieved and was ready to smile at what he deemed the fancies of the night. On leaving his room he went immediately to the landlord with kind inquiries after the sick man. "He is dead," was the reply. "Dead!" "Yes, he is gone, poor fellow; the doctor thought he could not survive the night." "Do you know his name?" "Oh, yes! he was from Brown University; a fine young fellow; his name was E——," mentioning the name of Judson's brilliant friend who had led him away from Christ. He needed no one to preach to him in that hour on the evidences of Christianity. He felt all his infidelity slipping away from him and he despised it as a lie. He went to his room and spent hours in a state of wretchedness bordering on stupefaction. The words, "Dead! Lost! Lost!" rang continually in his ears. He gave up his intended trip, and said, in the language of another poor prodigal who also found the husks bitter, "I will arise and go to my father." In the hour of his spiritual distress he could think of no place so good for him as the old home fireside, with his Christian father and mother. If he had gone on with his trip he would probably have grieved the Holy Spirit and would soon have hardened his heart against the gracious influences that had come to him, but his decision to go back home at once and tell his father and mother about his change of purpose was his salvation, and led to his happy conversion and glorious life.

If there are any who hear me at this hour to whom the Holy Spirit brings the message of warning and invitation, I implore you to follow Judson's example, and come home at once without delay. Do not try to seek the Lord secretly. Christ asks you for an open confession, and you owe it to him. How little it is in return for his great love!

At a religious meeting in the south of London a timid little girl wanted to be prayed for; she wanted to come to Jesus, and said to the Christian man who was conducting the meeting, "Will you pray for me in the meeting, please? But do not mention my name." In the meeting which followed, when every head was bowed and there was perfect silence, the gentleman prayed for the little girl who wanted to come to Jesus, and he said, "O Lord, there is a little girl who does not want her name known, but thou dost know her; save her precious soul!" There was stillness for a moment, and then away back in the congregation a little girl rose, and a pleading little voice said, "Please, it's me, Jesus; it's me." She did not want to have a doubt. The more she had thought about it the hungrier her heart was for forgiveness. She wanted to be saved, and she was not ashamed to rise in that meeting, little girl as she was, and say, "Jesus, it's me."

I invite you with all the tenderness of this blessed Gospel to come to Christ with the same childlike courage and simplicity.

A BREAKFAST WITH JESUS.

"Jesus saith unto them, Come and break your fast."—*John* xxi. 12 (*Revised Version*).

"So when they had broken their fast, Jesus saith to Simon Peter, Simon, son of John, lovest thou me more than these? He saith unto him, Yea, Lord; thou knowest that I love thee. He saith unto him, Feed my lambs."
—*John* xxi. 15, 16 (*Revised Version*).

THE Gospel according to St. John is the love-story of Jesus Christ and his disciples. Yes, it is more than that; it is the love-story of Jesus Christ and the whole lost world. What a sweet picture this is which we are to study together! We are on the shore of the little Sea of Galilee. It is in the beautiful Syrian springtime. The lake is clear and calm, lying there in the peculiar quiet of the early dawn. Away stretch the high-reaching slopes up to the lonely heights where the sheep are still in their folds, waiting for the shepherd to lead them out for the day's grazing. Here is a boat drawing nigh to land. Six excited and happy men are in it, for Peter has just jumped overboard, and swum ashore for a first word alone with his Master. There he stands dripping from his plunge in the lake, but glowing with joy and gladness at his conversation with the Lord. As the others draw near, they are astonished to behold a bright fire of coals there beside the water, and fish laid thereon, and bread. What an appetizing picture for seven hungry men! They have been fishing since yesterday afternoon, working all night long, and until just now, when they had cast their nets under the Lord's command, had taken nothing, and are in a good condition to appreciate such a sight.

Did you ever camp out? Did you ever pitch your tent beside a lake away from human habitations? Have you ever listened to the howl of the wolf or the boom of the night-hawk the last thing before you went to sleep, and awakened with the first flush of dawn to hear the birds sing their anthem of thanksgiving; plunged in the cool water and come out with every nerve tingling with life; watched the breakfast cooking on the coals in the open air and then ate it with an appetite such as no dining-room of man's construction ever gave? If you have not, there is a little touch of possible appreciation in this picture which you do not understand, and I extend to you my sincere sympathies.

As the other disciples gathered round the fire, Jesus said to them, "Bring of the fish which ye have now taken." Then Peter, generous, big-hearted fellow, willing to give the rest a chance to talk with the Lord and quick to do what would please him, went and drew the net to land. Fisherman that he was, he counted the fish and found there were one hundred and fifty-three by actual count.

There is a little touch right here that I like very much. Christ had already prepared breakfast for them, and the fish and the bread-cakes were all there smoking hot upon the coals; but he knows they will enjoy the breakfast far more if they have a share in getting it, and also no doubt desires to teach them that in his great mission he has need of their assistance, and so he tells them to bring some of their own fish which they have just caught that more may be cooking while they are eating what is now ready. So we may be sure Christ has need of us in his sublime work of feeding the hungry souls of men and saving humanity from starving for lack of spiritual food. He desires each one of us to assist him and to make our contribution of our own particular talent and ability.

Our good neighbor, Dr. Dixon, tells the story of a farmer some miles above Milton, Pa., who, when the ice was breaking up, got into one of his boats with the purpose of pulling it out of the river. But just then a floating mass of ice struck it, broke it loose from the bank, and carried both the boat and the farmer out into the current. A neighbor who saw the man's great danger mounted his fastest horse and rode as tight as he could run down to Milton. He scattered the news everywhere, and the people of the town hunted up all the ropes they could find and suspended lines of rope over the bridge, stretching clear across the river. They could not tell at just what point the boat with the farmer would pass under, so they put a rope down every two or three feet, clear across. By and by the farmer was seen, wet and cold, standing in the boat half full of water, drifting down the rapid current. When he saw the ropes dangling within reach, he didn't stop to ask any questions or make any conditions, but he just caught hold of the first rope he saw, the one that was nearest to him, and was drawn up and saved. Of course one rope might have been in the right place and have rescued him, but the people of Milton were not willing to take any chances when so much was at stake. So Christ wants us, every one, to have a hand in the salvation of lost souls. How aptly this illustration applies to the work in which we are engaged at present! In these revival meetings it is possible, of course, that the rope of salvation which I shall hang out in the sermon shall come near enough for some imperiled souls to grasp it and be saved, but if every member of this church would get out their tackle and by Christian devotion, by prayer and conversation, and personal seeking, would throw out their life-lines of hope, how the number of the saved would be multiplied!

There is in this lesson a very sweet thought of the rich joy of fellowship which God has made it possible for us to rejoice in. How sweet is the fellowship of the family and home! Among the many definitions of happiness there is one by Dr. Oliver Wendell Holmes that has become a favorite. "Happiness," said the sweet-souled Autocrat, "is four feet on a fender." The true poetry of the meaning can not be lost on any one who thinks. Holmes liked it so much that he often referred to it, and when his beloved wife who had been his lifelong companion had left him for a better world, and an old friend came in to condole with him, he said, with a shake of his good gray head, "Only two feet on the fender now." That is the shadow which falls over all the sweet fellowships of earth. The only silver lining to the cloud is the radiant promise of a happy reunion in the immortal life. The life of Jesus Christ, entering into the fellowship of our humanity as it does, brings to us the assurance of the divine fellowship with a sweeter realism than could ever have been possible without the incarnation. The possibility of personal friendship with Jesus Christ, of sharing with him life's sorrows and trials, as well as its work and its joy, is the dearest privilege of the Christian. How clearly Christ sets it forth in his invitation to all who are weary and heavy-laden to enter into a yoke-fellowship with him! Mark Guy Pearse tells how he once preached a sermon on the text, "Come unto me all ye that labor and are heavy laden. . . . Take my yoke upon you. . . . For my yoke is easy, and my burden is light." When the sermon was over, a man came to him and said: "I wish I had known what you were going to preach about, I could have told you something." "Well, my friend," Mr. Pearse said, "it is very good of you. May I not have it still?" "Do you know why his yoke is light, sir? If not, I think I can tell you." "Well, because the good Lord helps us to carry it, I suppose." "No, sir," he explained, shaking his head; "I think I know better than that. You see, when I was a boy at home, I used to drive the oxen in my father's yoke. Father's yokes were always made heavier on one side than the other. Then, you see, we would put a weak bullock in alongside of a strong bullock, and the light end would come on the weak bullock, because the stronger one had the heavy part of it on his shoulder." Then his face lit up as he said, "That is why the yoke is easy and the burden is light—because the Lord's yoke is made after the same pattern, and the heavy end is upon his shoulder." No wonder that in such fellowship men find rest unto their souls!

Altho Christ and the disciples ate of the fish and the bread, the sweetest food they had that morning was their tender conversation and their loving fellowship together. The true food of the Christian is fellowship with Christ and the saints in loving communion and service. How much of this delicious food the Bible gives us! As another well says, the power of the Bible over our hearts rests in the fact that it was history before it was a record; it was human life before it was a book. True men walked with God, and what was done in them and by them was set down; and as the result, the sacred Scriptures and their precious influence on the life and heart of mankind are a more wonderful miracle than any recorded in its holy pages. Its power over the hearts of men increases rather than decreases as the years go on. If you want your soul fed with honey out of the rock and with the finest of the wheat, acquaint yourself daily with the nourishing food of God's Word. A recent writer says that he once heard President Finney, the greatest revivalist of his time, in the midst of a lecture, read or attempt to read a few of the words of Christ which are recorded in the New Testament. He broke down with weeping, but instantly apologized, saying that since his sickness he could not trust himself to read the words of Jesus in public. The divine Savior had personally entered through his words into the deepest life of this man and had stirred in him emotions that tears alone could express.

It is doubtless true that more Christians die from starvation than from any other cause. They starve not for lack of food, but from neglect of eating. And one of the first effects of negligence to eat is the loss of appetite. The starving Christian never suffers from hunger. Many people on this account are self-deceived. They do not know their dangerous condition, and often persuade themselves that they are in good health when their spiritual life is really dying. The disciples of Christ were at one time greatly astonished when, in reply to an invitation to eat, he said: "I have meat to eat that ye know not of." They said among themselves, "Hath any man brought him to eat?" Then Jesus saith unto them, "My meat is to do the will of him that sent me, and to finish his work." This is the food for lack of which many professed Christians are perishing to-day. Doing the will of God, entering into fellowship with Jesus Christ, in service for the weak, in seeking after the lost, and in rescuing the perishing, satisfies the deepest hunger of the soul. It sustains life and gives strength, and there is nothing which yields so much in substantial joy. In the Christian life earnest, faithful work is food and idleness is starvation.

The invitations to Christ's round-table of fellowship are so generous and free that no one need count himself out. "Whosoever will may come." It is not a man's social position, but the hunger of his soul, the crying out of his great need, that recommends him to Jesus Christ.

As Sophie Schenck beautifully sings:

"He did not say—my Jesus never said,
    When, sick of sin, I sank upon my knees,
With streaming eyes and trembling hands outspread,
    Sobbing, 'Lord, help me, give my sad heart ease!'—
He did not say, 'Why empty come to me?
    Go hence and gather of the earth's rich store!
Pierce mines for gold, go search for gems the sea!
    When thou hast gained my price, return once more.'

"He did not say—my Jesus never said,
    'Laden with guilt, how darest thou come to-day?
Go cleanse thyself; do penance great and dread,
    Then scarred and bleeding kneel to me and pray!'
He said not so, my Jesus! to my feet
    He drew me, while my trembling hands he prest,
Then bending down he whispered 'Child, complete
    Thy pardon, come and on my bosom rest.'

A BREAKFAST WITH JESUS.

"He did not say, my Jesus, 'Go, thy sin
    Condemns thee!' But I heard him sweetly say,
'My blood effaced thy guilt! New life begin,
    Lean hard and watch, I will return some day.'
Each hour I feel his arms 'beneath me' still,
    My timid hands lie closely in his own,
To him I whisper low, when fearing ill,
    'Lord, help!' and straightway every ill has flown.

"He bade me 'watch,' and so for him watch I,
    But as days pass I smile, and count one less;
He will return, I know; but when, and why,
    And how, I know not! He will come to bless.
When birds and roses cheer may be that time,
    Or when ice-jewels gleam, and piles the snow;
It matters not! The heart's joy-bells will chime
    When Jesus comes, and I with him shall go."

Fellowship with Jesus Christ is a food which can make us strong for the highest and noblest service. All food is for strength. We eat not only that we may have continued existence, but that we may have strength to work and bring about results. How suggestively it is stated here that after they had had their breakfast, and the hunger of Peter's body was not only satisfied but the hunger of his soul had been fed with this loving conversation with Christ, the Savior immediately began to lay out Peter's work for him. "Simon," he says, in substance, "do you love me more than the rest of these? Is that the reason why you couldn't wait to come with the others, but jumped overboard and swam to the shore to meet me?" And when Simon had answered that the Lord, knowing his heart, knew that he loved him, Christ said, "Feed my lambs."

Divine food is given unto us not only that our own spiritual life may be made strong, but that we may feed the Savior's lambs. While this comes with force to every one of us, it ought to come with peculiar force to parents and to Sunday-school teachers. No one except the father or mother has a better chance than the devoted Sunday-school teacher to win young souls to Christ and feed them with the food from heaven. May the benediction of heaven fall upon all our Sunday-school teachers during this special season of revival interest! There is no more responsible position, no more honorable place, no trust more sacred or fraught with more glorious opportunities than the charge of a Sunday-school class and the opportunity to win young souls to a genuine and sincere Christian life. Neither those Argonauts who sailed according to the old Hellenic myth on the good ship *Argo*, nor those later travelers round Cape Horn, to California, in search of the Golden Fleece, dreamed of a treasure so rich and imperishable as that which is within the reach of every faithful, self-denying Sunday-school teacher. You are the Argonauts of the higher realm.

Fellowship with Christ and his people furnishes such food as makes heroes out of common material. An interesting incident is related of a flood in the Alabama River during the spring of 1886. The river overflowed its banks and spread desolation over great regions of country. The negroes in their little log cabins, so easily washed away, were the greatest sufferers. Relief expeditions were sent out from neighboring towns to rescue them. One day the news came that the negroes on a certain plantation had sought refuge upon a corn-barn, around which the water was rapidly rising, and so rendering their condition exceedingly dangerous. A boat came up to them just at night, when a heavy rain was falling. The top of the barn was covered with the poor people. When the boat struck against the frail log building, which was in the water to the edges of the roof, the poor creatures commenced to clamber hurriedly down to the boat. "Stop!" cried the man in command, "the women and children first." The men obediently resumed their seats. They took in all the children and then the women, and were about pushing off, telling the men they would hurry back for them as quickly as possible, or send the first boat they met, when an old woman seized the corner of the house and, looking anxiously into the leader's face, said, "Marster, ain't you gwine to take my ole man?" "No, auntie," he answered, "the boat is too full now, he must wait till we come back."

The words were hardly out of his mouth, when with a sudden spring she was upon the roof again. It shook as she scrambled on it, and took her seat by a little withered old black man, whose hand she seized as if she feared they would tear her away from him. "Come, auntie," the man cried, "this won't do. We can't leave you here, and we can't wait any longer for you." "Go on, marster," she answered; "I thanks yer, en I pray de good Lawd to fetch you all safe home; but I gwine to stay wid my ole man. Ef Simon got to git drowned, Liddy gwine git drown too. We dun bin togedder too long to part now." And they had to leave her, after throwing some blankets and a bag of provisions to them. As they rowed off in the rain and the night, a high falsetto voice, tremulous with age, came across the waters from the corn-crib, where they had left the almost certainly doomed group in the blackness of darkness, for they dared not have a light for fear of setting fire to their frail support. The pathos of that song as it came to them across the waters brought tears to the eyes of the rescuers. First Liddy's trembling voice and then a chorus of a dozen or more of the deep bass voices of the men:

> "We're a clingin' to de ark,
>   Take us in, take us in;
> Fur de watah's deep en dark,
>   Take us in, take us in;
> Do de flesh is po' an' weak,
>   Take us in, take us in;
> 'Tis de Lawd we gwinter seek,
>   Take us in, take us in;
> Den, Lawd, hol' out dy han',
>   Take us in, take us in;
> Draw de sinnahs to de Lam',
>   'Take us in, take us in."

Most fortunately, the first party came across a boat bent upon the same errand as themselves, which went immediately to the barn and saved all of its living freight. The building had apparently been held down by their weight, for, as the last one left, it turned over and floated away to the Gulf. The rescuers said that, as they drew near it, the first sound they heard was an old woman's voice singing,—

> "De Lawd is hyah'd our cry."

Answered by the men,—

> "Take us in, take us in,
> En he'll save us by en by,
> Take us in, take us in."

It is the joy of my heart to preach to you a divine compassion and a heavenly fellowship that can come into poor, ignorant, untaught human hearts, and make heroes like these of them.

THE GIFT OF POWER.

"But ye shall receive power, when the Holy Ghost is come upon you."—*Acts* i. 8 (*Revised Version*).

POWER is what we want—power to stay the tide of sin and iniquity; power to make men pause and consider the certain disaster of the downward path; power to arouse men who are asleep in trespasses and in sins; power to clutch the candle of the Lord that is lighted with the devil's fire and snatch it as "a brand from the burning;" power to turn a wrong world upside down; power to make Jesus live again in our lives; power to make him so real and so charming that men shall be drawn away from their sins and find freedom and purity in him. Jesus said to the disciples, "Ye shall receive power, after that the Holy Ghost is come upon you."

As we look into the New Testament we see that this was true everywhere during the ministry of Jesus and in the establishing of the Christian church. It was when Jesus was full of the Holy Ghost that he returned from Jordan and went up into the wilderness and won his great victory over the devil. On the day of Pentecost it was, when they were all "filled with the Holy Ghost," that Peter and his one hundred and twenty fellow-workers had such wondrous power in the presentation of the truth that the wicked, prejudiced Jews yielded to their preaching of the cross of Christ on every side, and three thousand of them were added to the church in a single day. It was when Peter and John were "full of the Holy Ghost" that they healed the lame man, and were so full of holy boldness that the people, perceiving that they were unlearned and ignorant men, marveled and "took knowledge of them that they had been with Jesus." It was when the early Christians were gathered together in prayer, and the place was shaken where they assembled together, and "they were all filled with the Holy Ghost," that it is said about them, "They spake the word of God with boldness. And the multitude of them that believed were of one heart and of one soul, . . . and with great *power* gave the apostles witness of the resurrection of the Lord Jesus: and great grace was upon them all." We are told in the description given of Stephen that he was "a man full of faith and of the Holy Ghost." We are not astonished after that to hear that he was full of power and "did great wonders and miracles among the people," and that the multitude "were not able to resist the wisdom and the spirit by which he spake." When Saul was stricken down with conviction of sin, on the way to Damascus, and Ananias came to him to lead him into the light, it is said that he was "filled with the Holy Ghost." After that it is only natural to read that he "increased the more in strength, and confounded the Jews which dwelt at Damascus, proving that this is very Christ." The same description is given us of Barnabas. It is said of him: "He was a good man, and full of the Holy Ghost and of faith;" and it follows then, as a matter of course, in the record: "much people was added unto the Lord." At Iconium "the disciples were filled with joy and with the Holy Ghost," and the result of the work carried forward in such a spirit was that "a great multitude both of the Jews and also of the Greeks believed."

The same power has been with the church in its days of triumph in every age. The men who have wrought wondrous things for the salvation of souls have been those who have received power because the Holy Ghost was upon them. Freeman Clarke well says that there is always a tendency in religion to relapse into mechanism—to multiply ceremonies and lose the spirit. Ever, as the winter of unbelief chills the soul and the river of religious life sinks in its channel, the ice of forms accumulates along its shores. Then the Lord sends a new prophet, to whom religion is not a form, but a reality; one who sees with his own eyes God as a heavenly presence in nature and life; who has the vision, the faculty divine. What a long and glorious procession there are of them—a line of torch-bearers who have kept the divine life aglow in the church! Such men as Paul, Augustine, Bernard, Savonarola, Huss, Wycliffe, Luther; and, in the later days, such men as Fox the Quaker, Whitefield and the Wesleys, Finney and Edwards, and Moody. Such men are divinely ordained to call people away from dusty books and dry forms to the open vision of a new heaven and new earth. Their power is not their own. It is not the power of genius, or learning, or logic, or eloquence. It is the power of the Holy Spirit. They see God face to face. They see him in Christ, as Whittier saw him when he sang:

> "Our friend, our brother, and our Lord!
> What shall thy service be?
> Nor name, nor form, nor ritual word,
> But simply following thee!"

This power we want!—a power that will make us irresistible as the messengers of the Son of God; a power that will melt down all our icicles of indifference and change our natures into impetuous torrents of loving enthusiasm. The disciples on the day of Pentecost were such marvels of fervor and earnestness that some of the people thought they were intoxicated with strong drink; but Peter replied that it was not the effect of wine but the power of the Holy Spirit working within them. They were carried away by that Divine Spirit; they were, to use a foreign phrase, "God-intoxicated men." When the people were astonished at the enthusiasm of Paul, he exclaimed, "The love of Christ constraineth us." Few men won more souls to Christ in his day than Richard Baxter. The secret of all his success was the power of the Holy Ghost which was upon him. That it was which gave him his unbounded enthusiasm. His biographer says Baxter would have set the world on fire while another was lighting a match.

"He preached as though he ne'er should preach again,
And as a dying man to dying men."

Dr. O. P. Gifford tells the story of a mighty revival which was in progress in a Wesleyan chapel. The rector of the Established Church dropped in one evening, as he was bound to do, the chapel being within the limits of his parish. Scandalized by the excitement, he rebuked the zealous Wesleyans, saying, "This is all wrong, all wrong.

When Solomon built his temple there was heard neither the sound of hammer, nor saw, nor chisel. You make too much noise here." The chapel preacher replied, "Oh, but that's all right; we are not building here, we are just blasting, getting out lively stones for the temple. Christ is the Master-builder." The preacher was right; he was using dynamite, destroying the kingdom of darkness. Something of this Paul must have done when his enemies declared, "These that have turned the world upside down have come hither also." A touch of the dynamic energy of the Holy Spirit shook the prison wherein Paul and Silas sung psalms and prayed to God. "Friends, this is what the Christianity of to-day lacks, what you and I lack—dynamic energy. Books as black as those of Ephesus need to be piled in the public squares, leaders as corrupt as Felix and Festus ought to be faced, hypocrisy as vile as that of Simon Magus ought to be unmasked, sins as flagrant as those at Rome and Corinth demand attention. Oh, for the promised dynamite of the Holy Spirit! This power which we lack, and which we may have because it is promised, has its source outside the church and human life altogether. 'Ye shall receive power'—not generated from within, not attained to by straining present powers, or enlarging present capacities. We can not whip ourselves into a state of power, as though we were eggs; strike the fire from ourselves by any flint and steel arrangement; lift ourselves into it by force of will; educate ourselves into it by culture of heart or head. The dynamic power is without; we are to receive it. Though itself such a mighty cause, it is also an effect; the power lies in the Holy Spirit. 'Ye shall receive power after that the Holy Spirit is come upon you.'"

Do you ask how we can receive this power? The answer is, by *obedience* and *prayer*. When Jesus came to be baptized of John in the Jordan he said to John: "Thus it becometh us to fulfil all righteousness." And it is recorded that "Jesus also being baptized, and *praying*, the heaven was opened, and the Holy Ghost descended in bodily shape like a dove upon him." Thus it was through obedience and prayer that Jesus passed from being Jesus the carpenter of Nazareth, to be Jesus the Christ, the Savior of the world. Then he began to do mighty works. We shall get power by following the example of our Lord.

At Niagara Falls for perhaps thousands of years a volume of water estimated at 275,000 cubic feet per second has been plunging over a precipice about one hundred and sixty feet in height, involving a daily force equivalent to that stored up in all the coal mined each day at the present time throughout the world. But it is only within a year that men have learned how to make this gigantic force do a part of the world's work. It has been flowing on through all the years, waiting for humble and obedient minds to take hold upon it and harness it to service. So the divine power of the Holy Spirit waits to be used by the prayerful, the humble, and the obedient. Everything in the way of winning men to Christ that was done in New Testament times can be done to-day if we have the same faithful prayer, and the same obedience of life. Men are more than a match for the devil to-day, as Jesus was in his day, when they are full of the Holy Ghost. Men are glad witnesses for Christ, and timid ones who have gone tongue-tied along the road speak the word with all boldness, when once the anointing of the Holy Spirit is upon them. As in Iconium multitudes believed under the influence of the ministry of the disciples, so in Brooklyn multitudes will believe when the power of the Holy Ghost is present with us as it was with Paul and Barnabas and their friends.

Let us not forget that the Holy Spirit, in answer to prayer, is able and willing to convict of sin even those who have long withstood his grace. In one of the Northfield meetings a year or so ago an account of his conversion given by a Christian merchant from Maine shows how marvelously the Holy Spirit can work in answer to prayer. During the revival that occurred in Boston in 1877 under the direction of Mr. Moody, this merchant came to that city on business. He was entirely indifferent to the Gospel of Christ. Hearing that large numbers crowded the Tabernacle every night at these evangelistic services, he suggested to a friend that they might attend on a certain evening after business hours. This friend was obliged to excuse himself owing to a previous engagement, but suggested that, to gain admittance, it would be necessary to be promptly at the Tabernacle at an early hour, as the doors were then closed. The merchant, actuated more by curiosity than anything else, determined to attend that evening. After tea he strolled leisurely on his way to the meeting, giving but little thought to the warning of his friend that the doors were closed at a certain hour. Arriving at the Tabernacle he found that he was five minutes late. The policemen stationed about the place were asked to admit him. He declared his willingness to accept even a standing-place within the building. He went to every door of the mammoth Tabernacle making this request, but was refused everywhere. The policemen said their orders were imperative and they could not admit him. After a moment's reflection he concluded to spend the evening at one of the Boston theaters. As he walked toward the theater he remembered that he had been distinctly told that the doors were closed at a certain hour, and that it was his own negligence that had shut him out. That was the chosen opportunity for the awakening of his soul to spiritual realities. The Holy Spirit in that moment suggested to his mind the sad condition of the five foolish virgins who were shut out of the kingdom of God. The Holy Spirit impressed upon him that he had been treating his soul's salvation with the same culpable negligence that he had shown on his way to the Tabernacle service. He had been often told that there was an hour for closing the door of grace; he had heedlessly disregarded the information. And now, if he were called suddenly to die, his condition would be that of the virgins who came to the door of heaven destitute of the necessary preparation and were denied admittance. And how terrible it would be to have the door of grace closed forever! These thoughts so fully occupied his mind that he was not able to recall afterward what scenes were presented that night in the theater. "The door is shut, the door is shut," was the voice of the Spirit speaking to his immortal soul throughout the entire evening. On reaching his home in Maine the following day, he announced that he had failed to hear Mr. Moody. His Christian wife was deeply disappointed. She had prayed that her husband might be brought to Christ in these meetings, and her pastor had united in the prayer. Little did they then know that the Holy Spirit was powerfully convicting him of sin; but not in just the way they had thought. The voice was constantly saying in his inmost soul, "The door is shut, the door is shut." The final outcome of his distress was most glorious. For three days and nights his soul was in agony. Opening the Bible when alone, he found just the words to meet his case; and at last in his own home, with praying souls about him, he surrendered himself in deepest penitence and accepted by faith the offered help of the Son of God. He lost no time in publicly confessing the Lord Jesus Christ. The years that have passed have shown the reality of his regeneration. He not only lives a godly life, but he devotes a large portion of his income yearly to the spread of the Gospel.

It may be that there are some who hear me at this hour who have been convicted by the Holy Spirit, and are at this moment conscience-stricken because of their sins. If so, I beg of you not to delay, not to grieve the Holy Spirit, but to yield to his gracious influence and accept Jesus Christ as your Savior.

WITNESSES FOR CHRIST.

"Ye shall be my witnesses."—*Acts* i. 8 (*Revised Version*).

I THINK it is very significant that immediately following the assurance that to the disciples upon whom the Holy Ghost was bestowed there should come mighty power, Christ said, "And ye shall be my witnesses." It suggests that the testimony itself is given added power and made effective by the presence of the Holy Ghost in the hearts of those who bear witness. Mr. Moody, telling the story of his own ministerial life, says that when he was first preaching at Farwell Hall, Chicago, he never worked harder to prepare his sermons; he preached and preached; but it seemed like beating against the air. A good woman used to say, "Mr. Moody, you don't seem to have power in your preaching." His great desire was that he might have a fresh anointing! He requested this woman and a few other people to come and pray with him every Friday at four o'clock. He himself prayed day and night that God would fill the empty vessel. One day about this time he was in New York, thinking on these things and longing for the Spirit's power to make his testimony for Christ effective; and as he was going into a bank on Wall Street, he felt a strange and mighty power coming over him. The glory of God came upon him so that he went up to the hotel, and there in his room he wept before God, and cried, "O my God, stay thy hand!" After that he never preached a sermon but somebody was converted. He preached the same sermons over again, word for word, that he had preached without effect in Chicago, and under the power of the Holy Ghost the dry bones were made to live, and these lifeless sermons became mighty instruments in the hands of God in winning men to believe on the Lord Jesus Christ. I am sure that one of the chief reasons for the great triumph of the early Christians was that they were not only preachers but witnesses. If the apostles had been only theorizers about Christ and his mission, Christianity would not have lived very long. But they were above all witnesses. This is true of every one of them. The greater part of their sermons were made up of testimony concerning what they had themselves seen and known of the power of Jesus Christ to forgive sin. They went everywhere bearing their witness to Christ. They were living witnesses. If they were summoned before a court to give an account of themselves, they glorified

God, for it only gave them the better opportunity to advertise their testimony to the life and death and resurrection of Jesus Christ.

What we need to-day above all is living witnesses to Christ—men and women full of faith and the Holy Ghost, who in season and out of season shall bear their glad testimony to what Christ has done for their souls. There may be learning and culture and eloquence in the pulpit, and large congregations to listen to earnest sermons, and yet no revivals and few conversions if the members of the church regard their religion as a matter of taste and luxury. Some people seem to think that when they have provided music and preaching as attractions to draw men to Christ, they have fulfilled all the obligations they owe to the Savior. They forget that while their pastor is an ambassador for Christ, that they are the witnesses who either uphold or belie by their own conduct the message he proclaims. It is not the pulpit only, but the rank and file of Christian men and women who are to shine as lights in the world, and who are to hold forth daily the word of life.

We have many instances given us in the Bible, and all of us who have had much experience and observation in winning men to Christ have seen the marvelous power of human testimony in bringing about such a result. How strongly this is set forth in that story Naaman and the healing of his leprosy, which is told us in 2 Kings. Rev. Mark Guy Pearse draws a very graphic picture of the contrast between Naaman and the little maid whose testimony for God was his salvation. There was the famous warrior who dwelt in the palace of the king, the commander of the king's armies, with authority to speak to the whole nation, and all men were ready to obey him; with troops of horses, and hosts of chariots, and servants that wait upon him and minister to him. In both the council and the military camp he was the leading man in Syria. And he was as brave as he was wise, and the whole country was full of his heroism and valor. His soldiers were proud of him, and his presence with them was worth an army. The people loved him, and called him the deliverer of their nation. There is an old tradition that it was he whose hand shot the arrow that smote between the joints of the wicked Ahab's armor, so that he fell down dead in his chariot. He was the kind of man that sometimes comes to the front in answer to the crying needs of every great nation— daring, wise, splendid in heroism, seeing the thing to be done and doing it swiftly and well. His name was an inspiration to his own forces, and a terror to his foes. In short, he was a great man. But it is very interesting to notice how alongside this word great there is set the word little; and alongside this mighty man of valor is put the story of the little captive maid. Poor little thing, her story is a very sad one. A troop of Syrians marching one day into Israel—fierce fellows, burning the homesteads of the villagers, before whom the frightened people fled to the mountains or caves—had come to some cottage, and there, it may be tending a sick mother, too feeble to escape, or guarding the little baby of the family, whom she would not forsake, this girl is taken captive and carried away by the soldiers. They sell her as a slave to Naaman's wife. A stranger in a strange land, with the memory of her bitter griefs, in thought and feeling and hope and religion severed from those about her, she must wait upon her mistress and do her bidding, with none to befriend her. We can think of her sighing in her loneliness, "Ah, me; if I were only king of Syria, or even this great general, I would set right the wrongs of the poor folks, and bid the cruel soldiers stay at home. I would have no burning cottages, no ruined homes, and no poor captive men or maidens, if I were king. How good it must be to be so great! But I am only a little maiden; what can I do? It is dreadful to be so weak and little." And yet this little maid it is who brings deliverance to the great man of Syria, because there are in her two things that are never little—a kind heart, and faith in God. Altho she was smarting with a sense of her own wrongs and sorrows, she was generous enough to think about the sorrows of her enemies, and of this great officer, her master. Day after day it made her little heart ache to see him grow white with the dreadful leprosy; and that, day after day, her poor mistress should carry so great a burden of grief. At last the little maiden could stand it no longer, and standing beside her mistress she sighed, seeing her sorrow, and timidly bore her testimony: "Would to God, my lord were with the prophet that is in Samaria, for he would recover him of his leprosy." And one went and told his lord what the little maid had said, and that word of testimony led to his healing and his conversion.

So there are none of us so little or of so little influence but that if we are faithful to God, and bear our testimony for Christ with a tender and loving heart, we may be of great blessing to those who come in contact with us. Paul may plant, and Apollos may water, but it is after all God who giveth the increase, and he alone can tell whose testimony is most powerful in winning the case for Jesus in a human heart. God often uses the weak things of this world to confound the strong and the mighty.

The story is told of a dissipated young man who one day entered a street-car in one of our large cities and sat down all unnoticed. He was so cast down and in despair that he did not heed or care who else was in the car. He had lost one job after another because of his dissipated habits, and now the extremity had come. He mumbled to himself: "If I can not get work, I can die; there's an end to all things. When one ceases to be useful, they ought to be out of the way." He then looked back to the time when he had come to the city, full of hope, ambition, and promises to his mother to be a pure, honest boy; but, alas! it was the old, old story. A sparkle came to his eyes as he thought of the fortune he soon hoped to lay at her feet. Then, as he realized his condition, a great wave of agony, shame, and distress swept over the once manly countenance. Now he found himself alone —the man beside him had just left. With downcast eyes he noticed a slip of paper. Slowly and thoughtlessly he picked it up and was about to throw it down when he thought the handwriting looked familiar. As he glanced at the script the words attracted his attention; he read and reread them until they burned themselves into his memory: "I thought on my ways and turned my feet unto thy testimonies." He was aroused to a sense of his surroundings as the car stopped and he saw they were at the terminus of the line. He got off because it seemed to make no difference where he was. So, without noticing what he was doing, he crossed the street and sat down on the grass in the shade, with head down, eyes fixed upon the ground, and as if seeing them there, again he repeated the words, "I thought on my ways and turned my feet." He was coming to himself as many another prodigal has done. He was thinking. He did not know he was being watched by a lady on the veranda across the way, and had not heard her daughter singing; but now the words floated out, through the open window—

> "Other refuge have I none,
> Hangs my helpless soul on thee,
> Leave, O leave me not alone."

"Alone, yes, alone," he said while he wept. He glanced up as a little child ran past him, then turned and looked at him with his countenance full of pity, and said, "Have oo 'ost anyfing?"

"Yes; I've lost my all, my manhood."

The lady missed the little child and called him, but he paid no heed. She came across the street for him. As she neared them the little boy said in tones of sympathy:

"Mamma, he 'ost somefing."

"Can I help you, sir?" she asked in the kindest,

sweetest tones he had heard since he left home and mother. And her Christian sympathy and kindly testimony of the willingness of God to stretch out a hand to those who are in trouble was the beginning of a new and noble life.

Is there anybody here who needs a word of testimony to God's grace and mercy? If there is anybody here who is heavy laden and weary, there are many of us that can bear glad witness that Jesus can give rest unto your souls. If there is any one here with a heartache, there are many present who can bear witness that in the deepest sorrows and tenderest griefs that ever surround or pierce a human soul Jesus Christ is a friend who can soothe and comfort. If there are those who are in the bondage of sin, who have tried to break asunder their chains and failed, there are those here who can bear glad testimony that Jesus can set the sinful soul free. Hear, I pray you, the testimony of your brothers and sisters who have known the same sorrows and sins that beset you, and who come offering you the blessed Christ who has been to them a glorious Redeemer.

THE ASCENSION OF JESUS.

"As they were looking, he was taken up: and a cloud received him out of their sight." *Acts* i. 9 (*Revised Version*).

No more poetic or beautiful scene has ever been conceived by the mind of man than the picture that is presented to us in the plain and simple story of Luke, the writer of the Acts of the Apostles, in narrating the incidents in connection with the ascension of Jesus. Glance for a moment over the record of the last forty-five days leading up to the ascension: The last supper of Christ with his disciples, with all its sacred solemnity; the scenes in the Garden of Gethsemane; the arrest of Jesus; the impetuous courage of Peter and afterward his denial and bitter grief; Christ's trial before Pilate; his condemnation; his crucifixion on the cross; the appearance in public of Joseph and Nicodemus as open friends of the Lord, and his burial in Joseph's tomb; the surrounding of the tomb with soldiers of Rome to insure the safe care of his body; the descent of the angel on the first Easter morning, the fear and flight of the soldiers, the rolling away of the stone from the mouth of the sepulcher, and the glorious resurrection of Jesus Christ; the coming of the women to the tomb early on that Sunday morning; their conversation with the angel and afterward their vision of and conversation with the Master; the appearance of Jesus to Mary Magdalene and his prediction, "Go to my brethren, and say unto them, I ascend unto my Father and your Father, to my God and your God;" his appearance to some of the disciples as they walked to Emmaus, his going in with them to see the other disciples, and breaking bread with them to the great joy of their hearts; his appearance afterward to them when Thomas was present, and his kindly condescension and love to Thomas, inviting him to touch the prints of the nails in his hands and thrust his hand into the wound made by the spear in his side, until Thomas, broken-hearted at his own past unbelief, and overwhelmed by the Savior's tender generosity to him, cries aloud, "My Lord and my God;" that lovely breakfast with its sunrise fellowship beside the Sea of Galilee, when Christ reinstates Simon Peter publicly in the most loving manner; and afterward his conversations with them in which he says many things to them about the kingdom of God. Not all of the words spoken at this time have been recorded for us, but we know that he assured them that they should receive mighty power after the Holy Ghost was come upon them; we know that he desired that they should tarry in Jerusalem—the very place of his crucifixion, the center of the prejudice against him—until, in answer to their prayers, the Holy Ghost should come upon them, and then go forth as witnesses to him, first in their own city, and afterward to the uttermost parts of the earth, preaching the Gospel to every creature, teaching and baptizing in his name, with the promise that he would be with them with spiritual power and comfort unto the end of the world.

Then he looks about the little group and says, "I would like to have you all come with me to Bethany." With loving fear, knowing that something of greatest interest to them is about to occur, they follow him to the holy spot. As they gather about him, picture to yourself the scene: Mary, the lovely mother of Jesus, is there; Mary Magdalene whose poor, sin-cursed life had been a burden to her until the Master met her and banished back to their native hell all the devils that tormented her soul, is in that little group; Thomas, doubting no more now or ever, has his deep-set eyes on the Master's face; James, clean-cut, holy man of integrity, stands near by; Peter, impulsive, full of vigor and life as ever, but now and ever after obedient to the will of Christ, crowds close to one side, while John, the beloved disciple, is near the Lord on the other. There is Jesus in their midst, the same Jesus who was born in Bethlehem, who was consecrated at the altar by Simeon, who argued with the doctors of the law in yonder temple, who worked as a carpenter over there in Nazareth, who was baptized of John in the Jordan, who for three years had gone about preaching and doing mighty works, healing the sick, cleansing the lepers, bringing the dead back to life; the same Jesus who stood before Pilate and was crowned by the cruel soldiers with the crown of thorns; the same Jesus who was crucified on the cross, dead and buried, and who on the morning of the third day rose in glorious triumph. Draw near and see that it is the same Jesus. There are the scars on his brow from the thorns; the prints of the cruel nails are yet in his hands and in his feet. If you will push back his garment, you will see the wound there in his side, made by the Roman soldier's spear. Yes, it is the same Jesus; but listen, he raises his hands over their heads to bless them. Methinks I hear him utter these words with which he had comforted them once before: "Peace I leave with you, my peace I give unto you: not as the world giveth, give I unto you. Let not your heart be troubled, neither let it be afraid." "Ye

THE ASCENSION OF JESUS. 185

believe in God, believe also in me." "I go to prepare a place for you. And if I go and prepare a place for you, I will come again, and receive you unto myself; that where I am, there ye may be also." Then gently he rises out of their midst, and as he rises a glorious chariot of cloud descends to receive him. He steps into the chariot, his loving face, always tender and gentle even in the dim distance, fades away in the glory of the illuminated cloud that wraps him about. There they stand, that little group of friends, looking upward into the place where they last beheld their Lord. The tears of loneliness are in their eyes, a great wave of fear is beginning to sweep over their hearts, when back from the cloud come two messengers, two glorious angels robed in white, who drive away their fear and arouse their hope by this triumphant exclamation: "Ye men of Galilee, why stand ye gazing up into heaven? This same Jesus, which is taken up from you into heaven, shall so come in like manner as ye have seen him go into heaven."

This declaration of the angels brought the disciples back to a consciousness that they had a great and glorious mission to perform as the representatives of Jesus Christ, and sent them back to Jerusalem to prepare for it. The story is told that some years ago a new clock was made to be placed in

Temple Hall. The clock-maker was instructed to wait upon the benchers of the temple when the clock was finished, to receive from them a suitable motto to be put under the clock. He applied several times, but without getting the desired information, as they had not determined on the inscription. Continuing to importune them, he came one day when the old benchers were met in the Temple Hall, and had just sat down to dinner. One of the benchers, who was indignant because the clock-maker came on such an occasion to trouble them, angrily replied, "Go about your business!" The mechanic, taking this for an answer to his question, went home and inserted at the bottom of the clock, "Go about your business!" and placed it in the Temple Hall, to the great surprise of the benchers, who, however, were greatly pleased, and decided that the accident had produced a better motto than they could have conceived; and ever since, the faithful Temple clock has continued to remind the lawyers and the public to go about their business. That was the mission of these two angels who came to the disciples on the occasion of the ascension. It was to remind them at once that they must be about the Lord's business. Oh, that some messenger from heaven would call us, and all God's people, to the great business which we have on our hands as the representatives of our Lord!

Joseph Parker, speaking of the upward look of the disciples, and of their return to Jerusalem with *uplifted* hearts, and of their choosing there an *upper* room where they were besieging the throne of grace for divine power to go out and *hold up* Christ before a dying world, recalls the very interesting fact that in ancient Madrid the rule was that, except there was a special stipulation to the contrary, the upper rooms of all houses belonged to the king. However humble your house, if it had been built in those days under the common law of Spain, the upper chambers were royal possessions. Is it not worth our while to ask our hearts the question, Is there any chamber in our house that belongs to the King? Do we keep a chair which he will turn into a throne by sitting in it? Do we keep one crust which he may turn into a feast by breaking it? Is there anything in all the house that is peculiarly and surely the King's? O brothers and sisters, let us make the whole house his from top to bottom; from garret to cellar let us furnish our whole house with such thoughts, such hopes, such purposes, such longing desires, that our house shall be pleasing to the King! If we shall do that, and linger in prayer and faith, God will make our house an antechamber to glory; he will make it a divine spot where the Holy Ghost shall come down upon us and from which we shall go out daily to be irresistible witnesses for him.

In the sixteenth chapter of John's Gospel there is recorded a conversation in which Jesus gives us the reason for his ascension. He had just been talking to them about his going away from them, and, noticing the gloom and sadness in their faces, he continued: "Because I have said these things unto you, sorrow hath filled your heart. Nevertheless I tell you the truth; it is expedient for you that I go away; for if I go not away, the Comforter will not come unto you; but if I depart, I will send him unto you." I think this is easy to understand when we consider a moment. If Christ had remained in the world in his human body, only one little group of people at a time could have had the joy of his presence; but now the Holy Spirit makes his presence known constantly the whole world round to every heart that opens itself to receive his comfort. How clearly this is suggested to us by the story of the death and bringing to life again of Lazarus, during the ministry of Jesus. After Lazarus was dead and buried, and Jesus and some of his friends drew near to that little home in Bethany where he had spent so many pleasant hours, Martha ran out to meet him, and the first words she said to him were, "Lord, if thou hadst been here, my brother had not died."

But, thank God! nowhere where Christ is proclaimed is there a poor Martha mourning for her brother who has need to make that wail now; for—in India, or China, or Africa, or Europe, or America—all may bring their necessities into the presence of Jesus and may know the consolation of the divine Comforter.

But we should not forget that in the very nature of things the Comforter can only give comfort to those who accept and love the Lord Jesus Christ. The Comforter is in this world to represent Jesus, and can not give comfort to those who hate the Lord except they repent and be forgiven. To those who do not love Christ he has another mission. In that same sixteenth chapter of John's Gospel, following the tender words concerning the Comforter in his relation to those who love Jesus, the Savior continues to define the mission of the Holy Spirit by saying: "And when he is come, he will reprove the world of sin, and of righteousness, and of judgment: of sin, because they believe not on me; of righteousness, because I go to my Father, and ye see me no more; of judgment, because the prince of this world is judged." So the Holy Spirit is in this world now not only to comfort those who love Jesus by the manifestation of his presence in their hearts, and sustaining them in every time of trouble and grief; but he is here also with a mission to every man and woman who has not yet come to know Christ as his or her personal Savior.

He is here first to convict of sin. If there are those present who have not yet made their peace with God, I pray God that the Holy Spirit may do the work of his great mission on your hearts now—that he may show you what a terrible thing sin is and how it has marred and hurt your own heart and character; that he may reveal to you how sad has been its influence on those who love you, and how ungrateful and wicked it has been in that it has shut up your gratitude which ought to have been returned to God for his great mercy and goodness to you. Oh, that he might make you see how mean and cruel a thing sin is in that it has made you to harden your heart, and refuse the invitations of the Christ, who was crucified for you. God grant that the Holy Spirit may convict you of sin now as never before!

He comes to convict men of righteousness—the righteousness of Jesus Christ. The righteousness of Jesus is more than simple morality. It is not only refraining from outbreaking and villainous sin, but an aggressive righteousness that seeks to make the stream pure by cleansing the fountain. The righteousness of Jesus Christ is superior to all other in that it does not consist in mere forms and ceremonies, but purifies the fountain of the affections and purposes. Oh, that the Holy Spirit might convict you of righteousness! that he might show you that the reason you have failed so many times when you have tried to be righteous, and to make yourself right, is because your righteousness has all been on the outside. You have been trying to send out a pure stream from a poisoned fountain. You have been shutting down under the hatches an unholy fire of lust, a burning, consuming appetite for wicked things, while in the mean time you are trying to present to the world a whitened conduct. The righteousness of Jesus Christ goes to the bottom of things. It goes down into the hull of a man's heart and drenches to death the unholy fire. Ah, yes, it does infinitely better than that—it not only drowns out the old appetites, but it loads the ship with a new cargo of hopes and aspirations and desires until it becomes the simple, practical truth to say about a man thus genuinely converted to God that the things he once loved he now hates, and the things he once hated he now loves. The old man with his deeds is put off, and the new man, created in righteousness after Jesus Christ, is put on. That is the reason there are no cases too hard for Christ. That is the reason he is able to save unto the uttermost all that come unto God by him. He can save the vilest sinner, because he makes him over again, and makes him a new creature in Christ Jesus. May there be many such blessed transformations to-night!

He convicts of a judgment to come. He calls to men's mind the fact that "it is appointed unto men once to die, but after this the judgment." He arouses careless hearts to appreciate the fact that their sins are not the playthings of an hour, but are solemn and awful things that must be accounted for. They may be covered up for a time, but just as sure as God is, they will be unmasked. God's word is just as plain and direct upon this subject as upon any other. Jesus himself says: "There is nothing covered, that shall not be revealed; neither hid, that shall not be known." And again it is plainly declared that the Lord shall bring to light "the hidden things of darkness." Do you remember that old legend of the man who murdered his friend and covered his body with leaves? He covered it carefully, and thought it was hidden forever, but the wind came and blew them all away. Then he took a huge stone and tied it to the body and threw it into the sea. But the sea gave up its dead. Then he took it once more, and dug a deep grave and put the body in it. But it was of no use. An awful earthquake cast it forth. It could not be hid. So shall it happen to all of us. If we are trying to hide evil things of darkness in our lives, we may be sure they will come out. Hugh Price Hughes, speaking of a man committing suicide, says that there could not be a greater delusion, for the poor sinner only rushes into the blaze of day. We can not hide ourselves in that way. God will make manifest the counsels of the heart, even the counsels that have never found expression in word or deed. He will judge the secrets of men. Some of you would consider it an awful thing if I had the power to bring you here into this altar, and have you sit here while, inspired of God, I should take down the record which is being written by the angel on high, and read to this congregation the story of your life—the unwritten story of your inner self and your hidden thoughts and imaginations and plans and deeds; yet that would be nothing in proportion to what is going to happen, for the whole universe shall hear it. Oh, that the Spirit of God might convict you of the certainty of judgment to come, so that you may repent of your sin and have it blotted out by the blood of Christ here and now, instead of having it forced out of your unwilling lips on the day of judgment, when it is too late for repentance.

I thank God that if any now are convicted of sin, of righteousness, and of judgment, Jesus, the ascended Savior, will, if you repent of your sins and come to him in faith, intercede for you in the court of heaven. Christ not only bore our sins upon the cross, but he has ascended unto the right hand of God, where "he ever liveth to make intercession for us." Stephen, the first witness for the Lord Jesus to give his life for the faith, was permitted to see Jesus in the glory that now crowns him at the right hand of God. When his enemies gnashed upon him with their teeth, and the stones were showering upon him, "he, being full of faith and the Holy Ghost," kneeled down, looked up, and the heavens opened, displaying the glory of God. He exclaimed, "Behold, I see the heavens opened, and the Son of man standing on the right hand of God!" Enraptured at the glorious sight, and in perfect fellowship with his Lord, he prayed for his enemies in his dying hour, saying in reply to their demoniac rage and their cruel treatment, "Lord, lay not this sin to their charge." Then, with a glance at his Master through the opening heavens, he said, "Lord Jesus, receive my spirit," and fell asleep.

O wanderer away from God, convicted of sin, longing for a righteous life, conscious you are unprepared to meet the judgment day, I pray you to accept the intercessions of Jesus, your ascended Savior and Lord, and through him receive the forgiveness of your sins.

THE SYMBOLS OF THE SPIRIT.

"The rushing of a mighty wind."—*Acts* ii. 2 (*Revised Version*).

"Tongues . . . like as of fire."—*Acts* ii. 3 (*Revised Version*).

"I will pour forth of my Spirit."—*Acts* ii. 17 (*Revised Version*).

"Ye have an anointing from the Holy One."—1 *John* ii. 20 (*Revised Version*).

LET us go back for a moment to Bethany, and see that little group of disciples who have just witnessed the ascension of Jesus, and whose hearts have been comforted and strengthened and aroused to high purpose by the words of the angelic messengers. They go to Jerusalem, and there for forty days they tarry in earnest prayer, waiting for the promised coming of the Holy Spirit.

We have revealed to us something of the conditions which obtained at the time of the descent of the Holy Ghost upon them. Luke says: "And when the day of Pentecost was now come, they were all together in one place." If we desire that the Holy Ghost shall come upon us with still mightier power to make us efficient witnesses for Christ, there must be in our hearts something of the same longing for the Spirit, and of the same harmony of feeling and purpose. It is not necessary that we should all believe alike about non-essentials, but it is necessary that we shall love one another as the disciples did, that we shall love Christ supremely, and that we shall be unselfishly united in our earnest prayer for the coming of the Holy Spirit upon us. Are we thus united? Do we thus ardently desire the presence of the Spirit of God in our hearts? Is there in our hearts a sincere willingness to give up everything that stands in the way of our being used by the Holy Spirit with the greatest possible effect in the salvation of souls? Are we cherishing in our hearts or in our daily conduct anything that interferes with our being efficient ambassadors for Christ to those who have not yet come to know him? These are very solemn and earnest questions. A man may pray until the day of judgment for the gift of the Holy Spirit and the anointing of power for service; and if all the time he is unwilling to sacrifice certain habits or pleasures that are nullifying his Christian influence, the power from heaven will not be given him. During this very week an earnest Christian worker was pleading with a young woman who attends this church, urging her to come to Christ. The reason given for delay was that there were certain enjoyments which she felt would have to be given up if she became a genuine Christian. And then she remarked upon the conduct of certain members of our own congregation, saying that they conduct themselves in regard to the theater and things of that sort just the same as though they were not Christians. Now the important point is this: Whatever may be said about any questionable form of amusement, every Christian is under obligation to God to ask first about his action, "What influence is my conduct to have upon my credibility as a witness of Jesus Christ?" It is not my present purpose to make a crusade upon dancing, card-playing, and theater-going church-members; but I am impelled to bear my testimony that in twenty years in the ministry I have never known among those given over to this sort of amusements one person whose influence was effective in winning others to Christ; I have never known one such in the church, either man or woman, that was regarded as a spiritual Christian. I repeat the question, then: Are we willing, as God gives us to see the right from day to day, to give up anything that stands in the way of our being for Jesus Christ the most influential witnesses possible? These questions are pertinent under this theme.

These people who, under God, won three thousand men and women to Christ on the day of Pentecost (just one day!) were people of this spirit. To them Christ was all in all. Would it please Jesus? Would it advance the cause of the Redeemer? Would it tend to bring glory to the crucified and risen Lord?—such were the questions that were in their hearts, and such was the devotion that made it possible for God to use them as channels for divine grace to the sinning souls who heard their message.

I desire very briefly to call your attention to four symbols of the Spirit for which we are praying. The first comparison is to the "wind." The record says: "Suddenly there came from heaven a sound as of the rushing of a mighty wind." Jesus, in his conversation with Nicodemus concerning the new birth, said: "Marvel not that I said unto thee, Ye must be born again. The wind bloweth where it listeth, and thou hearest the sound thereof, but canst not tell whence it cometh, and whither it goeth: so is every one that is born of the Spirit." Wind signifies life. It is the mission of the Holy Spirit to give us life. Do you remember that wonderful vision of Ezekiel? Ezekiel was a heroic soul, thoroughly loyal to the message which he received from God. In common with many other such preachers, his course did not always run smoothly. In the first years of the exile, before Jerusalem perished, his countrymen still clung to the hope that it would yet be delivered. To add to his difficulties false prophets who were seeking only popular applause deluded the people with visions of peace when God said there was no peace. We have not time to follow his history, which is of striking interest, but only to glance at one of the visions by which God encouraged his soul, and which illustrates our theme. Under the influence of the prophetic spirit he was carried in a vision into the midst of a valley full of human bones; like a place in which a fierce battle has been fought, and very great multitudes have been slain, and, according to ancient custom, the dead left unburied till the flesh is all consumed, and the bones dried, divided, and scattered about. When he had gone round and round, and after careful survey of the bones found them to be very many and very dry, the marrow from within as well as the flesh from without being utterly wasted, God inquired of him, "Can these dry bones live?" To which he answered, with humility and faith, "O Lord God, thou knowest." No created power could restore them to life; but if God should please to put forth his power they might be raised from the dead and live. The Lord then ordered him to "Prophesy upon these bones"—to predict their resurrection, to call upon them to hear his word, and to speak over them the promises that follow concerning their being united and restored to life, that they might know his power and God-head. Surely no other preacher had quite so hard a congregation as that. It must be very trying to have all one's audience asleep at once. It must have seemed more hopeless to the prophet than to prophesy the restoration of Israel to their ancient posterity. But he started no objections, and obeyed his orders. While he was speaking he heard a noise, and saw a great commotion among the bones; every one of them seemed in quest of his kindred bone. Under the divine direction and influence each speedily found its proper place, and was joined to those bones which belonged to the same body, until the whole were formed into a vast number of complete skeletons; and then, as he watched, sinews and flesh and skin covered them, and they became entire human bodies, yet without life. The prophet was next ordered to "prophesy to the wind," and to command it, in the name of the Lord God, to blow from the four quarters of heaven upon these slain men, that they might live; and while he obeyed these orders they were restored to life, and he was surrounded by a large and enthusiastic army. This vision is full of illustrative truth. The church lacks power oftentimes because the religion of many of its members degenerates into a ghastly form or creed, with no flesh on the bones, no sinews of influence or power, no unity of purpose, and no spiritual life and energy. Oh, for the breathing of God's Spirit upon every member of this church!

Again, the coming of the Holy Spirit was accompanied at Pentecost with tongues of fire. And in a spiritualized sense that has been true of every great revival of Christian life since that day. One of the certain characteristics of a genuine revival of religion in the church is the quickening into life of the speech of those who are the followers of Jesus. Those who lead in prayer do not usually pray so long as before, but it is because their tongues are aflame and they forget to pray by rote and form, which is always the recourse of the cold heart. They speak forth earnest words of petition which come with electric thrill from the heart and flash in lightning sparks from the tongue. The testimony takes on a different type. There is about it a keener sense of gratitude to God, a tenderer feeling of love for Christ, a deeper earnestness that it may produce conviction. Richard Sheridan said he liked to go and hear Rowland Hill preach because his words flowed hissing-hot from his heart. Oh, that the baptism of fire might come down upon us, so that our tongues shall learn new skill in speaking forth with simplicity and truth, but with blood-earnestness, what great things the Lord hath done for our souls!

Another comparison very often used is suggested by the promise, "I will pour forth of my Spirit"—suggestive of cleansing, refreshing, and abundance; the water of life which shall spring up in the saved heart like an artesian well, flowing on ever in undiminished supply. But it is not obtained like an artesian well, for that is gotten by boring deep into the earth itself. The Spirit of God is something which we will never obtain by digging in our own hearts; but God is able to fulfil to us the promise which Christ made to the woman at the well in Samaria—that his Spirit bestowed shall afterward be in us a well of water, springing up unto everlasting life. How greatly we need that God shall pour out upon us streams of divine grace, and overflow our dry and thirsty hearts with the fulness of his Spirit! Did you never notice along little inlets by the seashore, where the coast-line is low and the sea marshes are broad, how when the tide goes out the rank vegetation that grows in along these little tide streams lies down on the mud, flat and flabby and formless and soiled? But when the tide comes back from the great ocean, what a transformation there is! Then these flabby and soiled plants rise up under the buoying influence of the salt water, and are beautiful as they wave in the breeze, made strong by the vitalizing current which fills every stem and leaf and pore. Thus it is with us as Christians when the full tide of divine grace from the heart of God flows into our hearts and vitalizes our affections, our intellects, our wills, and fills us with the glory of our Christ.

There is still another comparison to the coming of the Holy Spirit, which John describes as "an anointing from the Holy One." Under the Old Testament dispensation prophets, priests, and kings were anointed with consecrating oil as a symbol of their calling and of their fitness for their special offices. Under the new dispensation every Christian is to be a prophet. Peter, on the day of Pentecost, called attention to that promise in his sermon: "But this is that which was spoken by the prophet Joel; and it shall come to pass in the last days, saith God, I will pour out of my Spirit upon all flesh: and your sons and your daughters shall prophesy, and your young men shall see visions, and your old men shall dream dreams: and on my servants and my handmaidens I will pour out in those days of my Spirit; and they shall prophesy." Every one of us is to be a prophet in the sense that we are to tell forth to the people the glad news of salvation. Every Christian, too, is to be a priest, in that he is to be, by pleading and persuasion and prayer, a mediator between God and men whom he would win to Christ. Oh, that God would anoint us for this purpose! This anointing from the Holy One makes us kings, also, who need not be ashamed of our monarchy. Solomon said, "Better is he that ruleth his spirit than he that taketh a city." Instead of being the slaves of appetite and passion, the bondmen of wicked habits, pursued by the bloodhounds of besetting sins, he who yields his heart completely up to the incoming of the Divine Spirit, who bows his head and heart to the anointing of the Holy One, is given power to become the son of God, and by God's grace becomes a king over the monarchy of his own nature.

And you that are not Christians, but are trusting in your own strength, following your own path—I call you to forsake your sins and accept the fulness of this rich and beautiful life which Jesus Christ offers to you. In the seventeenth chapter of Jeremiah there is a wonderful contrast drawn between the life that rejects God and the life that is open to receive all that he is willing to bestow. Notice the graphic strength of these two pictures: "Thus saith the Lord: Cursed be the man that trusteth in man, and maketh flesh his arm, and whose heart departeth from the Lord.

For he shall be like the heath in the desert, and shall not see when good cometh; but shall inhabit the parched places in the wilderness, in a salt land and not inhabited." But now notice the marvelous contrast suggested in the words that follow: "Blessed is the man that trusteth in the Lord, and whose hope the Lord is. For he shall be as a tree planted by the waters, and that spreadeth out her roots by the river, and shall not see when heat cometh, but her leaf shall be green; and shall not be careful in the year of drought, neither shall cease from yielding fruit." How true to life these pictures are! I beg of every one whose heart has departed from God and who is living in the desert of sin, where there can be no satisfying and permanent peace, but ever and anon the hot winds of unrest and remorse, to ask God's grace to transplant you and transform you so that you shall be like the tree planted by the rivers of water, where you may lean the weight of your needs, and cares, and sins, and sorrows, upon "him who careth for you."

PRICKED HEARTS AND THEIR CURE.

"Now when they heard this, they were pricked in their heart, and said unto Peter and the rest of the apostles, Brethren, what shall we do? And Peter said unto them, Repent ye, and be baptized every one of you in the name of Jesus Christ unto the remission of your sins; and ye shall receive the gift of the Holy Ghost."—*Acts* ii. 37, 38 (*Revised Version*).

AFTER the Sermon on the Mount by Jesus himself, this sermon of Peter on the day of Pentecost is the most famous in the history of the world. It is the first presentation of the Gospel to the multitude after the ascension of Jesus. We have, of course, but a condensed outline of the sermon, but enough to show us something of its scope and character. It was not a sermon that had been prepared very long beforehand, tho Peter had been preparing himself beforehand by a most earnest and faithful study of the Old Testament Scriptures. His quotations from the Prophets, and the Psalms, and his careful setting forth of the history of his people, clearly proving that Jesus Christ was the true Messiah, show that he was ready to give a reason for the faith that was in him. He had the still further preparation without which a knowledge of history and the Bible is unavailing —the anointing of the Holy Ghost.

A strong picture is presented to our imagination by this chapter: A great multitude of people surround the disciples, and the crowd constantly increases as the services proceed. There, in the midst of the throng, stands Peter, a strong, robust fisherman, with none of the graces of the schools, but aflame with earnestness and magnetic with the power of the Holy Ghost. There is no attempt made at elegance of rhetoric or oratorical finish, but just a big, blunt, plain-spoken man, trembling with holy passion, on fire to the very tips of his fingers, speaking out of the Scriptures, and still more out of his own heart history, what he knows about the life and death and resurrection of Jesus Christ. Such a man will never lack hearers. People may not be pleased with him always, but they will always want to hear him. He is absolutely fearless of everybody except God. He tells these people to their teeth that they themselves have taken the Lord Jesus, the Prince of Life, and by cruel, murderous hands, have put him to death upon the cross. If it had not been that the Holy Ghost was with him, and in their own consciences they knew he spoke the truth, they would have stoned him to death. Oh, that God will give us the power to speak to men's hearts! "I have an ear for other preachers," Sir John Cheke used to say, "but I have a heart for Latimer." George Whitefield went to preach once at Exeter. A ruffian went to the meeting with his pockets full of stones to throw at the preacher. He waited through the prayer, thinking it would be greater sport to stop Whitefield after he got to preaching. As soon as the text was named he pulled out a stone, and waited for a good opportunity to throw it. But the Holy Spirit sent almost the first sentences straight to his heart, and the missile fell from his hand. When the sermon was over, he went to Whitefield, and said, "Sir, I came to hear you, intending to break your head, but the Spirit of God, through your words, has broken my heart." The man was gloriously converted, and became an influential Christian. So as these men and women in the public street listened to Peter and the one hundred and twenty others who were scattered all through the crowd, everywhere, speaking the same message about Christ to everybody they could get to listen, the hearers were pricked in their hearts and began to cry out, "Brethren, what shall we do?"

Notice this—that it was their hearts, not their heads, that were pricked. The seat of sin is in the human heart. A while ago, when a notoriously wicked man was executed in this State for the murder of his wife, a committee of physicians examined the man's brain, and made a report that they were not able to find any cause of his crime in that organ. Why should they? They were altogether on the wrong track. They were looking in the wrong place. The man's brain was keen and bright. The trouble with him was that he had a desperately wicked heart. His heart it was, and not his brain, that was "a cage of unclean birds," "full of dead men's bones and all uncleanness." As a journalist said who commented on it at the time, he was bad not because the physical nature played bad tricks with the white matter of the brain, but because he chose to be. It is not strange that the man's downward career to crime could not be explained by the surgeons' scalpels. It is impossible to find the sources of such wickedness by cutting into a man's head, as you would search for a fountain of water by boring into the ground. The Bible explained it long ago a good deal better than the surgeon can ever explain it with his knife: "Whatsoever a man soweth, that shall he also reap;" he that soweth the wind, shall reap the whirlwind.

Universal human consciousness bears witness to the prevalence of sin in the human heart. As another said, not long since, the sense of sin is not something that we have been educated into by living in a Christian country. All the traditions and legends and records of humanity in every race and tribe of the world bear testimony that men have ever been conscious of sin, and that the sinful heart has ever been a stern fact of human nature which no people have ever been able to ignore or reason away. The leaders of every age and tribe of mankind have never ceased to think, and talk, and (if they knew how to write) record the consciousness of sin which has shadowed their pathway and burdened their hearts. A semi-infidel critic has had the candor to confess that "a guileless hero would be no hero for a drama." Take the thieves, hypocrites, liars, adulterers, conspirators, and murderers out of Shakespeare's tragedies, and who would go to a theater to see them performed? The result of Peter's sermon, accusing these people to their face of their sins, shows that there is in every man's bosom a court which weighs his conduct and pronounces judgment upon it, and convinces him that sin in his own heart is a terrible reality. The Bible says that "fools make a mock at sin." Ingersoll calls a conviction of sin "a nightmare—the result of too much appetite and too little digestion." But it was something more than a nightmare that made a far more honest infidel than Ingersoll say, speaking of the agony of his heart, "My principles have poisoned my friends, my extravagance has beggared my child, and my unkindness has murdered my wife! O God, is there yet another hell? But hell itself will be a refuge if it only hide me from thy face."

But, thanks be to God, the Gospel never warns and the Holy Spirit never convicts of sin without suggesting a remedy. And so Peter had something to tell them when, in his faithful preaching of the divine truth, he had by the aid of the Holy Spirit brought the multitude under conviction of sin, until their hearts were pricked and wounded, and they cried out, "Brethren, what shall we do?" In substance his reply was this: "Repent at once, cease your evil ways, turn to the Lord Jesus Christ whom ye crucified, but whom the grave could not hold; be baptized in his name, showing forth your obedience to him and your confidence in him, and you shall receive the remission of your sins." Simple obedience to Jesus Christ is the only cure for pricked hearts. O brother, sister! conscious of your sin, longing to be free from it, why will you not at once obey the simple conditions of salvation and publicly confess the Lord Jesus Christ as your Savior?

You remember the story of Naaman, the Syrian, who was a leper, and who had in the service of his wife a little maid, who spoke to her about

Elisha and that he would be able to cure her master of leprosy. I want to recommend to you the prompt action of that man who had so little light to guide him. He did not raise any objections at all. He did not despise the news of a possible cure because the doctor was over in Israel, a foreign country; but he was willing to have the cure at the hands of anybody that could perform it. Neither was he silly enough to despise the message because it came from the mouth of a little slave-girl. It is the letter that is important, not the particular postman who brings it. The people about that Syrian court were wise folks. Everybody about the place set to work as soon as they heard of the possibility of Naaman's being cured. The king of Syria wrote a letter to the king of Israel. They got together rich presents and made preparations for a quick journey. Naaman felt that everything was to be gained by promptness; while by delay he might lose everything. He not only went, but he went at once. The action of that Syrian general ought to rebuke some of you who hear me at this hour. How little light he had, and how much light you have! You have heard so much about Jesus Christ and his salvation that you are satisfied, intellectually, that no one is able to break the bondage of sin, cleanse your heart of evil, and give you the assurance of heaven and immortal life except Jesus Christ. Think of it! Naaman went to his cure on the testimony of one little girl who quite possibly had never seen the prophet at all. Naaman did not even know exactly where he lived; yet he starts at once, seizing and acting upon what little knowledge he has, as a drowning man clutches at a floating plank. But think of the testimony that has surrounded you all your life long! Many of your dearest friends, the people whom you have known and loved most, have been personally acquainted with Jesus Christ, and you have never doubted their sincerity. They have told you that the sweetest comfort of life has been the assurance of salvation they have found in Jesus Christ. And yet you hesitate and delay, and allow the foul leprosy of sin to spread in your heart and life.

Mark Guy Pearse surely does not speak too strongly when he says that there is only one word in the language that could have expressed the folly of Naaman if, instead of going to Samaria, he had sent for the little maid of Israel, and said: "Tell me all about your great prophet. What is his name? What is he like? What does he do? Where does he live?" And then, after half an hour's talk with her, he would send for her again in a week's time and hear something more about the prophet. How the little maid would have wrung her hands and cried, "Hear about it! No, my lord, you must go to him, and go quick!" Think if he should have told his musicians to sing of this Elisha and chant his greatness, and week after week should sit and listen to the story of the captive maiden. "I like to hear her," says he, "she is so much in earnest, and her gestures are so graceful, and her words so well chosen." O fool! and all the time the leprosy is eating into him with horrid cruelty, deeper and deeper, and every day he is growing more hideous and scarred, and his case becomes more desperate. And the longer he delays the more he questions about going at all.

One day the king of Syria comes to see him. "Well, have you been?" he asks.

"Been where?" says Naaman.

"Why, to the great prophet that can heal you of your leprosy," cries the king in astonishment.

"No," says Naaman; "I have not exactly been to him, but I have heard all about him, and have got quite familiar with his name and history, and know a great deal that he has said and done."

"But, surely," cries the disappointed king, "it were as well never to have heard of him if you do not go."

Naaman gets weaker every day, and one day the news goes with hushed voice through the palace and the city, "Naaman is dead; died of his leprosy. Dead! And he knew so much about the prophet!" And the little maid in the palace wails, "Would to God my lord had gone to the prophet that is in Samaria!"

Oh, no; Naaman did not do that way. It is only in religion that men play the fool like that; only in the more dreadful and deeper leprosy of the soul! How could there be any more terrible folly than to hear about Christ as your Savior year in and year out and yet never come to him? Oh, cease this unwise course. Drop everything else, and come to the Christ who is able to save you from your sins!

Do not let the devil cheat you of your soul's salvation by any cunning sophistry. Sometimes he says to a man, "You have waited so long, you have wasted so many opportunities, there is so little left, that it is useless to come now." Don't let the devil cheat you. The poor dying thief upon the cross had wasted a whole lifetime, yet Christ did not rebuke him for coming, but lovingly received him. Professor Henry Drummond tells the story of a young student in the university where he is a professor. He was a fine, manly fellow, a medical student, a very Hercules in strength; but he contracted typhoid fever and soon lay dying in a hospital. One of the physicians who attended him was an earnest Christian and a successful soul-winner, and he spoke to him about God and eternity. The young man listened, became anxious, and eagerly heard the story of redeeming love. "Will you give yourself now to Jesus?" asked the doctor. He did not answer for a while, and then, earnestly regarding the good man, he said, "But don't you think it would be awful mean just to make it up now, at my last gasp, with One I have rejected all my life?" "Yer, it would be mean; but, dear fellow, it would be far meaner not to do it. He wants you to do it now, for he has made you willing, and it would be doubly mean to reject a love that is pursuing you even to death." The dying man saw the point, and, appreciating the tenderness of the Savior's love, he accepted it with joyous thanksgiving. So I plead with you not to stay away because you have stayed away so long. The only return you can make for the past is to come now, at once, and from this moment give the Savior all your love and all your service.

PETER, JOHN, AND A CRIPPLE.

"In the name of Jesus Christ of Nazareth, walk. And he took him by the right hand, and raised him up."—*Acts* iii. 6, 7 (*Revised Version*).

THE historical setting of this picture is full of interest and suggestiveness. The glory of Pentecost had passed by. After such a marvelous day of victory, in which three thousand souls had been added to the church, the temptation was to despise small things and the routine duties of daily Christian life. But we see Peter and John on their way to the temple at the hour of the ordinary prayer-meeting. I am always alarmed about a man who is full of enthusiasm for special missions and times of unusual excitement, but can never be depended on for the regular prayer-meeting and class-meeting. A genuine, wholesome Christianity will make a man loyal to the every-day duties of Christian life. That church is rich which has many people who are humble enough and loyal enough to Christ to faithfully stand by the house of God and perform the ordinary duties which devolve upon them. Let us not get too large for following the example of our Master who went about doing good to humble people, in individual cases, and on common week-days. The temptation is to feel that nothing is worth doing unless it is something that makes a large show.

Dr. Williams, of Atlanta, Georgia, tells how he was struggling for a long time to get into a deeper religious experience. Finally, he was one day passing through a great Exposition and stopped in front of a potter at work. As he stood with a friend before the little stand and saw the workman fashioning the piece of clay, a great ugly lump, he thought of the words in the sixty-fourth chapter of Isaiah: "But now, O Lord, thou art our Father: we are the clay, and thou our potter; and we all are the work of thy hands." The potter fashioned the clay for a moment and then threw it upon the lathe, and, with a few quick turns of the foot, it came out before him the rough mold of a beautiful Corinthian vase. He turned to his friend and said, "How beautiful! Who would not like to be a Corinthian vase? How beautifully the potter understands his work!" The man turned it back into a lump again and dropped it on the lathe, and after a few deft touches it came out a vase of old Egyptian style. Anybody could afford to be an Egyptian vase, thought Dr. Williams; not quite as beautiful as the Corinthian, but valuable to a searcher for bric-à-brac. He threw it on the lathe again, and it came out a common table-plate. He did not like that so much. He threw it into a mass again, and it came out, to the doctor's consternation, a cuspidor. He said, "I don't want to be a cuspidor." But the clay found no fault with the potter. It seemed as well satisfied when a cuspidor as when it was a Corinthian vase. Then he looked at the beauty of the workmanship. "Well," he said, "the potter knows best." He turned away from the lathe and from the potter that day with some new thoughts, and said, "Now, Williams, you did not want to be a cuspidor. You would be a Corinthian vase; that is what you have been wanting to be all these days. You have been willing to be a piece of old Egyptian pottery, and have some one search you out and put you on the mantel, but you did not want to be a common table-plate, and you would not be a cuspidor for anything in the world." When he went to his room that night, the picture was still following him, and when he got down on his knees he said, "No, you would not, would you, Williams? But your Lord and your Master became a cuspidor for wicked men to spit upon; no! the servant wants to be greater than his lord." He wrestled there before God as Jacob did with the angel at the Jabbok ford, and when he got up from his knees it was with a holy joy in his heart that he stood again before God with his open Bible and bowed head, and said, "O Master, Savior, Jesus Christ, if you want to use me for a cuspidor or anything else, if it pleaseth thee, O thou great Potter, it is all I ask!" May that same spirit of humble consecration possess all our hearts! It is not how much show our lives make, but how much honest, faithful service there is in them for the Master, that is important. As the poet sings:

"Beautiful faces are those that wear—
It matters not whether dark or fair—
Whole-souled honesty printed there.

"Beautiful eyes are those that show—
Like crystal panes where hearth-fires glow—
Beautiful thoughts that burn below.

"Beautiful lips are those whose words
Leap from the heart like songs of birds,
Yet whose utterance wisdom girds.

"Beautiful hands are those that do
Work that is earnest, brave, and true,
Moment by moment, the long day through.

"Beautiful feet are they that go
On kindly ministry, to and fro,
Down lowliest ways, if God wills so.

"Beautiful shoulders are those that bear
Ceaseless burdens of homely care,
With patient grace and daily prayer.

"Beautiful lives are those that bless—
Silent rivers of helpfulness
Whose hidden fountains few may guess.

"Beautiful twilight at set of sun;
Beautiful goal with race well run;
Beautiful rest with work well done;

"Beautiful graves where grasses creep,
Where brown leaves fall, where drifts lie deep
Over worn-out hands—oh! beautiful sleep."

That is a suggestive sentence of Peter when the lame man asks of him an alms and he replies, "Silver and gold have I none; but what I have, that give I thee." Christianity is a giving religion. It is impossible that one should have the spirit of Christ and refuse to reach out his hand of help to those that need. If I speak to any who are specially tempted to selfishness, I entreat you to lose no opportunity to crush out that wicked and unchristian spirit. Mr. Moody tells the story of a wealthy farmer in this State who was converted. He had been a noted miser and a very selfish man. Soon after his conversion a poor man came to him one day to ask for help. He had been burned out, and had no provisions. This young convert thought he would be liberal and give him a ham from his smoke-house. He started toward the smoke-house, and on the way the devil tempted him and said, "Give him the smallest one you have." He struggled all the way as to whether he would give a large or a small one. In order to overcome his selfishness, he took down the biggest ham and gave it to the man. The tempter said, "You are a fool;" but he replied, "If you don't keep still, I will give him every ham I have in the smoke-house!" That is the wise spirit with which to resist the devil. Everything that we have belongs to God. It is only loaned to us. We are trustees and must give an account of our stewardship. Peter had no money to give to this man; but he had something infinitely better than money —he could restore to him his health. Some of you have not much money that you can give either to your neighbor or to spread abroad the Gospel of Christ; but you have hearts full of sympathy, you have the knowledge of your sins forgiven, you have the peace that passeth understanding; and these are riches for which our poor world is suffering more than for anything else.

There is another important thought here—that Peter entered upon the healing of this man with an entire personal consecration of himself. He not only demanded the man's attention to himself and commanded him in the name of Jesus of Nazareth to walk, but he acted as though he believed it was going to be done and that he was glad to have a hand in it. Notice the language: "He took him by the right hand, and raised him up." We want the consecration that will personally take hold upon people with all the power there is in us. You get interested in people for whom you do a personal service. Some poet says:

> "All's yours and you,
> All colored with your blood, or otherwise
> Just nothing to you. Why, I call you hard
> To general suffering.
> You weep for what you know. A red-haired child
> Sick in a fever, if you touch him once,
> Will set you weeping; but a million sick—
> You could as soon weep for the rule of three."

That is the true secret of the joy and glory of service for others. Coming into personal contact, sympathy is aroused, and if we are filled with the grace of God, divine virtue will go out from us.

Dr. Theodore Cuyler preached one Sunday in Dundee, Scotland, in the pulpit of Robert McCheyne. He asked some one: "Is there anybody living here who used to belong to his church?" The reply was, "Yes, that old gray-headed man." Dr. Cuyler introduced himself, and said, "What can you tell me about McCheyne?" This was the old man's answer: "I was a young man when he died, and a few days before he died he met me in the street and put his hand on my shoulder and said, 'Jemmie, how is it with your soul? I am going to see your sick sister.'" The touch of Mc-Cheyne's hand on that Scotch lad's shoulder made the blood tingle in his veins fifty years after, when he was old and gray. God help us that we shall not be afraid to reach out our hands to people.

But after all, these were only the methods of communicating the divine power. Peter was conscious that he had something to give this man; but the something was not his own, he was only the trustee of it. It was the magical name of Christ, which he was to speak in the man's ear, which was to do the work. "In the name of Jesus of Nazareth, walk." It would have meant nothing for Peter to have said that had his words not been accompanied by the Holy Ghost; but the divine presence in them made them words of living power. As he uttered them and stretched out his hand to seize the man's hand, there was that about his whole attitude, the flash in his eye, the glow of expectation on his cheek, the posture of his body, the firm, strong grip of his hand which made the man's blood boil to his very heart, and as he looked in Peter's eyes all things seemed possible. He never had walked, he had been crippled from his babyhood; but the spirit of Peter—nay, the living Christ that was in Peter—aroused a strange sensation of faith and hope in his heart, and he made the effort to get up. There was a tingling sensation in his ankles. The poor, crippled bones straightened and strengthened, and, wonder of wonders, he stood upon his feet. Everybody was astonished, a crowd gathered, but the healed man was only conscious that he could stand on his limbs. He takes a step or two to test it. It is no dream, for he can walk. Then his heart overflows and he goes wild with enthusiasm. He hops, and skips, and jumps, and leaps, and shouts praises unto God!

Oh, there are some here this morning who are crippled by sin, and are lying at the very gate of the temple—the beautiful gate arched over with the Savior's love. Some of you have been lying there for a long time. Oh, for the power of the Holy Spirit to come down upon me so that I may look in your eyes and grasp you by the hand and speak the magic words, "In the name of Jesus of Nazareth, walk!"

TURNING OVER A NEW LEAF.

"Repent ye therefore, and turn again, that your sins may be blotted out."—*Acts* iii. 19 (*Revised Version*).

REPENTANCE lies at the very first step toward salvation. It is the key which unlocks the outer gate. John the Baptist came preaching in the wilderness the doctrine of repentance. Jesus took up the message where he left off and preached, "Repent, for the kingdom of heaven is at hand." There is no other way into the fold. Men have sought easier ways, but they have always failed. The only way into the kingdom of God is through repentance. Thomas Moore, the poet, in his song of "Paradise and the Peri," illustrates this truth with great clearness. He says that,—

> "One morn a Peri at the gate
> Of Eden stood disconsolate.
> And as she listened to the springs
> Of life within like music flowing,
> And caught the light upon her wings
> Through the half-open portal glowing,
> She wept to think her recreant race
> Should e'er have lost that glorious place."

So sad was she about it that her broken heart expressed its sorrow in a song of touching grief which attracted the notice of the angel whose place of honor was to stand guard at the gates of light. He listened to her sad song until his eyes were suffused with tears, and he replied to her,—

> "'Nymph of a fair but erring line,'
> Gently he said, 'One hope is thine.
> 'Tis written in the book of fate,
> The Peri yet may be forgiven
> Who brings to this eternal gate
> The gift that is most dear to heaven.
> Go seek it, and redeem thy sin;
> 'Tis sweet to let the pardoned in.'"

A flash of hope came into the eyes of the exiled wanderer, and full of purpose sublime—

> "Rapidly as comets run
> To the embraces of the sun
> Down the blue vault the Peri flies."

She went everywhere, seeking earnestly to find what would be the most precious gift to carry back to the gates of light. She came at length to where an army of brave men were fighting against oppression, inspired by love of liberty and noble patriotism. In the midst of the cruel battle she saw a brave youth beset by his enemies. He fought nobly against overmastering arms, but finally fell bleeding and dying to the earth. The Peri flew and caught the—

> "Last glorious drop his heart had shed
> Before its freeborn spirit fled.
> 'Be this,' she cried, as she winged her flight,
> 'My welcome gift at the gates of light.
> . . . Blood like this
> For liberty shed so holy is.
> Oh, if there be on this earthly sphere
> A boon, an offering heaven holds dear,
> 'Tis the last libation Liberty draws
> From the heart that bleeds and breaks in her cause.'"

However we may honor patriotism and heroic valor in behalf of one's native land, or for a noble cause, history has proved to us that it has no power to cleanse a wicked heart, or to fit a sinful soul for the fellowships of the kingdom of heaven. Whoever shall trust in any record of works of righteousness which he has done to give him entrance into the gates of light, will be as disappointed as the Peri was when she heard the sad words,—

> "Sweet is our welcome to the brave
> Who die thus for their native land.
> But see, alas! the crystal bar
> Of Eden moves not. Holier far
> Than even this drop the boon must be
> That opes the gates of heaven for thee."

The Peri was greatly disappointed, but the sense of need in her famished spirit was so great that she gathered courage again and winged her way back to our poor earth. In her search she lights upon a city that is suffering from a deadly plague. Looking upon the misery of the people, she finds a young man who is dying from the loathsome and deadly disease and from whom all have fled except one, a woman who loves him and who, reckless of danger from the plague, has searched him out and has remained to comfort the one so dear to her, tho at the cost of her own life.

> "One struggle and the pain is past,
> Her lover is no longer living;
> One kiss the maiden gives, one last
> Long kiss, which she expires in giving.
> This farewell sigh of that vanishing soul,
> As true as e'er warmed a woman's breast,
> Softly the Peri stole, and then,
> Bearing to heaven that precious sigh
> Of pure, self-sacrificing love"—

she came once more to the guardian angel at the gates of light. She fondly thought that in that self-forgetful love of womanhood there was something so infinitely precious that before it the great gate would swing on its hinges. But, alas! how many of us have seen that priceless boon of a woman's love lavished upon the sinner's heart only to be trampled under his heel. How many a self-denying woman has followed the footsteps of a drunkard with the patience of an angel; given her money, her time, her love unstinted, to try to win the one so dear to her away from the loathsome bondage that enthralled him; but all in vain! And so we are not astonished that the guardian angel shook his head and said, "Not yet."

> "'True was that maiden, and her story
> By seraph eyes shall long be read;
> But, Peri, see; the crystal bar
> Of Eden moves not; holier far
> Than even this sigh the gift must be
> That opes the gates of heaven for thee.'"

Greatly discouraged and sadly cast down, but patiently persevering so long as there should be one ray of hope, Peri slowly wings her way back to earth again, seeking—

> "Where beneath the moon
> In earth or ocean lies the boon,
> The charm, that can restore
> An erring spirit to the skies."

While pursuing her almost hopeless search, she discovers a beautiful little child playing among the wild-flowers, himself the sweetest flower of them all. And after a while, tired at his play, he lies down amid the blossoms and the grasses and falls into an innocent, childish sleep. While he is sleeping, a rider who has had a long journey and is evidently very weary throws himself from his fagged steed to get a drink at a spring near where the little boy slumbers among the flowers. The man is fierce and repulsive-looking. His brow is haggard, and there is a certain sullen ferocity in his look—

> "A mixture dire
> Like thunder-clouds of gloom and fire,
> In which the Peri's eye could read
> Dark tales of many a ruthless deed:
> The ruined maid, the shrine profaned,
> Oaths forsaken, and the threshold stained
> With blood of guests were written; all
> Black as the damning drops that fall
> From the denouncing angel's pen
> Ere Mercy wipes them out again."

The man takes a long, deep draught of the cool water, and as he turns away from the spring his wicked eyes light by chance on the form of the innocent sleeper. Something in the sweet face of the child touches him deeply, and he stops to look again. While he is thus engaged, the vesper-bells in the distance ring out on the calm air of the evening, calling to prayer. The little boy awakes from his slumber and, dropping down on his knees among the flowers, lifts his childish voice in prayer. Memory carries the wicked man back over the wayward path of his life, and across the dark years he has spent in sin, to the time when he, too, was a little boy, innocent and simple and pure as the one kneeling there before him. He sees again the picture of himself before he had learned to take God's name in vain, but only used it in reverence and in prayer.

> "He hung his head ; each nobler aim
> And hope and feeling which had slept
> From boyhood's hour that instant came
> Fresh o'er him, and he wept—he wept
> Blest tears of soul-felt penitence
> In whose benign, redeeming flow
> Is felt the first and only sense
> Of guiltless joy that guilt can know.
>
> "And now behold him kneeling there
> Beside that child in humble prayer,
> While the same sunbeam shines upon
> The guilty and the guiltless one,
> And hymns of joy proclaim through heaven
> The triumph of a soul forgiven."

That tear of penitence it is that the Peri seizes upon with a new and more glorious hope than ever. As she flies toward the heavenly gate her track through the skies is illuminated with a

TURNING OVER A NEW LEAF. 233

light from the glory world. A radiance shines about her more beautiful than earth has ever known—

> "A light more lovely far
> Than ever came from earth or star.
> Ah! well the enraptured Peri knew
> 'Twas a bright glance the angel threw
> From heaven's gate to hail that tear,
> The harbinger of glory near."

Thank God! that picture is no mere poetic fancy; it is only an elaboration of the blessed declaration of the Lord Jesus Christ that "There is joy among the angels of God over one sinner that repenteth."

We have suggested to us in the language of the text the great characteristic of repentance in the words "turn again." There is a great deal of confusion in the minds of many people as to what repentance is. People get it mixed up with being sorry for sin. But repentance and sorrow for sin are very separate and distinct things. There is plenty of sorrow for sin in remorse, but no real repentance. As some poet sings,—

> "Repentance and remorse are not the same;
> That is a heavenly, this an earthly flame:
> One springs from love and is a welcome guest;
> And one an iron tyrant o'er the breast.

> Repentance weeps before the Crucified;
> Remorse is nothing more than wounded pride.
> Remorse through horror into hell is driven,
> While true repentance always goes to heaven."

Many people are sorry for their sins and imagine there is some virtue in their sorrow; but there is not unless it leads them to repentance, the very essence of which is "turning again." The Bible speaks of a "godly sorrow" which "worketh a repentance that needeth not to be repented of." The reason it does not need to be repented of is that it prompts the sinner that experiences it to change the course of his conduct and causes him "to cease to do evil and begin to do well."

Sometimes men who are convicted of sin, whose conscience tells them they are doing wrong, and whose judgment assures them that it is their duty to turn from their sins and confess Christ, hesitate and hold back because they think they ought to wait for some overpowering tempest of sorrow and grief before they act in the acceptance of the terms of salvation. Mr. Beecher used to illustrate it this way: Two children are quarreling; they have disobeyed their father and their mother, and they have come to blows, and they are both arraigned before the mother. One of them, as the mother looks upon him, bursts into tears and says: "O mother, I am sorry, I am sorry," and he rushes to her, buries his head in her lap, and is forgiven. The other says: "I am not sorry, and I am not going to be sorry," and the mother talks to him, but he pouts all the more. By and by she administers some punishment; that makes him more obstinate, and he fights it out all the afternoon and evening. Then he is sent to bed without his supper. Next morning he gets up and has nothing to eat. About noon, or toward night, he begins to come round, and finally he goes sneaking up to his mother and says: "Mother, I think I was wrong." Now which was the nobler of the two dispositions? The moment that one of them saw that he was wrong he gave up and confessed it; the other doggedly, obstinately, meanly, held out. Does not that illustrate the condition of some who hear me? You are satisfied that Jesus Christ is the Savior of the world. In your best hours you desire to be a Christian, and you are conscious as I speak that it is your duty to at once give yourself up to a Christian life. You are also conscious that you know enough about it to begin to change your life right here and now by openly confessing Christ, and, turning about, ask him to convert your soul and blot out your transgressions. Yet you are waiting for some greater influence, some powerful persuasion that you will not be able to resist. My brother, the noblest thing you can do is not to wait to be overwhelmed with the discipline of God or the persuasions of the Holy Spirit; but seeing that you are in the wrong, and have sinned against God, confess it at once, and turn about face, and begin to do promptly that which is right. Begin right where you are. Don't wait for anything else.

A professional diver has in his house what seems a very strange ornament for a mantel. It is a bunch of oyster shells holding fast a piece of printed paper. The possessor of this ornament was diving one day, when he observed, at the bottom of the sea, this oyster on a rock with the piece of paper in its mouth. The diver detached the oyster and held the paper up close to the goggles of his head-dress and commenced to read. It was a little gospel tract earnestly calling upon whoever should read it to repent at once and give his heart to God. It came upon him so unexpectedly and so impressed his unconverted heart, that he said: "I can not hold out against God's mercy in Christ any longer, since it pursues me thus." And down there at the bottom of the sea he repented, he turned again, he breathed out his heart to God in prayer, and when he came back to the top of the water it was with the glad consciousness that his sins were blotted out. Some of you who hear me here are clear down at the bottom of a sea of difficulties and perplexities and sinful entanglements that make it seem impossible for you to become a Christian; but, my friends, your part is simply to turn about and face the other way, and Jesus Christ will cut the whole net of your entanglements with one thrust of his glittering sword.

How splendidly suggestive is the word that is used here to express the complete annihilation of our sins if we honestly repent of them and turn to Christ in faith! It brings back to our minds the words of the Lord through the mouth of his prophet Isaiah: "Come now, and let us reason together, saith the Lord: tho your sins be as scarlet, they shall be as white as snow; tho they be red like crimson, they shall be as wool." They tell us that there is a little river in the island of Corsica which has the remarkable property of whitening anything that is thrown into it. Its waters are as clear as crystal, and every stone or other object seen on the bed of this wonderful stream is as white as snow. Any kind of metal, but particularly iron, when dipped into it, has the appearance of being plated with silver. That is very wonderful, but not so marvelous nor so beneficent as that—

"Fountain filled with blood,
Drawn from Immanuel's veins;"

where

"Sinners, plunged beneath that flood,
Lose all their guilty stains."

THE ONE SAVING NAME.

"And in none other is there salvation: for neither is there any other name under heaven, that is given among men, wherein we must be saved."—*Acts* iv. 12 (*Revised Version*).

THIS is the conclusion of Peter's splendid tribute to Christ when the multitude were marveling concerning the healing of the lame man at the gate of the temple. Annas and Caiaphas, who had had so much to do with the crucifixion of Christ, found that they had not put down this new religion by crucifying Jesus. It must have given those shrewd men much food for earnest thought when Peter, filled with the Holy Ghost, said unto them, "Ye rulers of the people, and elders, if we this day are examined concerning a good deed done to an impotent man, by what means this man is made whole; be it known unto you all, and to all the people of Israel, that in the name of Jesus Christ of Nazareth, whom ye crucified, whom God raised from the dead, even in him doth this man stand here before you whole. He is the stone which was set at nought of you the builders, which was made the head of the corner. And in none other is there salvation; for neither is there any other name under heaven, that is given among men, wherein we must be saved."

This question of salvation is as interesting to us as it was to Peter. Christ would not have come from heaven to share our sorrow and grief, to suffer loneliness and disgrace and shame, and die upon the cross for our redemption, unless there were something from which we have need to be saved. As has been well said, the very thought of saving suggests the most perilous and dangerous situations. When we hear the word saved applied to a fellow-being, it calls before our imagination the vision of the fireman climbing his ladder through the flames in a desperate attempt to rescue some poor man or woman or child who would otherwise be lost; or we think of the lifeboat amid wild winds and tumbling seas, striving to reach the wreck where, clinging to the mast or the rigging, are the half-perished crew, lost unless some one comes to save them; or we see a swimmer struggling desperately to reach a drowning man. Many times when we use the word we think of the doctor at the bedside in the sick-room, patient and alert, watching through the weary hours, making a brave fight for the life of the sufferer. And what joy there is when in a critical case the crisis has passed, and the few hours which must decide for life or death have gone, and you leave the room with the doctor, who with a sigh of relief says, "I think he is saved now, and we will pull him through all right." Those are the kind of things to which God compares the salvation of the soul from sin. Sin is not a small matter. It is so loathsome and terrible a thing that in order to save us from it, and its undying penalty, God in his great love gave Jesus to come and live and suffer and die—to be our Savior. Is it not significant that the most terrible, awful words spoken in the Bible concerning the punishment for sin are spoken by the tender lips of Jesus—the lips that drank the wormwood and the gall to save us? They are words that none of us should ever speak except in fellowship with the tenderness and grief of Jesus: "Then shall he say also unto them that are on the left hand, Depart from me, ye cursed, into the eternal fire which is prepared for the devil and his angels." There was need of salvation or Jesus would not have come to save us. There was no other way, and there is no other way.

Bishop Newman tells the story of one of the means of torture in olden Germany. There was a prison of exquisite beauty; its floors and walls were highly polished; it was roofless so that the inmates could look out upon the beautiful sky. A prisoner was placed therein, and for a moment congratulated himself upon the polish and splendor of his apartments: he could freely breathe the fresh air and see the stars that deck the brow of night, or the sun that rose in glory. But after a time he observed that the walls were gradually approaching him. Softly, noiselessly, as if by the force of gravitation, those walls grew nearer, inch by inch, and as they came closer and closer the cold sweat stood upon his brow, for he saw that they were soon to embrace him in the arms of death. There was but one way of escape, and that was from above; a friendly hand might possibly be put down, but there was no such friendly hand for him. That represents the condition of every one of us—the walls are approaching, there is only one way of escape, and that is from above. Jesus Christ from the throne of heaven is reaching down his hand of power into our dungeons; our only hope is to grasp it, or the walls of our own sins will crush us to death. Thank God! that hand is stretched down to us, and it is full of love and power to save sinners. No matter how helpless you are in your own strength, if you will just thrust your weak, trembling hand into the hand of Jesus he will lift you out of the pit into the sunlight of his forgiving mercy.

Luther tells us that once upon a time the devil

said to him, "Master Luther, thou art a great sinner and thou wilt be damned."

"'Stop, stop,' I said, 'one thing at a time. I am a great sinner, it is true—tho thou hast no right to say so. I confess it. What next?'

"'Therefore thou shalt be damned,' quoth he.

"'That is not good reasoning,' said I. 'It is true that I am a great sinner, but it is written, "Christ Jesus came to save sinners," therefore I shall be saved! Now go thy way.'

"So did I cut off the devil with his own sword, and he went away sorrowing because he could not cast me down by calling me a sinner."

But the only way we can escape being cast down by our sins is to accept the atonement made for us by the Lord Jesus Christ. It is left entirely to the choice of our own wills. Whittier sings:

"Tho God be good and free be heaven,
   No force divine can love compel;
And, tho the song of sins forgiven
   May sound through lowest hell,

"The sweet persuasion of his voice
   Respects thy sanctity of will.
  .   .   .   .   .

"A tenderer light than moon or sun,
   Than song of earth a sweeter hymn,
May shine and sound forever on
   And thou be deaf and dim.

THE ONE SAVING NAME. 243

"Forever round the Mercy Seat
   The guiding light of love shall burn;
But what if, habit-bound, thy feet
   Shall lack the will to turn?

"What if thine eyes refuse to see,
   Thine ear of heaven's free welcome fail,
And thou a willing captive be,—
   Thyself thine own dark jail?"

It only remains for me, then, to again invite you to come to Jesus, and find in him salvation. Do not let any bugbear such as a lack of feeling or lack of deeper sorrow for sin, or anything of the sort, keep you from just coming to Jesus himself. I tried to tell you last night that the essence of repentance was not in sorrow for sin, altho that might work a repentance, but in turning to God. Dr. Rainsford tells an interesting story of a case which came in his own personal experience. He had in his parish a young doctor who interested him very much. Tho he went about his business and did not give in that he was ill, it was plain to everybody that while he was healing others he was a dying man himself. It was consumption—a clear case and a quick one. The young man never allowed any allusion to his state of health, but the disease galloped on all the same. The minister tried to get acquainted with him. He called again and again at the house, but only once had a chance to talk with him and make a bare acquaintance. After that he always dodged the preacher, fearing something would be said to him about his spiritual condition. But finally, one morning about daylight, a messenger came and said in an excited voice:

"It's Bailey that wants you, sir—Dr. Bailey. For God's sake, come at once!"

He went over as quickly as he could. It was a dark winter morning in the shortest of days. Poor Bailey had burst a blood-vessel and was very low—dying they feared—gasping for breath, so that he was nearly speechless.

"Oh," he breathed in whispers, as the minister bent his ear over him, "Oh, I thought you would never come!"

"It's the words of God you want now. Just listen to them: 'Him that cometh to me, I will in no wise cast out.' Do you hear it? Him that cometh; him that cometh! Will you come?"

"He'll not have me to come without repentance," gasped the sick man.

"Oh, don't be putting a stumbling-block in the way! The way is all open to Christ. He is the way himself. Just start in the way the first step, and you are at him already."

But, poor fellow, he did not seem to be able to take it in. He groaned in anguish and looked hopelessly up into the minister's face. Ah, few of you know what a minister lives through in a time like that! I have been there, again and again, when it seemed if all the interest of the universe centered in the decision of the next fifteen minutes.

The minister said to him, "Do you know about the prodigal son?"

"Not much. I have never read my Bible, nor gone to church, nor cared for any such thing."

So he repeated to him the parable of the prodigal. He had left his Bible at home, but he knew all the sweet words. When he came to the place— "He came to himself"—he stopped a bit there.

"Now what brought him to himself?"

"Oh," gasped the man, "I suppose he knew he had nothing but husks, and he—"

"No," the minister replied, "that was not it, Bailey. You have known for a long time that there is nothing but husks in this world. Now what brought him to himself?"

"Tell me the story again," he whispered.

Dr. Rainsford began and told it over till he came to the same place.

"Now what does it mean, Bailey—'He came to himself'?"

"Well," groaned he, pitifully, "well, he found out that he was a bad one,—"

"Oh, no, that was not it! You've always known you were a bad one. He always knew he was a bad one. Now what was it—'he came to himself'?"

"Would you just tell me the whole story once more from the first?" he gasped.

He was not doing this to make time. There was no time to be made! He was about through with time. But his mind was toiling with the subject.

So the minister repeated the story again, and stopped at the old spot with the old question: "Now what was it he did when 'he came to himself'?"

At this point a strange thing took place. It was an ill-lighted place; the muggy twilight of a sullen, cloudy morning was struggling in at the windows, and only partially dispelled the shadows of the room. But there flashed a sudden light from the pallid face of poor Bailey that was fairly a glory-gleam from the face of God.

"What was it, Bailey, when 'he came to himself'?" said the minister, coming close, with his own heart in his throat.

"*He remembered that he had a father.*"

And at that moment poor Bailey knew that he had a Father!

"Did he tell his poor boy to stand off and **repent** before he came near the house?"

"Oh, no!" breathed the boy, with a smile.

"Did he tell him to stay away till he had better clothes, till he was clean and tidy?"

"Oh, no!"

"Oh, but he ran, he ran—the father did—when he was a great way off, and fell upon his neck, and kissed him; and he brought out the best robe; and put a ring on his hand—all he needed for his comfort and cleansing; and more and above—things he didn't *need*—things that were just for beauty and joy."

But there was no use talking any farther. Bailey knew all about it, with his face so full of rapture, and shining so as no painter ever could paint it. The same light that shone in the face of Moses and of Jesus, the light we see shining in the face of many an old saint, was beaming from Bailey's face the instant "*he remembered he had a Father.*"

It was six weeks before Bailey crossed over the river—six weeks of glorious testimony for Christ. A day or two before his death the minister called to see him and found a young lawyer, a friend of his, with him. The young lawyer was not a Christian, and when he saw who it was coming in, he tried to slip away, but the minister called him back, hoping to win him too.

"Well," he said, "it is not so bad a thing to say

good-by to Bailey since he knows just where he is going. Ask him where he is going; he'll tell you. Ask him yourself."

So the young lawyer stiffened up his voice—tried to, at least, but he did not make out very well.

"Where is it, Bailey?" he said.

Oh, how that face lit up! Oh, how clear was the whispered answer, with the beautiful upward glance:

"*To Father!*"

"Ask him how he knows it; he'll tell you; he knows. Ask him how he knows it," said the minister to the lawyer.

"How do you know it, Bailey?" said he, with a half sob.

The wonderful look grew more intense on the illuminated face.

"*Father never lies!*"

"And so," says Dr. Rainsford, "he went home to glory, with the light shining upon him even before he crossed the river."

So I beg of you to let nothing keep you from simply coming to the Savior. With childlike simplicity accept his loving invitation and trust him as your all in all.

CHRISTIANITY, A RELIGION OF JOY.

"Philip went down to the city of Samaria, and proclaimed unto them the Christ. And the multitudes gave heed with one accord unto the things that were spoken by Philip, when they heard, and saw the signs which he did. For from many of those which had unclean spirits, they came out, crying with a loud voice: and many that were palsied, and that were lame, were healed. And there was much joy in that city."—*Acts* viii. 5-8 (*Revised Version*).

CHRISTIANITY is a religion of joy. The prophets for three thousand years before the coming of Christ declared that it should be so. The angels that sang to the shepherds the anthem at the Savior's birth declared that they heralded a time of good tidings and great joy. The ministry of Jesus brought comfort and blessings and joy to the people wherever he went. The blind men who begged by the wayside, the leper who drew near with fear and trembling, the sick man by the healing pool, the mother following her son to the grave—all felt the heavenly kindliness of his presence. About every home he entered he might have said, as he did of the house of Zaccheus, "Salvation is come to this house." For while there were some that did not yield to him, and whom therefore he could not save, to all who opened their hearts to receive him he was healing for the sick, forgiveness for the sinful, hope for the discouraged, joy and gladness for the doubting and the sad. One of his sweetest promises to the disciples was that his joy should remain with them and that no one should be able to take it away from them. And so with the opening ministry of those first Christians, one of the chief characteristics of the result of their preaching was that it brought great joy to the people.

Philip went down to Samaria and proclaimed Christ unto the people, and the result was that there was great joy in that city. And why should there not have been? One of the deepest longings of the human soul is to feel sure that the heart of the God who reigns over the universe cares for us and sympathizes with us and loves us. Philip went down to Samaria to preach the glorious truth that God so loved the world that Jesus Christ had come among men to show forth God's heart to us; that the love of the Savior was so great that he had given his life for a world lost in sin and iniquity.

There had never been any such conception of love as that. The greatest love the world had ever known is described truly by Jesus when he says: "Greater love hath no man than this, that a man lay down his life for his friends." We have some wonderful illustrations, now and then, of such love. During the civil war, in a great naval battle when the Union squadron under Farragut entered Mobile Bay the monitor *Tecumseh* was struck by a torpedo and began to sink. The only way of escape from the room where the captain and pilot were was by a narrow ladder and a small door through which only one could go at a time. The pilot and captain both sprang instinctively for the ladder at the same moment, but the instant Captain Craven saw that another man was seeking life, he stepped back with a courteous cry, "After you, pilot!" And the brave man went down with his ship into the sea. That was a glorious deed, but the pilot was his friend. Philip went down to Samaria to preach about a Savior who died for his *enemies*.

A few weeks ago in a neighboring city a house was on fire in the night, and there was great danger that the family in the second story would burn to death. The father had gone out to see if the fire could not be extinguished before he knew the danger was so great, and he was cut off and could not return to them. He shouted from the outside, and as the mother threw up the window he begged her to throw the children to him. It was dangerous, of course, but it was the only hope.

There were five of them. She helped the oldest out first, and then held him in her arms, feeling as only a mother can, and dropped him down the side of the wall. The father caught him safely in his arms and that encouraged her; but they were in a fearful plight, the room was full of hot, blinding smoke and they were almost suffocated. She dropped three others, one after another, safely; then the flames burst through into the room; but a little two-year-old, where was he? The poor little fellow was suffocating on the floor in one corner of the room, and could not even answer her cry; but the mother would not leave without him. In that awful hell of fire she searched until she found him, and carried him to the window and dropped him unharmed into his father's arms. Then, burned and blinded by smoke and flame, she herself jumped from the window. It cost her her life, and she died in a few hours. It was a heroic, glorious deed; but it was for her children that she gave her life. But Philip went down to Samaria to preach about a Savior who was rich, and who became poor that those who were sinful and unworthy might become rich; a Savior who wore a crown of glory, and put it aside and came down to earth and wore a crown of thorns, that he might save from their sins wicked men; a Savior who came to seek after the lost, after the unlovable, after hopeless ones. Oh, no messenger ever carried news that was more likely to give joy to a city than that!

Another great longing of the human soul is for a consciousness of safety: to be assured that whatever happens to us is going to bring us blessing. There is no greater source of joy than to be sure that the everlasting arms of God are beneath us; that we are at peace and harmony with him whose hand is over all; that all things work together for our good, because we love him.

Dr. A. C. Dixon tells the story of a gentleman who was going through the Zoological Gardens in London, when the rules were not so strict as they are now, having with him a little unruly dog. Coming to the lion's cage he said to the keeper, "You may throw that dog to the lion." The keeper chased the little animal around until he caught him, opened the door, and cast him into the cage. The big lion looked at the dog as it lay trembling before him; then reached out one paw and stroked its head, and then the other paw and stroked it; and finally drew the trembling little creature up to himself. They made friends. A few weeks afterward the owner of the dog, passing through the garden, thought he would go round and look at the cage into which his dog had been cast; and there, looking through the bars of the cage, was the little dog, walking around as independently as the lion, perfectly safe. Said the man to the keeper, "I have repented of my angry fit; I believe I will take that dog home again. The children have missed it." "Well, here are the keys," said the keeper, "help yourself." But he dared not open the cage. That dog, under the protection of the lion, was perfectly safe. The lion with one stroke of his paw could have crushed him to death; but when he saw fit to throw the strength of that paw over the dog for protection he was safe. Philip went down to Samaria to preach to men and women who had thought with dread and fear about a God who would punish them for their sins. There is among all peoples such a conception of God. In heathen lands the old idols are often equipped with instruments of torture and cruelty. But Philip went to preach about the God who loved the world, and had given the Lord Jesus Christ to be their Savior, and if they would accept his salvation the strong arm of his love and power should be about them and give them peace. Was that not enough to give joy in the city of Samaria?

Another great longing of our souls is to know something of our own nature and to be sure that we are of a high and noble race. Make a man believe that he is of no higher order than the ox or the dog, that he is only a chemical combination of earthly things, that he has no kinship with heaven, and it is impossible that he shall be capable of deep and abiding joy. His horizon is too little for that. A man can not afford to risk anything or to deny himself anything for the sake of love or hope or any of those noble sources of highest joy, if he is only an animal with but a few days to live, and even those few uncertain.

Some years ago, when wages were very low, a Vermont farmer attempted to increase the small income of his farm by a contract of lumbering. He had for an assistant a tall, lank youth of eighteen. In the late fall the trees were cut and drawn together in a pile on the brink of a steep hill where, when there should be sufficient snow, they could be easily loaded on a sled and drawn to the mill. A large pile had thus been accumulated when the blocking that held them in place suddenly gave way and the logs began to roll down the steep incline. The young man was standing at the moment directly in their path, and the farmer shouted to him to run for his life. Instead of this, he dropped into a little hollow that chanced to be near, and the huge logs came down and buried him several logs deep. The farmer supposed that he had been instantly killed. The logs were too heavy for him to remove alone, and with much difficulty he secured the assistance of several men. When the logs were rolled away, the youth crawled out unharmed. "Why didn't you run, you idiot, as I told you?" said the angry farmer. "Do you s'pose I am going to run for ten dollars a month?" was the indignant reply.

In the boy's stumbling wit is a great and important truth. You can not get a great life, full of nobility and courage, entering into sympathy with the highest and holiest things, capable of a well of joy that shall spring up in the heart, buoying one up under all circumstances, unless there is the consciousness of something nobler about the soul than the things of earth. Well does David say to the Lord, "I will run in the way of thy commandments, when thou shalt enlarge my heart." Philip went down to Samaria with the glorious news that they were the children of God, and that the Father loved them so much, even in their waywardness, that he had given their Elder Brother to come and suffer and die to win them back to their lost inheritance.

And the best of it was, under the preaching of Philip every one that tested the glorious news that he brought to them, and who turned from sin and accepted Christ as a personal Savior, found the good news true. Men who had been possessed by evil spirits, who had been the skeleton in their home closets or the open shame and sorrow of those that loved them, coming to Christ in response to Philip's earnest appeals, saw the devils cast out, the awful power of evil habit broken; and they became joyous and peaceful members of the community. No wonder there was great joy in that city! There is no way that you can bring so much joy into any city as to bring the blessed presence of Jesus Christ in saving power into the hearts and homes of the people. Suppose to-night I had the power to go into every home in this city where there is a drunken father, or a drunken husband, or a wayward son, or a wilful daughter, and I could take Jesus with me and so introduce him to the hearts of these fathers, and husbands, and wives, and sons, and daughters, that they should come to love him, and the power of strong drink under his love should be cast out, and the wilful, disobedient spirit should be dispossessed, and every one of these hearts should, under the influence of Christ, be transformed as I have seen thousands of hearts transformed. Oh, what a heaven there would be in Brooklyn to-night! What watch-nights of joy and reunion there would be before morning! What tears of gladness would flow, what words of love would be spoken, what glorious hopes would come where despair has been a steady visitor! And up from tens of thousands of homes in Brooklyn there would go a great glorious wave of joy to the very throne of God! God has not seen fit to give any man that power. It must be one heart at a time, one home at a time; but, thank God! whosoever will may come and enter into this deep, abiding joy of salvation here and hereafter.

I never have any sympathy with the people who talk about what they had to give up to be Christians. The story is told of an old couple who, early in life, had been very, very poor. But the husband became a Christian, and God blessed their industry, and they were living in comfort, when one day a stranger called on them to ask their subscription to a charity. The old lady had less religion than her husband, and thought he lost money sometimes by being so very strict about keeping the Sabbath so closely in business matters. So when the visitor asked their contribution she interposed and said: "Why, sir, we have lost a good deal by religion since we first began. Have we not, Thomas?" she inquired, turning to her husband. After a solemn pause Thomas answered: "Yes, Mary, we have. Before I got religion, Mary, I had an old slouched hat, a ragged coat, and holes in my shoes and stockings; but I have lost them long ago. And, Mary, you know that, poor as I was, I had a habit of getting drunk and quarreling with you; and that, you know, I have lost. And then I had a hardened conscience, and a wicked heart, and ten thousand guilty fears; but all are lost and like a millstone cast into the sea. And, Mary, you have been a loser, too, tho not so great a loser as myself. Before we got religion, Mary, you had the privilege, in order that we might not starve, of going out to wash for hire, when I was drunk, but since then you've lost that chance. And you had a gown and a bonnet, much the worse for wear and very shabby; but you have lost them long ago. And you had many an aching heart concerning me at times; but these you happily have lost. And I could even wish that you had lost as much as I have lost; for what we lose for religion will be an everlasting gain." The old man had the true secret of wisdom in regard to all our losses for Christ's sake. Christ once said to Peter that every one that gave up anything for his sake in this world should have here a hundredfold and in the end everlasting life.

My dear friends, I beg of you to bring your selfishness, along with any wicked habit you may have, any cross or ugly temper you may possess, every sin that mars and hurts your soul, every wearing care and sorrow that weighs you down—bring them all to Christ to-night, and in exchange obtain a heart made pure, a pardon for your sins, peace with God, and a hope which shall be an anchor to your soul, sure and steadfast, and reaching within the veil.

PHILIP AND THE FIRST GOSPEL WAGON.

"The Spirit said unto Philip, Go near, and join thyself to this chariot. And Philip ran to him."—*Acts* viii. 29, 30 (*Revised Version*).

It must have seemed a strange providence to Philip, after his marvelous success in preaching the Gospel in large cities, where his word had been so blessed by the Holy Ghost that great revivals had followed his ministry and waves of joy had swept over the communities where he proclaimed the word of God, that he should suddenly be called to a halt, taken away from the midst of this success where he was the instrument of so much good, and sent out across the desert. But Philip went at once on the path of duty, and went without any grumbling. He had grown strong in the Lord by bestowing upon others every good gift God had given him. And I want to say to every Christian here, and to every one beginning now this Christian life, that the way to a joyous and strong Christianity is not by hoarding up any of the treasures which God gives you, but by carrying to others in a spirit of helpfulness and sympathy the joy and comfort that come to your souls.

A mother down by the seashore one summer remarked to a friend: "I don't know what to do with my little boy. He hasn't been well, and the doctor told me to take him to the seashore and let him play all day in the sand. But how am I going to make him play when he does not feel like it? He hides from the merry children and sits and mopes by himself."

"I know a prescription much better than your doctor's," said a strange lady who was sitting near by.

"What is it?" asked Will's mother.

"Call him here and let me try it," was the reply.

"Will, O Will! Come here a minute, my son," called the mother.

Will got up slowly, leaving his bucket and spade in the sand. "They are just going to tease me about not playing," he grumbled to himself. "I wish everybody would let me alone."

But they did not say a word to him about playing.

"Will," said the strange lady brightly, "if you are not too busy, I wish you would help me a little."

Will pricked up his ears. It had been a long

time since he had been allowed to help anybody but himself.

"You see that little yellow cottage away off there?" asked the lady. "It's about a mile up the beach. There is a lame boy in that cottage, and I want to send him an orange; will you take it?"

"Yes, ma'am, certainly," said the small boy.

"And, Will," she continued, "if you can do anything to amuse or cheer him, it would be a good thing, you know; he can't get out of the house by himself, but he might with you to help him."

Will was done moping now for good. He forgot all about himself in doing things for lame Lucien. His appetite increased, his zest for life came back, and he was soon as robust as anybody.

If you want to be a robust and rugged Christian, full of abounding hope and joy and courage, quit thinking about yourself, and put yourself to giving out every precious thing God gives you to those who are in need. God does not want us to act as tho we were stinted, and if we will give away the comfort and joy he gives us, he will give to us yet more abundantly.

I have heard a story of a woman who had been very poor herself, but she married a very wealthy man. He put ten thousand dollars into the bank for her personal use, and at the end of the year he said to her, "Do you wish me to put in any more this year?" He meant to ask if ten thousand dollars a year was enough for her. She said, "No, I have only spent a hundred." "Why didn't you spend it all?" "Why," she said, "I thought it wasn't right to spend such a lot; you see I am poor." "But I am rich." "Oh," she replied, "I thought there might come a day of need and I had better keep it."

That grieved the husband very much. He said, "My dear, I meant you to spend it, and there is more whenever you want it; I have more than I can spend; take it and use it; I meant you to give away what you did not need." Our Heavenly Father is rich. He abounds in riches of goodness and love and heavenly peace and comfort; and the more of it we give to needy souls the better he will be pleased and the more abundantly he will be able to endow us. God is seeking after men and women with hearts big enough to just take all the love and mercy which he is willing to give them, and to carry it to the wandering and the lost and bring their hearts out of despair and darkness into his marvelous light and joy.

Philip was a man of the Spirit. He found his joy in following the commandments of God and carrying heaven's gladness to dispel earth's sorrow. The kingdom of God does not consist of earthly things, but of "joy in the Holy Ghost." And since Jesus has told us that the Holy Spirit is in the world to represent him, we know that the joy of the Holy Ghost is the joy of working with Christ for the salvation of our fellow men. Oh, it is the most precious work in the world! So Philip went gladly and willingly on his way across the desert to Gaza. It was a wicked city; he did not know what was before him; but he was doing the work God had indicated to him, and he went on his way rejoicing. As he went trudging forward a chariot came along. It paid no heed to him, but the Spirit of God impressed Philip that the man in the chariot, who was the treasurer of the Queen of Ethiopia, had need of him, and that he must not let the chariot pass by, but must go to it at once. You know how it is if you are walking, and a carriage comes along going the same way with a splendid team of horses—they soon pass away and leave you in the dust, and if you are going to climb into that carriage you have to be in a hurry. And so the moment Philip was impressed that he had a duty toward the man in this passing chariot, he ran as fast as he could; and as he came up alongside of the chariot he heard the man reading in the prophecy of Isaiah; and, running beside him, Philip shouted to him, "Understandest thou what thou readest?" And the treasurer looked up astonished, and replied, "How can I, except some one shall guide me?" Then he stopped the chariot and begged Philip to come up and sit with him. So they rode along together. "Now the place of the Scripture which he was reading was this,

> He was led as a sheep to the slaughter;
> And as a lamb before his shearer is dumb,
> So he openeth not his mouth:
> In his humiliation his judgment was taken away:
> His generation who shall declare?
> For his life is taken from the earth.

And the eunuch answered Philip and said, I pray thee, of whom speaketh the prophet this? of himself, or of some other? And Philip opened his mouth, and beginning from this Scripture, preached unto him Jesus."

You may see the secret of his success in the way Philip at once seized hold of his opportunity and preached Jesus to this man. That's what you and I want to do everywhere we go—carry the message of Christ as the only name whereby we can be saved. John Ruskin, in his "Notes on the Construction of Sheepfolds," says that it is the business of every Christian man, whether he be minister or layman, to be constantly and incessantly talking Christ, not only indirectly, but directly, to the people in his own home, to the men he meets in travel, to the people with whom he is thrown in touch in his work; that, indeed, it is our one business as Christian men and women to talk Jesus Christ, and so set forth his helpfulness, the glory of his person, the kindness of his friendship, the tenderness of his sympathy, that we shall win everybody that we know to desire him and love him.

Doubtless some who hear me say to themselves: "That is all very well to people who have gotten accustomed to it and are not backward, but I am so timid about these things that it is not possible for me." Thank God, he does not expect impossibilities of us. But if we will begin trying to do his will, he will help us, and we shall grow in this ability to confess him everywhere. In Patterson Du Bois' little book on "Beckonings of Little Hands," he tells the story of one of his children who has since died, whom he could with greatest difficulty get to mention the name of God or of Christ. The child was born with this holy awe and hesitancy, and the timid little fellow never came to a place where he was able to overcome that feeling. When the child had died, they found a little note-book which had been given him by his nurse, and there printed in great sprawling baby letters, right across the page, were these words, "God is love; he loves lambs." If the child had lived he would have grown up into fellowship with God and would have been able to have talked about him who loves lambs. I speak to many who have this hesitancy about voicing their inmost feeling in regard to Christ; but I pray for his dear sake, and for the sake of those who are strangers to him and whom he loves, that each one of you will cultivate every day the gift of using every opportunity to speak about him in love and tenderness to all with whom you come in contact.

As Philip preached Christ to the traveler the man's heart was convinced that Jesus was the Savior of the world, and therefore his Savior, and so he determined upon a public confession of Christ then and there; and as in their drive they came to where there was some water, he said to Philip, "Behold, here is water; what doth hinder me to be baptized?" And he ordered the chariot to stop, and Philip went down with him to the water and baptized him in the name of Jesus. After he was baptized the Lord carried Philip away to other work, and the Ethiopian treasurer saw him no more; but while he no doubt regretted this, it is said of him, "He went on his way rejoicing."

I commend to every one of you who have heard the message about Jesus Christ and are convinced in your heart that he is the Savior of the world, that you do not hesitate or delay any longer, but give your heart to him at once. More souls are lost by delay than anything else. Luther is said to have had a dream that there was great commotion in hell; one of the devils came down and said to Beelzebub, "Tidings, my lord, from earth; Luther is going to preach the doctrine of justification by faith to-morrow." Beelzebub said, "What shall we do?" One devil said, "I will go into the congregation and move from soul to soul and say, 'It is all a lie; there is no need of justification, there is no devil.'" Beelzebub answered, "You fool, every man knows there is a devil; he has only to look within and see that he is there." Another said, "I will go and say there is a God, and there is a devil; but God is too kind to punish sin, and there is no hell." Beelzebub replied, "You fool, every man knows that sin must be punished and there must be a hell." Another said, "Let me go; I can deceive the whole congregation. I will say to them, 'There is a God, and he is very just and holy; there is a devil, and he is very strong and wicked; there is a hell, and it is everlasting, and very bitter, but you do not need to go there; you will have time to repent some time in the future; if no sooner, at least when you are dying. Do not repent to-day.'" "You may go," said Beelzebub. "You will succeed." Alas! how often he has succeeded! And how many there are here who have been deceived again and again, waiting for some convenient season which has never come. No opportunity can ever be better than this. Accept Christ now, and register your decision once and for all to stand with Jesus Christ here and forever. If you shall do that, it shall be with you as you go out from this church to-night as it was with the Ethiopian treasurer after his decision—you shall go on your way rejoicing.

ÆNEAS, A MAN WHO WAS HEALED.

"And it came to pass, as Peter went throughout all parts, he came down also to the saints which dwelt at Lydda. And there he found a certain man named Æneas, which had kept his bed eight years; for he was palsied. And Peter said unto him, Æneas, Jesus Christ healeth thee: arise, and make thy bed. And straightway he arose. And all that dwelt at Lydda and in Sharon saw him, and they turned to the Lord."—*Acts* ix. 32-35 (*Revised Version*).

How much of suffering and sorrow is represented in the opening of this scene, and what great blessing and joy in its conclusion! Here was a man who had been sick eight years, who had no doubt lost hope of being healed until the news had come to him of the healing of the crippled man at the gate of the temple, by Peter, in the name of Jesus Christ. You may be sure Æneas had heard that story. I have often been greatly impressed in visiting sick people, especially those who have been ill a long time with some chronic and lingering disease, by learning how well-informed they are about the many things that are suggested as remedies for their disease. And while the crippled man at the gate was not afflicted in exactly the same way as Æneas, yet he would naturally reason that it would be no harder to cure a man with the palsy than to heal a poor cripple who had been helplessly lame all the days of his life. No doubt Æneas had many times said to himself and to those with whom he had a chance to talk, "If only I could get to see that man Peter, who healed the lame man up there at the temple, I believe he could do something for my palsy." But then the poor fellow would sigh and say, "Alas! I am too helpless to go to him." Had he been as fortunate as that poor man who had four friends who carried him to Christ, and let him down through the roof, and thus secured his recovery, it was yet too great a journey for such an attempt to be made.

But one day strange and wonderful news came to Æneas. Some neighbor came along and exclaimed, "Æneas, have you heard the news?"

Poor Æneas, he was in the dumps that morning, helpless and weak and almost hopeless; and I see him as he lifts his weary eyes to his neighbor. Without any especial curiosity in his voice he inquires, "How is a poor fellow like me to hear any news? But what news do you mean?"

"News? why, good news, I should think, for you. Don't you remember how interested you were a while ago about a lame man that had been a cripple from his birth, and for the last thirty years or more had lain at the Beautiful Gate of the temple, who was cured, sound and well, by a man called Peter, a fisherman, who has been preaching the glory of the Nazarene who was crucified in Jerusalem, and whom he says was raised from the dead? Well, the news is that this man Peter is in town. He came this morning."

There is no lassitude about Æneas now. He is all interest and excitement. He must somehow see Peter. He feels sure that it is the one hope of his life-time, and so he begs his neighbor, "Please, neighbor, go ask this wonderful man to come and see me. It may be the only chance I'll have. You see, I can't do anything, I can't walk. I have no one I can send. Take mercy on a poor fellow, and go and tell Peter that there is a poor sick man in here who can't get out to see him, and beg him to come and heal me here."

Away goes the neighbor and finds Peter and tells him about Æneas. Peter, always impulsive, never putting off till to-morrow the duty for to-day, jumps up and says, "Certainly, if there is a poor fellow here who wants to see me, then he's just the man I want to see." And in a little while Peter came, led by the neighbor into Æneas' room where he had lain sick and helpless for eight long years. Æneas heard them coming, and as the steps grew near, how his heart did thump against his ribs! And then Peter comes in at the door and the sick man's eyes, flashing now with expectancy and hope, look into the face of Peter—a face that has been mellowed by association with Jesus Christ until the gruffness has gone out of it and much of the gentleness of the Great Physician has found lodgment there. And Peter does not wait to torment him with questions, he just cries out to him with a cheery voice, "Æneas, Jesus Christ maketh thee whole! arise, and make thy bed." And Æneas did not wait at all on the order of his obedience, for he felt a new thrill of life and vigor in his veins. In that moment he did believe on the Christ, that there was power in the name that Peter had invoked to give him new life, and he arose up immediately.

How this man's faith ought to rebuke many who have so much greater light, and yet are waiting, and considering, and thinking, and failing to be made whole. Many of you that are listening to me have heard ten thousand times more about the power of Jesus Christ to heal the guilty soul, to give men power to resist temptation, and break the power of sinful habits, than Æneas had ever heard about him in any way. Yet his sense of need was so great that he seized the first opportunity of being healed. Oh, I would that God would show you your great need of a Savior! If you only knew what a terrible thing sin is! If you could only look at the cross of Jesus Christ—see the Savior hanging there, nailed to the shameful tree, and realize that it was your sin that helped to make necessary; if you could only realize how your sinful thoughts and imaginations, your ingratitude of heart and life toward God, are separating you from the richest comfort and blessing that immortal souls can ever know—I am sure you would be anxious and aroused to seize the first opportunity of coming to the Great Physician of souls.

I want to impress upon you as clearly as I may the concluding sentence of this Scripture, which shows that none of us can live unto ourselves, but that the influence of our yielding our hearts to God and being made whole may be a great blessing to many others. The record says that the healing of Æneas had this result: "And all that dwelt at Lydda and in Sharon saw him, and they turned to the Lord." Why should you not regard the influence which your life has upon others? It is a terrible thing to occupy such a position that others, following your example, are restrained from accepting Christ and are lost. If you would only come to Jesus to-night and throw your whole life and soul on his side, no doubt there are other hearts to whom it would bring great joy.

Dr. Guthrie tells the story of two women who lived not far apart, though in widely different circles of society, whom the Lord Jesus Christ had healed of all their sins at about the same time. One of these women had been very wicked. She had neither feared God nor cared for the good opinion of the community, and was bringing up her children in evil ways. "One evening," to use Dr. Guthrie's quaint description, "she happened to be within ear-shot of a preacher; as he was emptying his quiver among the crowd, an arrow from the bow drawn at a venture was lodged in her heart." And right there, that night, in the street, she was converted. It was a case of sudden conversion, like the thief on the cross, the jailer at Philippi, or Saul on his way to Damascus. This woman was confronted with Christ. Her heart was broken with contrition for her sins and she immediately accepted him as her Savior. As soon as this wonderful transformation had been wrought in her heart she thought of her children at home, and into what danger she had led them by her own sinful life. She hurried home. She found the family asleep, but in the new light that had come to her she saw in each one of her children an immortal soul that she had led in the path of ruin.

So intense was her desire to undo her awful work that she rushed on the sleepers as if the house were in flames, and shook them, crying, "Arise, call upon thy God!" And there at midnight, with her children kneeling around her, her eyes streaming with tears, her voice trembling with emotion, did that poor mother cry to God, that he would have mercy upon her children and pluck them as brands from the burning.

Near by, in the most respectable circles of society, lived another woman. Her husband was a Christian and had often in the dead of night prayed for her salvation. At last she, too, was smitten with anxiety; the Holy Spirit convicted her of sin; but she could find no peace; she walked in darkness and had no light; when she lay down beside her husband at night she would say, "If you should die before to-morrow it would be happy for you; but if I should die, it would be an everlasting farewell!" Her husband's pastor came to see her. She was in the garden. Her husband left the house to call her. "Who seeks me?" she asked. Without forethought, as if the words had fallen from heaven on his lips, he replied, "Jesus Christ seeks you!" It came to her as the voice of God. She followed him into the house, and in the prayer that followed she was made whole, and filled with great joy.

Dr. Guthrie, talking with the husband about the incident, inquired, "And what did you do?" "Do, sir?" he replied; "I sprang to my feet; I clasped her in my arms; I exclaimed, 'This is our marriage day;' and unable to restrain my joy I cried, 'Hosannah to the Son of David! Praise him, all ye his angels; praise him, sun, moon, and stars; praise him, all ye orbs of light!'"

I know families that have been long divided, tho usually it is the wife who has been a Christian and has been praying to God in some cases for many years, and if her husband would only come to the Lord her soul would go out in gladness like that.

I appeal to this highest possible motive to-night. Not only for your own soul's sake; not only because of what you owe to God and the gratitude due to the Lord Jesus Christ; but because of your influence upon others and the salvation it may bring to them, or the gladness with which it may fill their hearts, delay not your coming to God, but come to him now.

CORNELIUS, THE TRUTH SEEKER.

"A devout man."—*Acts* x. 2 (*Revised Version*).

CORNELIUS is a signal illustration of the great truth of the unity of the human race. God loves all his children. The people of one nation are as dear to him as are those of another. He is not afar off from any of his creatures. Altho Cornelius had but little opportunity indeed to know about the true God, and knew still less, perhaps, of the Jewish Messiah, yet he was a man of devout and reverent soul who followed the leadings of the Holy Spirit and was a consistent and earnest seeker after truth.

The Bible gives us the record of many such cases. Job is a very striking illustration of the same kind. He was not a Jew and, so far as we know, had no knowledge of Jewish literature. There is no reference to Job at all in Jewish history. He was an Arabian, and yet he was a sincere and honest servant of God, and there is no book in the Bible, unless it be the Psalms of David, that so unlocks the secret chambers of the human soul and holds up before the eye the unwritten and hitherto undescribed struggles of an aspiring soul that seeks to live a noble and holy life in the midst of earth's sorrows and temptations, as the book of Job. God spoke to Job and brought him unscathed out of all his sorrows, and shows us in the story of his life that the Arab in the desert is as dear to the heart of the Great Father as the prophet or the priest in the Holy City.

Similar examples have been found among far more untaught and simple peoples, those destitute of literature and the arts of civilization. Men were found among the North American Indians who held communion with God before any message of Christ came to them. Brainard found a wild Indian who was living apart from his people, coming out among them occasionally as a preacher of righteousness, trying to restrain their wicked passions and to persuade them away from their wretched vice of drink; and when he was unable to accomplish his beneficent purpose he would run away into the woods in tears and grief and anguish which he could not repress. "Ah, there must be some one," he would say, "who thinks like me; where shall I find him?"

So in the depths of Africa the missionaries found a woman who had been praying many years to "The Unknown God," and who, as soon as the story of Jesus was given her, exclaimed, "Oh, that is he, the same that I have found, and now have always with me!"

Cornelius' was a case like these. He was a devout man, reverent toward God, and seeking earnestly to find the truth. His spirit is illustrated in his conversation with Peter after his arrival from Joppa, when he says to him, "Now therefore are we all here present before God, to hear all things that are commanded thee of God." This shows his reverence and his earnestness. He feels that Peter has not come to amuse him or to entertain him; neither is he there to satisfy some curiosity he may have; but he recognizes that Peter comes as the messenger of God, and he desires him to speak clearly all the message which God has given to him.

It would be well indeed for every one of us to recognize that that is exactly our condition to-night. It is not my business here to simply amuse you or to entertain you, but to bring you as clearly and simply as I can, by the aid of the Spirit of God, the message of God to your hearts; to bring you the invitation of Christ, and to urge upon you that you shall accept it at once.

If your house were on fire and your property in danger of being consumed, and the fire company which had been summoned should come and locate the engine in the street before your house, and, instead of pouring a stream of water upon the fire and trying to drench out the flames as speedily as possible, should go through a dress parade drill in the street for your entertainment, and seek to amuse you and excite your admiration by showing you how high or how far they could throw a stream of water in some other direction, how indignant you would be! You would rush up to the superintendent in a frenzy of despair, and cry out, "Man, are you crazy? Don't you see my house is burning down before your eyes? Our home is being consumed. What do you suppose we care for all this parade? Turn your stream of water on the fire before it is too late!"

Or suppose your child were very ill and the doctor should come and, neglecting the patient, should enter into long and curious conversations about the discoveries of medical science and seek to amuse and entertain the family, would you not say, "Doctor, put these things away for some other time; our child is suffering, he will die if he does not get help soon; we have no taste for curiosity or amusement until he is safe."

How much more when you come here to this house of God to hear of the divine remedy for sin should I bring you at once the message of the Great Physician, and deal earnestly with souls that are in danger of eternal loss. While besetting sins are dogging your pathway; while the chains of evil habit are strengthening their hold upon you every day; while evil imaginations and thoughts are evolving evil deeds, and these are earning the deadly wages of sin, I have no heart to mock you by simply trying to entertain you for the hour. Instead, with all the earnestness of my soul, I bring you God's message and preach unto you Jesus Christ as the only Savior from sin.

We have suggested in the story of Cornelius that a man is only safe who lives up to the light as God gives him to see it from day to day. There is salvation in the truth, but it is not enough to know the truth and admire it, and even to praise it—we must embrace it in faith. There are many men who praise the light, but still love the darkness. Many that know the truth, still refuse it in its application to their own lives and perish in their sins. The Bible records of such an one, " His own iniquities shall take the wicked, and he shall be holden with the cords of his sin. He shall die for lack of instruction; and in the greatness of his folly he shall go astray." Cornelius' salvation was that as fast as he knew more truth he put it all into practice. He had been a prayerful man before. He had brought up his family according to the best of his ability. He had been a generous man and helped to feed the poor. But he did not fall back into wicked self-complacency as many such people do. He recognized that he owed everything to God and sought to do his best according to every new light that came to him. And so when Peter came and preached Jesus Christ as the Savior of the world, and as God's atonement for sin, Cornelius did not fall back on his alms or his good deeds, or even his prayers, and say, "I have been doing the best I could and I guess it will be all right with me without my doing anything farther." He at once accepted Christ as his Savior, and made the most public and open confession of Jesus that he could make. There is your consistent and honest truth-seeker! Many men pretend to be seeking after the truth who live and die in their sins. But Cornelius was made free by the truth because the moment he came to know it he accepted it and acted upon it.

I am sure that there are those here who need just this message. You know very much of Gospel truth. You have to a greater or less extent followed the example of Cornelius in prayer and in doing good, but you have not admitted the great and supreme claim of the Lord Jesus. You have not given to him your open and unreserved confession. Some of you say, "I would do that, but I fear I would not be able to hold out." So long as you stand in that attitude you are refusing to give Christ your trust and your confidence. You can not expect that God will reveal himself to you in assurance that your sins are forgiven until you are willing to obey the Lord Jesus and without any reference to your feelings or emotions follow the right as God gives you to see it. We are to walk by faith, and not by sight.

The story is told of Alexander the Great that he had a physician who was his bosom friend. One day there came an anonymous letter on a waxed tablet to the king. The letter ran like this: "Oh, king, there is treachery in thy home. Thy physician purposes to kill thee by the draught which he gives thee to-morrow, under the plea of healing thee." The king put that waxed tablet into his bosom and the next day, when the physician came to give him the draught, he put out his left hand and, taking the cup with his right hand, handed the tablet to the physician and said, "Friend, I trust thee," and drank the potion without stopping a moment to see the effect upon the physician. That is just what some of you need to do. You wish you were a Christian, you are longing for salvation, but you want to get it without trusting Christ. It is not enough to believe historically that Christ is the Great Physician of souls, but you must trust him. Step right out on his promises and declare openly your purpose to take Jesus here and now as your Savior.

Cornelius came into the assurance of salvation by implicit obedience to Christ. The same spirit of obedience to the Savior will bring all here to the same blessed assurance that they are the children of God, that their sins are blotted out, that they are heirs of God and joint heirs with the Lord Jesus Christ. John wrote his first epistle with the one purpose, he says, of showing people how they may know that they are accepted of God. In the fifth chapter of his first epistle he says, "These things have I written unto you that believe on the name of the Son of God; that ye may *know* that ye have eternal life." One of the most significant things John says about knowing whether we are Christians or not is this: "We know that we have passed from death unto life, because we love the brethren. He that loveth not his brother abideth in death." "Well," you say, "how in the world can I love people if I don't?" Well, begin at once to obey Christ and try to set matters right with anybody toward whom you have angry or wrong feelings. You must forgive them in your own heart. Jesus says in the Lord's Prayer that we can ask God to forgive us only as we forgive others who have wronged us or trespassed against us. If there is anybody you are not on speaking terms with, or have strained relations with; anybody toward whom you are sure you don't feel right and who you know doesn't feel right toward you, write a letter before you sleep and ask forgiveness, and try to make it right. No matter if you think the other party is more in the wrong than you are. It is better to ask a man's forgiveness a hundred times when you are the party sinned against, than to let one arrow go on rankling in your heart and poisoning the spirit of love that ought to reign there supreme.

Mr. Moody relates that he was once preaching in Scotland on the subject of forgiveness, and in the course of his remarks he said, "If any one here has had any trouble with any one, and wants to go off and have the thing settled to-day, go now; we will excuse you." One Scotch woman got up and started; she pressed through the aisle, elbowing her way and making the people stand aside. That night she came and brought her husband, and they were both converted. She said, "I have wanted to be a Christian for years, but I had trouble with my mother-in-law, and hadn't spoken to her for years; so this afternoon I went right off and saw her, and she forgave me." After that the woman had no trouble finding Jesus, and it was the salvation of her husband as well.

The great lesson of all this story of Cornelius is to act at once obediently to all the light God gives us. I am sure there is no one of you that can go up to the judgment seat at last and say, "I would have been saved, but no one was faithful enough to my soul to warn me of the danger of my sin, and tell me the simple story of salvation through faith in Jesus Christ." You have light enough. If you never heard the Gospel before, hear it now: "The wages of sin is death, but the gift of God is eternal life, through Jesus Christ our Lord." "Except ye be born again ye can not see the kingdom of God." "If we confess our sins, he is faithful and just to forgive us our sins, and cleanse us from all unrighteousness." "And the Spirit and the bride say, Come. And let him that heareth say, Come. And let him that is athirst come. And whoseover will, let him take the water of life freely."

THE GOLD MINE OF HUMANITY.

"Unto me hath God shewed that I should not call any man common or unclean."—*Acts* x. 28 (*Revised Version*).

THE greatest lessons are learned slowly and oftentimes painfully. Peter had been for three years a disciple of Jesus Christ. He had had the great privilege of close and intimate acquaintance and fellowship with him who is the Light of the world. And yet that bigotry which was a part of his inheritance as Jew in that age he had not been able to get over and outgrow. He did not yet understand that God loved the Gentiles as much as he did the Jews.

After the healing of Æneas and Dorcas, Peter remained for some time in the house of Simon the tanner. One morning he went up on the housetop to pray, but he became so hungry that he told the folks about it, and while they were making ready a meal for him he fell into a trance and had a strange vision. The heavens opened before him, and a great sheet knit at the four corners was let down to the earth, and in this enormous sheet were all manner of four-footed beasts, and wild beasts, and creeping things, and fowls of the air. And a voice commanded him, "Rise, Peter; kill and eat." But Peter replied, "Not so, Lord; for I have never eaten anything that is common or unclean." But again the heavenly voice spoke to him, saying, "What God hath cleansed, make not thou common." As if to impress the lesson on his mind, this was repeated three times; and then Peter came out of his trance, and while he was much perplexed to know what it could mean, the message came to him from God "Behold, three men seek thee; arise, therefore, and go with them, doubting nothing: for I have sent them." Peter went down at once to meet the men and inquired why they sought for him. The men replied that they came from Cornelius, a Roman centurion, who lived at Cæsarea. This man Cornelius they represented as a devout and reverent man who feared God and sought to live up to the light that God gave him. An angel had appeared to this Roman soldier and had commanded him to send for Peter. Peter went with the men at once, and on the next day, when he arrived at the house of Cornelius, his host came out to greet him and fell down at his feet and worshiped him; but Peter took him up, saying, "Stand up; I myself also am a man." And then Peter enters into conversation with Cornelius, and shows at once that he understands the meaning of his vision. "Ye know," he says, "how that it is an unlawful thing for a man that is a Jew to keep company, or come unto one of another nation; but God hath shewed me that I should not call any man common or unclean." And a little later, when he begins his sermon to the household that are gathered together, he opens his discourse with these words: "Of a truth I perceive that God is no respecter of persons; but in every nation he that feareth him and worketh righteousness, is accepted with him."

Peter seems to have learned this great lesson once and for all at this time. It is the most revolutionary characteristic of Christianity. It takes the average person longer to learn it than any other lesson which Christ teaches us. There is no nation under heaven where the class spirit and the spirit of caste of some kind does not work oppression and separate the children of God from each other, to the great loss of all. We call this a democratic land; we boast of the democracy of our republican institutions; yet there are multitudes of instances that might be pointed out where our practical conduct shows that we believe that certain classes of people are common and unclean and are not the children of God in the same sense that we are. Many people that would not admit this live as tho it were the creed upon which their lives were built. I want to call your special attention to the fact that Jesus Christ throughout his entire ministry acted as tho wealth and social position and power were accidents or merely incidental conditions that were not worth considering in comparison to manhood or womanhood. He went in his ministry to the suffering to the house of a rich man just as readily as to the hovel of the poor, but he did not show in any way that he regarded the rich man's case to be any more interesting or important than he did the pauper's. Once when he was on his way to heal the daughter of a rich nobleman, a poor, beggared woman who had been sick twelve years pressed through the crowd behind him that she might touch the hem of his garment and be healed; and the Savior stopped and held a considerable conversation with her while the nobleman must have been almost crazy to have him hurry forward; but that poor woman was as important to Jesus as tho she, too, had lived in a palace. If the special mission of Christ had been to set before the world the worth of the individual soul, the inexhaustible riches of humanity itself, tho it be stripped and naked of everything that ornaments it and beautifies it, he could not have acted differently than he did. He never let down his standards one iota to persuade a rich man to enter the kingdom of God; neither did he thrust any suspicion or bar into the way to keep the vilest of sinners from coming into closest fellowship himself, and proclaiming themselves openly his disciples. Zacchæus, the rich tax collector, got into the kingdom; but he made restitution of four dollars for every one he had gained by cheating, and he shared his wealth with the poor. On the other hand the poor demon-beggared man of Gadara, with money and reputation and everything gone, was received with open arms and sent to tell everywhere what the Lord had done for his soul.

Look at the kind of people of whom Jesus Christ made a great deal, and with whom he always conversed with the most perfect naturalness and simplicity, never for a moment indicating that it was condescension on his part to do so. One morning a company of scribes and Pharisees brought to him a woman upon whom they had heaped curses and maledictions, and whom they were preparing to stone to death. She stood before the Master trembling and terror-stricken, her face buried in her hands. Shame and grief and despair possessed her. These self-righteous accusers pointed at her with fingers of scorn and said, "Master, Moses commanded that such an offender be stoned." They were trying to catch Jesus in his words. At first the Savior seemed to pay no attention to them. He seemed in meditation, and bent down and appeared to be writing in the sand. But they became all the more rabid in their denunciation of the poor sinful woman, and cried out again to him: "Master, Moses commanded that she be stoned. What sayest thou?" Then Jesus straightened himself up, and looked on them with those heart-searching eyes that read men's souls, and said: "He that is without sin among you, let him first cast a stone at her." And again he stooped and wrote in the sand. That single sentence struck them dumb. They stood self-convicted before the judgment seat of righteousness. Ashamed and conscience-stricken, they looked into each other's faces, and then, loosening their clutch of the stones they had meant to hurl at the shrinking woman, they dropped them one by one, and silently withdrew. No Gatling gun ever dispersed a mob quicker than that. When they were all gone the Savior looked kindly and pitifully on the poor sinner and inquired, "Hath no man condemned thee?" "No man, Lord," she replied, no doubt in great astonishment. Then came the tender words that must have been a revelation of the very heart of God to the woman's soul: "Neither do I condemn thee; go, and sin no more."

Or go with the Master again as he passes out of Jericho on the way to Jerusalem. A poor old blind beggar named Bartimæus sits by the wayside begging, and he inquires what the noise is. He is told that Jesus of Nazareth passeth by. As soon as the old beggar knows who it is, he begins to shout at the top of his voice, "Jesus, thou son of David, have mercy on me!" And the people tried to stop him. They told him to keep still. Why did they try to stop him? Because he was poor—that was it; because he was an old blind beggar, that they did not consider of any account. They stopped him from exactly the same motive which sways many people now who would rather have some rich man that is well dressed, or it may be has some official position, come to church and sit with them in their pew than some poor fellow who is out of work and has a hard time to keep soul and body together, and whose clothing is worn shabby. Those people that tried to stop Bartimæus were not such different sinners from ourselves that we can not understand them. But what was Christ's attitude? That is the thing that is interesting to me, and ought to be interesting to you. For we are the disciples of Jesus and it is not our business to ape the hangers-on that tried to block the way for poor old Bartimæus when he wanted to get to the Master. When Jesus heard the cry he stood still, and commanded his disciples to bring Bartimæus to him. How quickly their tune changed then! The very people who had been telling him to keep still said to him now, "Be of good comfort, rise; he calleth thee." And Bartimæus got up as quickly as he could and came to Christ. The Savior inquired of him: "What wilt thou that I should do unto thee? The blind man said unto him, Lord, that I might receive my sight. And Jesus said unto him, Go thy way; thy faith hath made thee whole. And immediately he received his sight, and followed Jesus in the way." I want you to take notice of those last words—"he followed Jesus in the way." He became a member of Christ's church. And I haven't a doubt that Bartimæus was one of the one hundred and twenty that tarried in that upper room in Jerusalem after the ascension of Jesus, and that on the day of Pentecost there was not a more effective exhorter than Bartimæus who used to be the blind old pauper down by the gates of Jericho.

Bear with me, I pray you, while I urge the necessity of being watchful over our own hearts to see that we do not lose the spirit of the Master in seeking after the poor and the despised and the discouraged, for whom the world has contempt, to preach to them the Gospel of the Lord Jesus and to welcome them to this blessed fellowship. I am sure that the greatest reason why the Christian church is not controlling for Jesus Christ and for righteousness in our modern cities is because, to a great extent, it is getting away from the poor. I know we have many missions to the poor. We have many institutions and societies to carry charity and help to those who are in need. I do not underestimate their value nor their importance, but I do say that it is important that the poorest of men and women shall not only be welcome but sought after and desired in every church that bears the name of Jesus Christ. If every church in Brooklyn, of every denomination of Christians, could point with glad satisfaction, as one of the signs of fulfilling the mission of its Lord, to the fact that within its walls "the poor have the Gospel preached unto them," it would produce a mighty reformation in this city. We must seek for a new baptism of this spirit if we hope to be greatly blessed of God in the salvation of men. I would rather go back to the old log cabins where I began to preach the Gospel, in the mountains of Washington and Oregon, than to preach in any church, however rich or famous or splendid, that does not open its heart and its fellowship to welcome the poorest of God's children.

I thank God that Jesus Christ has not lost his power to pick the gold out of the quartz of common human life. Over in a New England village, a few years ago, a man queerly dressed and ill at ease and seemingly anxious to escape observation came up to the gate at the outskirts of the town where a woman, the mistress of a little cottage, was standing. The stranger said, taking off his hat with shy politeness, "Madam, have you any work that I could do?"

"I am sorry," she answered, "that I have not any. Will you come in and rest? My husband will be here directly."

"Thank you," he said after a moment's hesitation, "I have walked far to-day. I am tired and hungry and have little money. I will accept the first kindness that has been shown me in twenty years."

Mrs. Armstrong led the way into her little parlor, and offered her guest a chair by the window, then went into her kitchen. Just then her husband came in, crying, "Belle! Belle! I sold the meadow lot at a splendid bargain; I have the money here in my pocket—three hundred dollars in hard cash. What do you think of that?"

"Sh-sh-sh!" said the wife. And then drawing him away she told him about the stranger who had looked so tired out and discouraged that she had invited him in.

"It was all right to do it," he said; "still, I wish

this money were safe in the bank and not in my charge to-night with a man like that under our roof. If only I hadn't shouted my news out as I did when I came in."

But Armstrong was a brave Christian man, and there came to his memory at the moment the text they had read at family worship that morning, "There shall no evil befall thee." So he went in and gave a hearty hand-shake to the stranger, and showed him to the little dainty upper room, kept fresh and neat for company, and when presently the man came down, washed and refreshed, the three sat down to their evening meal.

The food was abundant and the poor foot-traveler partook of it with great zest. Under the influence of Mr. Armstrong's agreeable manner, the odd guest thawed, and became friendly and social. Once he laughed, but checked himself quickly as if he were not accustomed to it.

When it came bed-time Mr. Armstrong remarked, "It is our custom to have family worship, and we will be glad to have you join us." The wife sat down to the little melodeon, and their voices blended in—

> "Sun of my soul, thou Savior dear,
> It is not night if thou be near;
> Oh, may no earth-born cloud arise
> To hide thee from thy servant's eyes.

"If some poor wandering child of thine
Have spurned to-day the voice divine,
Now, Lord, the gracious work begin,
Let him no more lie down in sin."

Tears blurred the stranger's vision. He put up a slender but work-worn hand and furtively dried his eyes.

Mr. Armstrong read a few words from the Gospel of John, then they knelt, and a hearty prayer was offered.

The worship over, the guest was escorted to the spare chamber and left to his night's repose.

Next morning, after a good breakfast, he bade his kind entertainers farewell, and was about to proceed on his way. Mr. Armstrong inquired his direction, and, finding that he was bound eastward, gave him a lift for some miles in his wagon, and finally parted with him, with a cordial God-speed, and after depositing his money in safety in the bank, returned to his home.

"Belle," he said, "that man is a discharged convict. For some crime or other he has spent the best years of his life in prison. I knew it by many little signs, most of all by his step, and that way of acting as if watched."

"Jonathan! and you let him sleep here, when we had three hundred dollars in the house, and he might have robbed and murdered us both. Why, how could you sleep as you did, knowing that?"

"I trusted God. And I hope a new life will begin for that poor fellow, but he's got a hard row before him. I wish I could have helped him better than I did."

Two weeks later, Mr. Armstrong received a letter from a distant city. It ran thus:

DEAR SIR:—The stranger who ate your bread and slept in your house some days ago was a poor Ishmael, his hand against every man and every man's hand against him. He had spent twenty years in State prison, and, coming out, felt he had not a friend in the world. You and your wife have saved him. He went from your door straight to the house of a kinsman whom he had feared to meet. He has work and friends now, and has begun an honest life. But let him tell you that he was tempted to steal the money you brought home from the sale of the meadow lot, and perhaps he would have done it but for your great goodness and your family prayer. He is a saved man, thank God, and he owes it to you."

God help us to weigh human nature in the scales of Jesus Christ. He is able to inspire in the hearts of what seems the poorest possible material an enthusiasm and courage that will dare to seek for the loftiest and holiest things. Carroll

D. Wright tells a little story which shows the power of God to flash his divine spirit through one of the most lawless and useless of men. It was in the army. The man in question was a bummer in every sense of the word. As a soldier, he was for a long time a complete fraud. It was almost impossible to get him on a detail of duty. He constantly played the rôle of being ill. But one day when the regiment was going into battle this man, of no great intellectual power, of no particular strength of moral spirit, was placed next the color-guard in a post of honor. As the waves of battle swayed back and forth, and men went down, and the color-sergeant was shot, and the next man to the color-sergeant raised the flag, to be shot down immediately, and the third, and the fourth, and the fifth man fell, and all the colors of the whole division were down, and there was not a single rallying-point on which to assemble the charge, this man, this bummer, whom his comrades had considered a mean, contemptible soldier of no spirit, seized the staff and raised the stars and stripes in the center of the brigade, and made a rallying-point for the whole division, and carried the flag fearlessly through the fight; and from that hour he has been a man of grandeur, a man of character, a man of moral force. Afterward he told Mr. Wright that it came upon him as a call from heaven. Suddenly, there in the turmoil of battle, the Spirit of God spoke to his inmost soul and awoke him out of the deadly lethargy in which he had lived. Like a lightning flash it was revealed to him that there was something Godlike in him, and in seizing the colors he consciously surrendered his heart to a spirit he had never realized before—the spirit of duty, the spirit of sacrifice.

If I speak to any one who is discouraged about himself, who has fought on the whole a losing battle, I pray God that in the midst of your discouragements you may hear as never before the call to give yourself wholly and completely to the service of Jesus Christ. All things are possible to him who walks in fellowship with the conquering Christ.

THE CONVERSION OF A FAMILY.

"While Peter yet spake these words, the Holy Ghost fell on all them which heard the word."—*Acts* x. 44 (*Revised Version*).

THE place is the house of Cornelius. We do not know how large a family he had, but they were all gathered together. It is probable that not only his children, but some of his neighbors and friends, possibly some of the soldiers under him, as well as the servants of the family, may have been present. Anyhow, it is stated that all of his house were there. Peter preached to them a very plain and straightforward gospel. Like all the preaching of Peter and the early evangelists, it was almost entirely about Jesus Christ. First he told them about the life of Jesus, stating that "God anointed Jesus of Nazareth with the Holy Ghost and with power: who went about doing good." I suppose only the pith of the discourse is given in this mere outline of the sermon. Peter, no doubt, gave many incidents that had come under his own personal observation of the kindness and tenderness of Jesus toward people who were sick and in trouble. Possibly he told them his own experience. It must have broken any man's heart to have heard Peter tell the story of his own relations with Jesus Christ. Then Peter told them about the death of Jesus, how he died upon the cross; or, as he described it, "Whom they slew and hanged on a tree." And then he tells the story of the resurrection—"Him God raised up the third day, and shewed him openly." And with this story of the life and death and resurrection of Jesus as a foundation, he proceeds to preach Jesus as a present and personal Savior from sin, and declares to his attentive hearers, "Whosoever believeth in him shall receive remission of sins." As Peter preached, "the Holy Ghost fell on all them which heard the word." And Peter's friends who had come with him, who were Jews and had not yet absorbed the great lesson which had been taught to Peter, that God is no respecter of persons, were amazed and astonished at the conversion of these Gentiles, and at hearing them shout the praises of God. But Peter was thoroughly converted now to the new order of things and said, "Can any man forbid water, that these should not be baptized, which have received the Holy Ghost as well as we? And he commanded them to be baptized in the name of the Lord."

But the thought which I wish especially to emphasize is the happy fact that Cornelius in accepting Christ was able to bring his entire household with him. It is impossible to overestimate the blessedness of religion in the family. I fear that there is a decadence in the custom of family worship. I think there is reason to believe that the family altar is not so common among homes professedly Christian as it has been sometimes in the past. The *Advance* printed, recently, from the pen of a distinguished missionary, a letter in which he states that before his departure from this country, in 1859, he does not remember to have been in a Christian home in which family worship was not the daily custom. He declares, however, that on his recent visit he noticed a marked change that made a painful impression on his mind. On the first occasion when he was entertained in the household of a Christian layman, he did not know what to make of it that there was no gathering, either morning or night, for the reading of God's Word and prayer. Since then he has received the hospitality of many families, East and West, and now has come to be somewhat surprised when, in apparent contrast to the prevailing custom, the parents and children come together for family worship. There could not be a greater loss than this. There is no surer way to promote individual and domestic piety than daily worship in the home. It is not astonishing that people who have no family worship, who arise in the morning without thanksgiving to God, publicly expressed, for his care over them, who gather the household flock together at night and retire to be wrapped in sleep (twin brother to death) without any word of gratitude or any appeal for the Divine protection, lose the keenness of their anxiety for the conversion of the individual members of the family. Fathers and mothers in such homes grow accustomed to the sight of their children growing up with their minds absorbed in worldly things, but with no thought for the great spiritual interests of their souls.

Cornelius showed great wisdom in seeking to bring his household with him when he came to Christ. In that union of family worship, in that Christian fellowship one with another, there was great power. A reporter for one of our daily papers was standing on the rear platform of a car on the elevated railroad in New York city a few evenings ago, when the guard pointed suddenly and said, "Did you see that, Mister?" "Yes." "Well, then," added the guard, "you saw my three little children. They were kneeling on a trunk in front of the window of that house we passed. Behind them stood their mother. She was about to send them to bed, but before they go she teaches them to pray for me. Yes, and she brings them there so that I can see them." Then with a manly attempt to stifle a sob that swelled up in his throat he added, "She has told me what she tells them to say." "What is it?" inquired the now deeply interested listener. "I hope you won't think me foolish, sir; but as I guess you are a married man and a father you may care to hear it. You see, it is this way: The children, they go to bed at nine. That's about the time my train goes by the house. It's right on the line. So, just about that moment, she brings the little ones up to the trunk in their night-gowns and makes them kneel down with their hands clasped on their faces. And then they pray—" "For you?" was the interruption. "Yes, you're right. They pray that papa will be good and kind and bring home all his money and not drink any more, and—" The big guard's voice trembled. "But," he continued, with an effort, "I've been a rough man, and I have a hard place and many temptations— but I love my wife and I love my children. They are the only ones on earth that keep me straight." What a divine power there is in the consciousness that the dear ones of the family group are praying for us and that we are buoyed up by their tender sympathy in our efforts to live Christian lives!

By their carelessness concerning their own lives while their children are growing up, many parents plant thorns in their pillows for their later years. I speak to some at this time who have little children growing up in the home. God has put them into your hands as a sacred trust, and you fully intend, I am sure, to be true to that trust. Yet you are not Christians yourselves. You think that somehow you shall be able to bring up your children to love God and live a Christian life while you remain outside of the church of God and refuse your heart's devotion to Jesus Christ. It is impossible. And your children will not be very old before they will know that father and mother are not Christians, and the more they love you and admire you and trust you, all the more determinedly they will say in their little hearts, "We will not be Christians, either." I have never known more terrible grief than I have witnessed in the sorrow of some parents who, having neglected to seek salvation until their example had led their children astray, had at last been aroused and awakened, come to God and been forgiven, but were unable to bring their children with them. I trust there are none who hear me to-night who shall make this terrible mistake!

Some of you are toiling hard to give your children earthly advantages; but, after all, they will be useless to them unless they have the spiritual riches which alone can glorify a human life. If you want to have a powerful influence for good over your children, do not let them have any reason to doubt the genuineness of your religion or the sincerity of your desire for their salvation.

The story is told of a young infidel who one night in bed was contemplating the character of his mother. "I see," said he within himself, "two unquestionable facts: First, my mother is greatly afflicted in circumstances, body, and mind; and I see that she cheerfully bears up under all by the support she derives from prayer and the reading of her Bible. Secondly, she has a secret spring of comfort of which I know nothing; while I, who give an unbounded rein to my appetite and seek pleasure by every means, seldom or never find it. If, however, there is any such secret in religion, why may I not attain to it as well as my mother? I will immediately seek it of God." Thus it was that the Christ which shone in his mother's life led the brilliant Richard Cecil to know the Savior himself, and to glorify him by a life of most successful devotion to his service.

I thank God that the message is just as simple and plain to-day as it was on the day when Peter preached it in the household of Cornelius. Then, as now, it is simply to take Christ at his word and trust him as our Savior. Many years ago, on a snowy winter evening, a homeless boy found himself standing before a chapel at Colchester, England. Altho he was very young, there was a great burden of distress upon his mind. He had committed no crime; but he had been searching for months for salvation. Tired with his search, the boy stepped into the chapel and sat down in an obscure seat. It was such an unpleasant evening that there were less than twenty people in the audience. The preacher was in very ill health and near to death. He wondered at first whether it would pay to preach to so few. But perhaps conscious that he would not much longer have the opportunity of preaching the glorious Gospel, he stood up, pale and thin as a skeleton, and announced his text, "Look unto me, and be ye saved." "Why, that's just what I am after," thought the boy. Then the preacher turned and gazed upon him, and his piercing eyes seemed to penetrate his heart. "Young man," he cried in a loud voice, "you are in trouble!" "Sure enough, I am. How does he know it?" murmured the boy to himself. "You will never get out of it unless you look to Christ," said the preacher. Then with uplifted hands he exclaimed, "Look, look, look! It is only look!" This phrase, which may not have meant anything to anybody else in the house, meant everything to the troubled boy. His heart bounded. The simplicity of the words carried him straight to Christ. That troubled boy was Charles Spurgeon, who became the greatest soul-winner of his time. So I say to every one here to-night who is out of Christ, who is without God and without hope in the world; I invite you, nay, I plead with you, to look to Christ and be saved!

HEROD, THE KING WHO WAS WORM-EATEN.

"Herod arrayed himself in royal apparel, and sat on the throne, and made an oration unto them. And the people shouted, saying, The voice of a god, and not of a man. And immediately an angel of the Lord smote him, because he gave not God the glory: and he was eaten of worms and gave up the ghost."—*Acts* xii. 22, 23 (*Revised Version*).

WHAT a wonderful contrast there is in the story of Herod between the opening and the closing of this chapter! At the beginning he is in great seeming prosperity, and stretching forth his hands to destroy the Christians; but before the chapter closes he is eaten up by worms, as was one of his forerunners. Joseph Parker says that these Herods were a bad stock, and the worms were ill-fated that had to live upon them.

This particular Herod was a man of great egotism, fond of display, and willing to sell his soul for popular applause. Josephus tells us that he was accustomed to wear a robe that was wrought of solid silver, which glittered and shone in the sun as he moved. No doubt, on this festal occasion, when he came forth before the people in his silver robe and sat down to make his oration, he presented a very dazzling and splendid appearance. The multitude, knowing where his soft spot was, doubtless having contempt for him the while they did it, greeted him with thunders of applause; and Herod, blinded by his own vanity and wickedness, gulped it all down. Even when they cried out, "It is the voice of a god, and not of a man," the sensual bigot more than half believed it and was willing to take to himself even the honor due to the Almighty.

But the cup of Herod's iniquity was full. The applause had scarcely died away before the angel of the Lord "smote him." So it has been with many a man who has defied God and scoffed at righteousness. Silly lookers-on have said, "It is vice that prospers. It is the men that do not care about God and about righteousness that get on in the world." Wait till the story's done before you come to any such decision as that. Herod is not the only man whom worms have gnawed to pieces under his silver robe.

We may see in this case the delusion of those who believe that it is possible to permanently prosper by disobeying God. There is a strange chapter in the book of Revelation, where we are told that the bottomless pit was opened and out of it came a great smoke, and out of the smoke there came forth locusts upon the earth; and the remarkable thing about these locusts was that they were dressed up to represent the most terrible creatures of war. They had sham crowns on their heads that looked like gold, they had faces like men, and teeth like lions, and breastplates that seemed to be made out of iron, and when they flapped their wings they made a great sound like chariots running; but they were only locusts after all, and their power was for but a few months, and they vanished away. All the promises of sin are like that, and they come from the same place—the bottomless pit. Sin promises great things, but it never gives what it promises. The crowns of sin are never real solid golden crowns, but, like those on the mystical locusts, they are only sham; they are crowns "as it were." As Dr. W. L. Watkinson says, sin always acts by an infernal magic; it is full of illusions, imposition, and mockery. The prizes of sin and worldliness are always cruel shams. They look well, they seem splendid, they shine from afar, they captivate the imagination, they kindle ambition and desire, but they lack reality; when you lay hold upon them they are tantalizing vapors. Sinners never get any of the grand things for which they sell themselves. They get these things only as the locusts did their crowns—"as it were." There is a terrible irony in sin. It promises a great deal, and, in a sense, it fulfils its pledges, but in a satiric, mocking way. Its promises are—

> "Juggling fiends,
> That palter with us in a double sense;
> That keep the word of promise to our ear,
> And break it in our hope."

The devil promised Adam and Eve that on partaking of the fruit of the tree of wisdom they should be as gods and have the knowledge of good and evil; and so we have had the knowledge of good and evil, but with it the flaming sword, the thorns, and aches, and pains, and sorrows that have cursed our race. The devil promised Achan a wedge of gold and a beautiful Babylonish garment, but when he got them he had to bury them in his tent, and then, like Eugene Aram's victim, they could not be hid, and in the end they buried him. The devil promised Gehazi a scarlet robe. He sold his soul to get it, and when he got it he became a leper. That is the history of the promises of sin. Sinful ambition promised Napoleon universal conquest and glory, and he lived the last years of his life a prisoner. It is not only the great Herods and Napoleons and Nebuchadnezzars who are eaten of worms, or sent to eat grass like oxen. God is no respecter of persons, and it is as true now as it was when Paul wrote it to the Galatians: "He that soweth unto his own flesh shall of the flesh reap corruption; but he that soweth unto the Spirit shall of the Spirit reap eternal life." A man may think he can deceive God, but he is certain to be mistaken in the end. "Be not deceived; God is not to be mocked: for whatsoever a man soweth, that shall he also reap." Men who give themselves up to acquiring success in a worldly way for their own selfish ends, without regard to God or his claims upon them, lose all the beauty and glory there is in success after it is achieved. To a man who labors and plans to win prosperity and gather money or influence and power with noble purposes in view, holding his ability and talent as a loan from God, regarding himself as a trustee, a steward, of every treasure that comes into his hands, purposing to use everything for the benefit and blessing of all God's children, to such a man prosperity has an unfading glory. But when a man has built up his prosperity on pride and vanity and selfishness, by sharp tricks, caring not what the result shall be save only that he shall succeed, all the glory dies out of it, and it becomes disgusting. "The burglar seizes property, but in his hands it is no longer property, but pillage. The sensual man seizes love, but beautiful love thus seized instantly dies and becomes a ghastly corpse that we call lust. The ambitious man seizes greatness, but the moment that he touches it in the spirit of egotism and pride the splendid crown becomes tinsel. The coveted thing, whatever it be, loses its essence when the lawless lust has got it." Anything that you obtain by sinning against God and doing violence to your conscience you may be sure will lose all its preciousness and sweetness.

Some of you are refusing the Lord Jesus Christ and his claim to your open confession and service because you want pleasure, and yet I do assure you that real, abiding, satisfying pleasure will never be obtained by those who stifle their convictions of right and duty in order to purchase it.

The wise old Hassan sat in his door, when three young men pressed eagerly by.

"Are ye following after any one, my sons?" he said.

"I follow after Pleasure," said the eldest.

"And I after Riches," said the second. "Pleasure is only to be found with Riches."

"And you, my little one?" he asked of the third.

"I follow after Duty," he modestly said. And each went his way.

The aged Hassan in his journey came upon three men.

"My son," he said to the eldest, "methinks thou

wert the youth who was following after Pleasure. Didst thou overtake her?"

"No, father," answered the man. "Pleasure is but a phantom that flies as one approaches."

"Thou didst not follow the right way, my son."

"How didst thou fare?" he asked of the second.

"Pleasure is not with Riches," he answered with a sigh.

"And thou?" continued Hassan, addressing the youngest.

"As I walked with Duty," he replied, "Pleasure walked ever by my side."

"It is always thus," said the old man. "Pleasure pursued is never overtaken. Only her shadow is caught by him who pursues. She herself goes hand in hand with Duty; and they who make Duty their companion have also the companionship of Pleasure."

Learn the lesson of the old fable. You are cheating your soul when you stay away from Christ because you want pleasure, or happiness, or joy, or whatever name you give it. In doing so you are running after delusive phantoms and cheating visions and turning your back on the only real fountain of joy.

I would to God I knew how to bring to your mind in some new and startling way, that would arouse you and cause you to see clearly, this truth—

that there is no more deadly peril to an immortal soul than to become ensnared with worldiness. To a great extent people look with many degrees of allowance upon this sort of sin. It hardly seems sin to them. Yet God's Word calls it idolatry, and our own observation shows us that the insidious meshes of worldly pleasure, and worldly desires, and selfish interests, draw more souls away from the high and holy life to which Jesus Christ calls us than almost any other sin. This sin of worldliness, which is causing some of you to refuse and neglect this great salvation, can only be overcome by striking at its very center, by surrendering your whole heart and life to Jesus Christ and his service.

Two brothers were out fishing off the Farallones on the Pacific coast a few weeks ago, when they felt a tremendous strain on one of their lines. They were fishing for rock cod, but the fisherman who lay back and braced himself to meet the strain on his line knew that he had hooked something very different. He shouted for his brother to help him, and, each wondering what kind of a creature was making such a desperate fight at the other end, they hauled in the line inch by inch. At last, the waving tentacles of a huge devil-fish shot through the water and the fishermen knew they had hooked something they did not want. They twitched the line away, and tried to escape, but it was too late. The angry devil-fish clapped a powerful feeler over the side of the boat, and in much less time than it takes to tell it, the men were fighting for their lives. The fishermen knew that their only hope was to stun the creature. One grabbed an oar and the other a hatchet, and, keeping out of the reach of the long tentacles, they watched for an opportunity to get in a good blow. The one with the hatchet struck off a section of the tentacle nearest him, but that did not do much good; there were plenty more tentacles and an abundance of fight in possession of the fish. All the while the boat was rocking at a furious rate. For a time it looked as if the waves might help the devil-fish in his efforts to either upset the boat or clamber into it. For the first few minutes, in rocking strife, the devil-fish had it pretty much his own way, for the men found they had their hands full in trying to keep their places in the boat. Suddenly a lunge of the boat sent one of the men rolling head first right past the blazing eye of the enraged fish. A tentacle shot round him, and the next moment he was tangled up in three of the monster's hideous defenders and fighting the hardest fight he ever fought in his life. Indeed, his life would have ended then and there but for his brother. While the devil-fish was busy getting a good grip on the chest and neck of his victim and a satisfactory purchase on the boat, the other fisherman picked up a short club and managed to put in a smashing blow on the head of their foe. That did not do much good, and he looked about for the hatchet to cut the gripping tentacles from around his brother. "The knife, the knife!" shouted the man in the toils. "Stick him with your knife!" The man was yet free who wanted to slash off the tentacles, but the poor fellow who was fighting hard against them still had breath enough left to tell his brother to cut into the throat. And the other, watching his chance, plunged his knife deep into the soft pulp of the creature's neck. That settled the fight. Gradually the feelers relaxed, and the fisherman drew himself out from their loathsome grasp, thankful for his life.

You may see illustrated in that gruesome incident the fatal mistake which many people make in trying to save themselves from evil habits, from worldly tendencies, from unholy appetites that are pulling them into sin and iniquity and threatening them with ruin. Ever and anon, seeing their danger, they arise up in some sudden impulse for reform or some resolution to do better, and, like the fisherman with his hatchet, try to slash off some of the tentacles of evil that have wound their loathsome folds about their lives. Alas! the monster evil itself is not attacked. The iniquity of the sinful heart is left, and so long as it remains new tentacles will grow again, and it is only a question of time when the soul will be destroyed beyond the reach of remedy. He is the wise man who is like the fisherman in the toils of the devil-fish when he shouted to his brother not to waste his time cutting off the feelers of the monster, but to stab him in the throat, and thus destroy his very life.

It is to such a complete conquest that I call you to-night. I do not ask you to register another of a thousand attempts to do better, or cut off some one besetting sin, or break loose from some peculiarly uncomfortable vice; but I call upon you in the name of the Lord Jesus Christ, who came down from heaven and died on the cross to redeem you not only from the guilt but from the power of sin, to break loose from all sin and give your whole heart to him who is able to cleanse and keep you pure.

A LIGHT IN THE PRISON CELL.

"Behold, an angel of the Lord stood by him, and a light shined in the cell."—*Acts* xii. 7 (*Revised Version*).

THIS is one of the most sublime and beautiful pictures in all the portrait-gallery of the Bible. Herod, cruel and wicked, willing to build himself up by popular applause gained by shedding innocent blood, had already killed James, the brother of John. And for no other reason than to gain popular applause he seized upon Peter and cast him into prison. To human eyes Peter's is a hopeless case. He is already condemned in the Emperor's mind. But any such conclusion leaves God out of the account. Outside the prison there was a prayer-meeting where day and night unceasing prayer was made by the servants of Christ, pleading with God that Peter might be released. We do not know how many there were at that prayer-meeting. Barnabas was there, a rich man who had consecrated his wealth to the service of the Master; Mary, the mother of Mark, was there, who opened her house to the people of God and counted it an honor that the church meetings were held in her home; John Mark was there, a young man who had nothing else to give, and so gave himself to the Lord Jesus. And then there was a little girl, Rhoda. Who else we do not know, but there were others who were friends of Peter and they gave themselves up in prayer to God. They were praying all night, for to-morrow, unless God shall interfere, Peter will be led out to his death.

Christian friends, learn the great lesson of this midnight prayer-meeting. If you have dear ones who are in the dungeon of sin, who are held in bondage by the cords of iniquity, and there seems to be no hope for them, do not despair, but give yourself up to God in prayer for them. Get somebody else to join in with you, and keep them constantly before the Throne of Grace.

In the mean time, how fares it with Peter? He is in a cell made of massive rock, and sixteen armed soldiers, all answerable with their lives for his safe-keeping, keep guard over him. Not only so, but he is fastened with two chains, and there are three great bolted gates, each guarded by armed soldiers, to keep one unarmed, defenseless preacher of the Gospel. Dr. March says that the care with which Peter was kept was a confession that even Herod was afraid of him. And how about Peter himself, who expects to die on the morrow, a martyr to his Lord? How is he spending the night? Why, bless your soul, he is sleeping as sweetly as a little child, lying on the prison floor. There is no sleeping draught in the world like the consciousness of sins forgiven, the assurance that one is doing right, the confidence that one is working together with God to build up the cause of righteousness in the earth. Peter slept so soundly there on the stone floor, with each hand chained to a soldier on either side, that the light which shone from the presence of the angel that came to rescue him did not awaken him. The angel had to speak to him and shake him in order to wake him up from his sound sleep. A man with a conscience void of offense toward God and man can sleep in the face of peril, knowing that "all things work together for good" to him because he loves God. But the angel arouses Peter, and says to him, "Rise up quickly." Peter was not unaccustomed to marvelous manifestations of the power of God in behalf of his children, and yet it is not astonishing that at first he thought it was only a heavenly dream. There stands before him the beautiful angel. A voice gentle but firm calls him, and as he seeks to obey it the chains fall from his hands. Again the voice sounds in quick, earnest tones: "Gird thyself, and bind on thy sandals." He clothes himself as in a dream. There the armed soldiers lay on the floor in their heavy sleep. "Follow me," says the angel, as he moves toward the bolted door, and Peter follows as tho walking in a maze. How they got through that door Peter does not remember, but he finds himself outside, still following the angel. The guards outside also slumber on as they pass. They cross the prison court and come to the second gate. But nothing stands in the way of this celestial messenger and his follower. At last they come to the outer iron gate, but the angel has keys for everything, and the great gate swings on its hinges, and the two pass out into the public street. Peter follows his guide, wondering what is to come next, when suddenly he finds himself alone. He has come to himself now, and he sees it is no dream. His garments are about him, he has his sandals on his feet, the walls of the prison are behind him, he stands in the public street, and immediately proceeds to the prayer-meeting to tell them of his glorious release.

I have chosen our theme this evening to call your attention to the great truth that God sends the light of hope and mercy into the darkest prison cells of earth. Peter was not dearer to God than is any one of you. He is seeking after you with the light of heavenly sympathy and of tender, pitying love. There is no dungeon so dark but that the light of that love can penetrate it and lead the imprisoned soul out to new liberty and freedom. There is no comparison for sin which more aptly illustrates its baneful influence than when it is likened to a bondage. The prisoners of sin are the saddest prisoners in the world; but, thank God! there is no bondage of iniquity so cruel, and no prison of sin so dark, that the light of God's mercy does not shine into it and offer to lead the prisoner out to freedom.

A brother minister tells this story: In an inn in a small village, where the chief business was to sell strong drink, the proprietor died a death of hopeless despair. The old man whose soul had been ruined by his business had at the last told his only son, to whom the business fell as an inheritance, the terrible story of his own life. It was a tragic story that came from those poor, death-blanched lips. It began with the pure love of husband and wife in a new and happy home; the first-born boy; then the mother's sickness and early death; hard work on the part of the father, and growing zeal to do well, especially for his child—the "do well" meaning to get money; the arguing with conscience till, offended, it almost ceased to speak; quibbling with evil till it seemed goodness; coveting the devil's ways till they seemed paths of brightness. Finally, he traded the cottage home for the village inn, in order to make money. The voice of blasphemy soon choked the voice of conscience. The love of sin cast out the love of God. The boy grew up used only to this life of money-getting by moral losing. He had a sweet, sweet memory of something brighter, and it grew real by the dying father's bedside. The dew of death was on the old man's brow, and the finished life of earth, like a horrid nightmare of crushing defeat, made him cry out, "Get out of it, my lad, get out!" The young man like a little child knelt down for the first time in his father's presence, also the death presence, and he prayed: "O God, O God, help me, help me, for my own sweet lassie's sake. Brighten her life as mine was darkened when it is easy to forget. O God, help me, help me, for it is hard to change!"

Two weeks passed by. It was a dark winter evening and only two spots shone out with strong light —the church and the inn. It was Sabbath evening, and the church folks were speaking, thinking, praying about their greatest outward hindrance in their service of the Christ. The preacher, knowing that the dying man had besought his son to get out of his wicked business, went to the prodigal in the inn, to plead with him to come to God's house. He spoke of his dying father's charge, and of his own child's safety. He spoke to him tenderly of his own vow, which he seemed to be forgetting. At first the young man seemed only sorrowfully sullen, saying: "I can't come to-night, I can't possibly." The devil had again made his slave a coward. He went with the preacher to the door, and then suddenly shut it with them both outside. Seizing the arm of the puzzled minister, he hurried him across the village street, on to the village green, under a wide-spreading chestnut-tree, where they were hidden. Then, falling on the preacher's neck, he wept like a broken-hearted boy, and cried out like a fast-bound slave of sin: "Oh, I do want to get out before I lose the wish! For my child's sake I want to get out. But the landlord will not free me at once. It makes me almost swear to hear him say he knows a good tenant when he's got one. I do want to get out! Let me go to church with you. But no, I can't! Oh, that hell-shop yonder! I won't go back! It's impossible to be good in there."

That young man found God's minister who led him out of his business into new and wholesome associations to be as surely the messenger of heaven as was the angel who struck off Peter's chains and opened for him the iron gate.

Possibly I speak to some this evening who are not only chained by their evil habits and guarded by their besetting sins, but are walled in by sinful associations and friendships from which they must be separated if they are to be saved. Many a man has had to break with all his old associations, and permit the angel of God to lead him from the dungeon of sinful friendships into the fellowship of the saints in the prayer-meeting, before it was possible for him to lead the new life in Christ Jesus. Make up your mind here and now that nothing shall stand between you and an open and joyous Christian life. Pray God that all the prison doors of your heart may be thrown open and that the light of heaven may shine in. Some one sings:

> "Open the door, let in the air,
> The winds are sweet and the flowers are fair;
> Joy is abroad in the world to-day,
> If our door is wide open he may come this way.
>   Open the door.
>
> "Open the door, let in the sun;
> He hath a smile for every one;
> He hath made of the raindrops golden gems,
> He may change our tears to diadems.
>   Open the door.
>
> 'Open the door of the heart; let in
> Sympathy sweet for stranger and kin;
> It will make the halls of the heart so fair
> That angels can enter unaware.
>   Open the door.

"Open the door of the soul; let in
  Strong, pure thoughts, which shall banish sin;
  They will grow and bloom with a grace divine,
  And their fruit shall be sweeter than that of the vine.
      Open the door."

And you may open the door to all these by opening the door to Jesus Christ.

Do not to-night cheat your own soul by summoning your pride and saying, "I am not a very great sinner, after all." Be honest with your own heart, and do you not know that there is sin in the mastery that temper, and self-will, and passion have over you; in the unsafe habits of your lives? These things make you to know as well as God knows that your heart is wrong and wicked. As Dr. McLaren says, we do not need to go to inebriate homes where there are people who would cut their right hands off if they could get rid of the craving, and can not, to find instances of this bondage. People who pride themselves on their respectability have only to be honest with themselves, and to try to pull the boat against the stream instead of letting it drift with it, to know the force with which the current runs. A tiny thread, like a spider's, draws after it a bit of cotton a little thicker, and knotted to that there is a piece of pack-thread, and after that a two-stranded cord, and then a cable that might hold an ironclad at anchor. That is a parable of how we draw to ourselves, by imperceptible degrees, an ever-thickening set of manacles that bind our wills and make us the servants of sin. "His slaves ye are whom ye obey." If ever you are to know the joys of salvation, if ever you are to have peace with God, if ever you are to join the blood-washed throng in heaven, these chains of sin must be broken off. I come to you at this time as the messenger of God, and in the words of the angel to Peter I say, "Rise up quickly!" Remember that the first step toward your salvation—since Christ has made atonement for you, and the Holy Spirit has convicted you of sin, and I, as the ambassador of Christ, bring you his invitation—must come from you. Do not wait thinking that some marvelous operation of the Divine Spirit will save you without your action in the matter. As Dr. Wayland Hoyt points out, in commenting on this very Scripture, God never does for us what we can do for ourselves. Peter *could not* get himself out of prison; so God sent his angel. Peter *could not* smite off his chains; and the angel smote them off for him. But Peter *could* bind on his sandals; that the angel did not do for him. Peter *could* cast his garments about himself; that the angel did not do for him. Peter *could* follow the angel; and the angel did not carry him. Peter **could not** open the prison's iron gates; and they were divinely opened for him. Peter *could* go through the gates; and he was not carried through. Nobody doubts that if Peter had refused to do what he could do, God would not have given him help to what he could not do. That is the message of God to your souls. Rise up quickly and follow the light you have, gird up the loins of your will, and God will smite off the chains of sin, and open the prison doors, and lead you out to glorious freedom.

THE LIVING HOPE.

"Blessed be the God and Father of our Lord Jesus Christ, who according to his great mercy begat us again unto a living hope by the resurrection of Jesus Christ from the dead, unto an inheritance incorruptible, and undefiled, and that fadeth not away, reserved in heaven for you."—*1 Peter* i. 3, 4 (*Revised Version*).

HOPE is the mainspring of human life. When the mainspring is broken, the watch ceases to run. When hope is dead, the man ceases to act. There is no medicine that science has ever discovered so powerful as hope. There is no elixir of courage that will so inspirit an army and send it to victory as hope. No man is defeated so long as hope lives. No man can be victorious after hope is gone. An Indian on Lake Erie, who had taken to his canoe after being worn out by the chase, fell asleep and drifted into the rapids above Niagara. He did not awake until the current was sweeping his frail boat swiftly to destruction. At last he was aroused by the shouts of horror-stricken spectators on the shore. He sprang to his feet and saw at a glance that his doom was inevitable. He did not touch the paddle, nor make a single cry, but with the stoicism of his race and the calmness of despair resumed his seat, folding his arms across his breast, and was hurled to his horrible death. Hope had died out of his heart.

It was a feeling something akin to that despair of the Indian that the disciples had when they saw Jesus die on the cross and carried his mangled and wounded form and laid it away in Joseph's tomb. Their hopes fled. This is illustrated in the language of the two disciples whom Jesus overtook on the way to Emmaus. When he asked them why they were so sad they told him about the crucifixion of their Master, and how they had hoped that he was to have been the Redeemer of Israel. But all this darkness of doubt and fear and despair was dissipated by the resurrection of Christ; and Peter declares that to be the foundation of "the living hope" of the Christian.

It is this living hope which I wish to present to you to-night. Christianity is ever new and full of vitality because it centers about the personal, living Christ. Jesus says, in the Revelation, "I am he that . . . was dead, and . . . am alive forevermore." The living personality of Christ is the vitalizing power of Christianity everywhere. And every one who takes hold upon Christ by faith is electrified by the life-giving current and stimulated to noble purpose and holy living as truly as were Peter and John who came in personal contact with him while he dwelt in the flesh.

There is everything about Christianity and about the Christ who is its center and its heart to attract youth. Young men and young women who are attracted by life and activity, and whose hearts, unless prematurely withered and dried by artificial surroundings, open naturally to heroic and daring appeals, can surely find nowhere such inspiring leadership as in Jesus of Nazareth. "Ian Maclaren," the writer of those sweet Scotch stories which everybody is reading, draws attention in a most graphic manner to the fact that Jesus drew about him during his early ministry a group of young men who were full of courage, and who were inspired with hope by the vitality which filled the personality of Jesus. There was about Christ an atmosphere of enthusiasm that constituted his first attraction. His kingdom was to do away with artificial distinctions, to embrace all kinds of people, to bring every wrong to an end, to award the crown to goodness alone. And we must fight toward that glorious ideal. Wo be to the man who pulls down the standard of Jesus Christ and makes compromises with the world, the flesh, and the devil in order for seeming and temporary success. It is the glory of Jesus Christ that he makes no compromise with anything that is wrong. His sublime appeal to the youthful heart is to struggle toward the very mountain-top of nobility of life. When Jesus was on earth he naturally gathered about him daring souls who loved life and heroism. Following Jesus meant high spirit, and that had died down to gray ashes on the cold hearthstone of worldly hearts; it meant risk, which is often abhorrent to people with an assured capital, either in money or reputation. But those are the very arguments that ever win brave souls. There is an age when the love of danger is in a man's blood, and he is ready to woo hardship as a bribe. I speak to some here who have read of heroic deeds of other days and who have been conscious of something within the heart which has responded to the heroism of those early times. You have said, "There is something in me that could do deeds like that under certain conditions and opportunities." Jesus Christ appeals to that romantic spirit which, to some degree, is in every human heart, and especially in the heart of youth. The very exertion and unflinching moral courage, the opposition to the world, the battle with sin—all these appeal to everything that is heroic, romantic, and splendid in human nature.

I impress this upon you because I am trying to

uproot the false opinion which you may have had that religion is in some way unnatural to you. Nothing could be farther from the truth than to suppose that to become a Christian is to dry up and narrow the streams of life which God has bestowed upon us. Instead, no one lives fully until his whole nature is aroused by coming in contact with Jesus Christ. To become a Christian is not a mere negative affair. It does not mean that in some arbitrary, artificial way the heart shall be fenced off from the natural joys and pleasures of human life. It means, rather, that a nature that has been only partially developed, and it may be has been marred and hurt by sin so that some of its divinest faculties have lost their power to take in joy and gladness, shall be so thoroughly restored that the whole man or woman shall have all faculties complete under the control of a purified and noble spirit.

Christ came to give us life; and not only so, but more abundant life than can be had any other way. He stands before the young man or the young woman who is conscious of vitality and a desire to do, and dare, and be something that is worth doing, and daring, and being among their fellows; wishing in their best moments that they might rise out of the dusty commonplace and be of some real power and force and blessing to humanity; Christ stands before all such, and says: "What you want is life in mind and heart—life to give power and joy. Religion is not only morality and doctrinal statements; it overflows all such boundaries; it is life. Begin to live at once, there in your place, by hearing my call and obeying it. You have existed for yourself; now forget and deny self and live for others. This is my cross—accept it, carry it, rejoice in it. The moment you lift it, you will feel the exhilaration of life; and the longer you carry it, you will have life more abundantly."

Oh, that I knew how to inspire you with the spirit of that appeal which Christ is making to you! In him is the living hope that never fades away. Riches may take wings and fly away, but they have no power to check the upspringing fountain of that inner life which was not born of them, did not depend on them for sustenance, and is not impoverished by their loss. Friends may misunderstand or prove unfaithful, or grow cold and neglectful; but the spiritual friendship with Jesus Christ, which is the most helpful and inspiring of all the friendships humanity can know, will seem all the nearer and more precious in such a time of trial. The tide of physical health may run low. Sickness may lay its hand upon the house in which we live, under the withering touch of disease the hair may grow prematurely gray, and the trembling weakness of the worn-out frame may tell of shortened life on earth, and prophesy the speedy end of the mortal career; but the inner life, the living hope, the immortality, born of sonship to God and fellowship with the conquering Christ, runs all the more fully in its current, glistens the more brilliantly in the sun, and grows brighter and brighter unto the perfect day.

I thank God that our Christianity is something so vital and full of living power that any poor wanderer who has strayed from God and lost hope may find in Jesus Christ a hand strong enough to lift him out of the Slough of Despond into which he has fallen and set his feet on the way of safety.

Mrs. Ballington Booth relates an interesting little story about her little boy. The *War Cry* once had a picture of a boat in the midst of the sea, and all around it were struggling, gasping, sinking men and women. In the rear of the boat was General Booth reaching out his hand to the drowning. His little grandson, who is only a few years old, looked and looked at the picture, deeply interested in it. At last, he said, "Mamma, what is grandpa doing? Is he trying to get people into the boat, or is he just shaking hands with them?" Jesus Christ did not come, and does not come to-day, on simply a mission of entertainment, or even of moral improvement, but as a divine rescuer of the lost and the perishing. It is a real hand of rescue—kind, and tender, and loving, but strong and powerful as kind—which he reaches forth to every one sinking beneath the waves of sorrow and sin.

This theme ought to have in it a message of encouragement for all who have striven and failed, or for those who have neglected until the tempter has whispered: "It is too late." The living Christ calls you to-day out of your lethargy with the assurance that all things are possible with God, and that if you will courageously accept the invitation of Christ nothing shall be able to stand against you in your struggle for a new and glorious life. As Paul Hamilton Hayne sings:

" 'Tis the part of a coward to brood
    O'er the past that is withered and dead;
  What tho the heart's roses are ashes and dust?
    What tho the heart's music be fled?
    Still shine the grand heavens o'erhead,
Whence the voice of an angel thrills clear on the soul,
'Gird about thee thine armor, press on to the goal.'

"If the faults or the crimes of thy youth
    Are a burden too heavy to bear,
  What hopes can re-bloom on the desolate waste
    Of a jealous and craven despair?
    Down, down with the fetters of fear!
In the strength of thy valor and manhood arise.
With the faith that illumes and the will that defies.

"Too late! Through God's infinite world,
  From his throne to life's nethermost fires,
Too late is a phantom that flies at the dawn
  Of the soul that repents and aspires.
  If pure thou hast made thy desires,
There's no height the strong wings of immortals may gain
Which in striving to reach thou shalt strive for in vain.

"Then up to the contest with fate;
  Unbound by the past which is dead!
  What tho the heart's roses are ashes and dust?
  What tho the heart's music be fled?
  Still shine the fair heavens o'erhead;
And sublime as the angel that rules in the sun
Beams the promise of peace when the conflict is won."

It is to this new life of dauntless hope I call you at this hour. It is the only hope that can glorify human life and cause it to grow more beautiful as the years go on. As Dr. Lyman Abbott recently said, let a man live under the impression that the horizon of this present time is the horizon of his life, and I do not see how he can help, at times, asking himself, Is life worth living? and shaking his head sorrowfully in reply. It is only the glorious assurance that life here and now has its roots in immortality, that here and now we have close kinship with heaven, and that the purposes and hopes that animate us to-day instead of being destroyed by death shall find their completion and fruition in the realm beyond death, that makes life a sweet and glorious benediction. "Life is like an ocean voyage. The man comes out in the morning from his cabin, and starts to walk the deck. Whether it is a little boat or a big one does not make much difference; for after a few years he has traversed the whole deck from stern to stem, stands on the bow and knows all the life that is. What then? Lie down to sleep, wearied one, in the morning thou shalt wake in harbor, a new continent before you, and your friends there waiting to receive you. This is the anchor that you are to throw out while you wish for day: weeping may endure for a night, but joy cometh in the morning."

Blessed are those whose illuminated hearts bear witness to the morning! I invite you to the Christ, "the Light of the World," who can dispel earth's darkness, and who himself shall be the glory of the morning.

THE DRIED-UP SPRINGS OF LIFE.

"These are springs without water."—*2 Peter* ii. 17 (*Revised Version*).

THIS is Peter's characterization of certain people who live for the senses, and are devoted to the pleasures of a worldly life. It is a very striking picture. To appreciate it one must have lived or traveled some time in a mountainous or hilly country where the treasures of the snow are gathered in the great reservoirs of the mountains, and, when the springtime comes, and the sun is high in the heavens, and the days are long, the snow melting on the long mountain slopes finds its way down through the fissures in the rocks, and, following underground channels, comes out down the mountain-sides and among the foot-hills in bubbling springs of pure water. I was born among the hills, and on my father's farm in my childhood there were a number of these springs. Some of them were ever-living. Summer or winter seemed to make no difference to them. In hot or cold they poured forth their full, fresh tide of cool, sweet water from some great reservoir so inexhaustible and so protected that it could not be reached by the cold or checked by heat. But on the same farm there were other springs that, when the warm rains came in the early springtime, gushed forth an abundance of water. A stranger passing through the country might have thought that these were the most valuable springs on the farm; but later in the season these fountains which did not draw their water from any channel from the mountains, but from some little local watershed among the hills about them, gradually narrowed their output until by the time the hot days of July had come they were dried up entirely, and the channel where the promising stream had run in April was dry and bare.

This is the picture which Peter sets before us as a portrait of the man or woman who, instead of drawing hope, and courage, and strength from the high hills of righteousness and the lofty reservoirs of the Bible and prayer, depends upon the local watershed of the earth. Tell me the source from whence you get your strength and pleasures, and I will tell you how long they will endure and when your spring will run dry.

Let us inquire for a moment what are some of the springs of life that are necessarily temporary, and must in the nature of things soon dry up, and refuse to give us joy and peace.

The first is youth. It is a spring, a source of pleasure and joy to every one who makes the journey of life. There is a certain hopefulness, an elasticity, an abounding optimism about youth which finds joy of some sort in almost everything. It is a period when it is delightful simply to be alive, to breathe the air, to look upon the trees and the sky, to scent the flowers, to sleep, to dream, to grow, to peer toward the mysterious future and wonder concerning the hidden possibilities of this new developing life. Yes, youth is a spring, a fountain of joy and pleasure. I speak of mere physical youth; the fact that life is yet to be lived and that one may make it what he will. But delightful and glorious as this fountain is, it is certain that it comes from the local watershed of life and will soon have poured all the waters from its slender reservoir. Its springtime has already passed for most of us, and for many it has passed altogether. Youth is a spring that will dry up for every one.

Health is a spring of joy and strength, a natural source of gladness and delight. To stand out in the broad sunlight of God's day and feel that your physical and intellectual manhood is strong and complete, that all the organs and faculties of body and mind work harmoniously together, and that you have in all its wholesome roundness the power to do among your fellows what a man or woman can do, is a bountiful source of joy and delight, and a cause for profound thanksgiving to God on the part of every one that possesses it. But this, too, is a spring that will dry up. No man's body is so perfect but that it may be wounded and mangled by some accident or misfortune before to-morrow night. No woman's figure is so graceful or features so beautiful but sickness may distort the one and blight the other with scarcely a moment's warning. Disease lurks in the very air we breathe and waits for us morning and night, and soon the strongest arm must tremble and the most giant-like form recline in weakness and lose the grace and beauty of health. Yes, our health and strength and beauty are springs that will dry up.

Another great fountain of joy and delight is human friendship. God has given us wondrous power of comforting and making glad each other by kindly fellowship. And many a person who has not much strength or beauty, and has passed beyond the vigor and enthusiasm of youth, still counts himself firm in an impregnable fortress because of the friendships that gird him about. And yet all friendships that are of this world alone are perishable springs. It is not only that we have to run the risk of the frailties of human nature and take the chance that some cruel misunderstanding shall separate us from the love of our friends; but they, too, are subject to all the laws of weakness, and sorrow, and affliction, and death that threaten, and many times within a single year a soul that looked upon strong friends like bulwarks on every side has seen them vanish away like mists before the morning sun, until they stood friendless and alone. Yes, friendship is a spring that will dry up if it has no higher source than earth.

But, somebody says, you have left out one source of joy and pleasure—What of riches? Alas! that, too, is a spring that will dry up. But you argue with me that money will purchase servants to care for you when you are weak; it will minister to your taste, and give you power to surround yourself with many protections and shelters; and all that is indeed true. But money can not keep alive in you the vigor and enthusiasm and power of enjoyment of youth. Wilberforce, in speaking of the Richmond villa, belonging to the Duke of Queensbury, whose wealth was many millions of dollars, says that once on dining with the Duke in company with a party of celebrated guests, altho the dinner was sumptuous, the views from the villa most enchanting, and the Thames was in all its glory, the Duke looked on with indifference. In reply to Wilberforce, who, then a young man, had made some appreciative remarks on the beauty of the scenery, the Duke protested almost angrily, "What is there to make so much of in the Thames? I am quite tired of it. There it goes—flow, flow, flow, always the same." All his wealth could not keep for that sensual old man the bright appreciation of nature, and of beauty everywhere, which had been the natural inheritance of his youth. Money can not bribe disease to stay away, and it can, after all, do little to stay its ravages. Money can not keep our friends alive, it can not stay the coming of the white horse and its rider. It is proverbial that shrouds are without pockets, and Scriptural that we brought nothing with us into this world and we can take nothing out of it.

Count them over, the great sources of joy and pleasure for the worldling: youth, health, money, friends. They are all there; everything that the worldly man can know is grouped under some one of these four, and there is a limit to the reservoir which each of these springs draws upon, and they shall all dry up, and leave the soul that trusts to them naked and bare, bankrupt and hopeless at the last.

Ah! you say, it is a sad sermon you are preaching to us. I wish I had stayed at home. But I thank God you may give it a bright side if you will, for there are possible to the human soul springs that draw upon the higher watershed of the hills of God, whose streams flow on with ever-abounding fulness through youth and manhood and old age; streams that are only sweetened by affliction and weakness, that can not be frozen up by poverty, nor scorched and dried out by any lack of human fellowship. Jesus said to the woman at the well of Sychar that she had been drinking of that well only to thirst again, but he was able to give her living water which should be within her soul a fountain springing up unto everlasting life. Paul, in the thirteenth chapter of his first letter to the Corinthians, said that there are some springs that abide, "But now," he says, "abideth faith, hope, love, these three; and the greatest of these is love." The Psalmist says, in a grateful tribute to God, "All my springs are in thee." I call you from the lowlands of worldliness, where all the springs of life shall dry up, up to the treasures of the highlands where there are streams of joy that shall flow forever. Frances Ridley Havergal sings:

> "Hear the Father's ancient promise!
>   Listen, thirsty, weary one!
> I will pour my Holy Spirit
>   On thy chosen seed, O son.
> Promise to the Lord's anointed,
>   Gift of God to him for thee!
> Now, by covenant appointed,
>   All thy springs in him shall be.

"Springs of life in desert places
  Shall thy God unseal for thee;
Quickening and reviving graces,
  Dew-like, healing, sweet, and free.
Springs of sweet refreshment flowing,
  When thy work is hard or long;
Courage, hope, and power bestowing,
  Lightening labor with a song.

"Springs of peace, when conflict heightens,
  Thine uplifted eye shall see;
Peace that strengthens, calms, and brightens;
  Peace itself a victory.
Springs of comfort, strangely springing,
  Through the bitter wells of wo;
Founts of hidden gladness, bringing
  Joy that earth can ne'er bestow.

"Thine, O Christian, is this treasure,
  To thy risen head assured!
Thine in full and gracious measure,
  Thine by covenant secured!
Now arise! his word possessing,
  Claim the promise of the Lord;
Plead through Christ for showers of blessing,
  Till the Spirit be outpoured."

Do you ask how to obtain these springs that shall never dry up? My answer is that the woman of Samaria obtained for the asking, not only for herself, but for many others who believed on Christ through her word. The same gracious terms are extended to you to-night. Christ is seeking after you with as great tenderness as he sought after her. When Moses held up the brazen serpent in the wilderness before the dying Israelites, whosoever looked upon it lived. And so to-day it is "look and live." It is Christ's own illustration. Let us not try to make hard what he has made easy. Do not let the simplicity of the Gospel keep you away from this great salvation, but rather thank God that he has made the path so easy that the youngest and the weakest may come.

PETER'S CONFIDENCE IN OLD AGE.

"We did not follow cunningly devised fables."—*2 Peter* i. 16 (*Revised Version*).

THERE is an exceedingly sweet flavor about this chapter. It is fragrant with thanksgiving to God arising from the heart of a saintly man, like perfume from a vase of flowers. It is written by a man who is conscious that he is very near to the end of his earthly pilgrimage. There is a charm about such writing that is indescribable. In the presence of death all disguises are thrown off. There is a naturalness, a simplicity, about statements made at such a time that give them great effect. Peter is writing for the benefit of those who shall come after him, that their hearts may be established in the faith, that they may go on their way rejoicing in confidence, knowing that they are not following "cunningly devised fables."

More than eighteen centuries have gone by since then, but the power of Jesus Christ to comfort the human heart and to rescue it from the bondage of sin is as effective as ever. All along the way there have been philosophies and religions that have sprung up for a time and have had their little day, and, like a hunter's camp-fire built of pine knots, have soon burned themselves out and left only a heap of ashes behind them. But Jesus of Nazareth is still the Day Star of human hope.

In Christ alone is there a strength that abides through all the changing scenes of time. A traveler tells these two stories: There was a storm at sea during which a sailor on watch at night was swept overboard. There were two men on watch together, and it was the one least exposed that the wave, leaping over the bow, swept away. When the captain was asked how that could be he said: "Because the second man had nothing to hold on to." Many a storm shall sweep over the deck in the course of the voyage of life. Be sure you lay hold upon the one Hope that is as an anchor to the soul, sure and steadfast, and reaches to within the harbor.

The other story is about climbing the Gornergrat. The Swiss guide, seeing the traveler was exhausted, said: "Sit down, and rest upon this rock." It was a hard, jagged thing, and he asked: "Why not rest on the snow?" The guide answered: "Because I know the rock will not slip with us; it is anchored underneath." In climbing the mountain steeps of human life there are many slippery places where a false step may start an avalanche that will sweep you over the precipice or into the deadly crevasse below. Be sure you plant your feet on the Rock of Ages!

There ought to be in our theme great comfort and encouragement to every one who has been delaying his return to God and putting off his acceptance of Christ because he fears his own nature may be so uncertain and unreliable that he will not hold out in his attempt to lead the new life. Peter was just that kind of a man—a man with many good impulses, but a man who, after three years of close association with Jesus Christ, deserted him in the hour of his greatest trial. But instead of throwing him away because he had failed, and casting him out on the waste-heap, Christ kept his hold on Peter and by patience and sympathetic care and love made him the Peter who was like adamant in his rugged fidelity.

Mrs. Maud Ballington Booth says that in a certain city she saw something that was a wonderful advertisement and a wonderful lesson. There was a great fire, a tremendous blaze; an entire block of buildings worth a million dollars was entirely destroyed; all was one mass of charred ruins and only one thing was standing—a great brick wall. And on this wall was written, where everybody could see it: "This is a wall built of fire-proof bricks!" with the name of the brick-makers below. Everything else had gone, but that wall had stood. Some of the buildings were constructed of stone and marble, and made a very imposing appearance, but the fire brought them down in three hours. Jesus Christ is able to build a character that will stand. The fire of persecution or trial may rage about it, but if it has been humbly and lovingly entrusted to the building and keeping of the divine Christ, it shall stand the test and come out of the fire stronger than ever.

Paul, in speaking of the mighty struggles and conflicts which come to us all in the course of our lives, says that we should have on the whole armor of God, "Withal," he says, "taking up the shield of faith, wherewith ye shall be able to quench all the fiery darts of the evil one."

Mr. W. J. Leonard, a Brooklyn carpenter, has invented a bullet-stopping shield. The material is a combination of cotton, wood, wool, and felt, treated chemically. There are three plates of the composition in the shield at a little distance apart from each other. At a trial of it a short time ago, in the presence of friends and newspaper reporters, the inventor removed all doubt as to the truth of his assertions by putting on one of the plates and allowing himself to be shot at. After the trial it was seen that the bullet had penetrated the shield about three quarters of an inch. The inventor said that the shot felt as if some one had poked him lightly with a stick, but the bullet fired into the shield was mashed flat and almost torn to pieces. So it is with the shield of faith. The missiles of the enemy are themselves destroyed, but he who wears that shield walks in safety.

Frederick the Great, of Prussia, when he was in the height of his prosperity, built a beautiful cottage where he could retire from the cares of state, and find perfect relief from all the troubles that beset an emperor. This dainty little cottage-palace was surrounded by beautiful gardens and was as near an earthly paradise as money and taste could make it. Over the door the monarch had written in gold letters, "*Sans Souci*"—"Without care." There he was determined to get away from all annoyances. But he was doomed to disappointment. Frederick found, like many another man, both on the throne and off it, that it is impossible to fence out the troubles of life by any earthly wall. Once when the same monarch was traveling he sent forward word to a worthy clergyman whom he knew that he would stop with him. The house was made ready, the royal party arrived and were entertained, and when they left the emperor made a handsome present of money to the clergyman. On coming back the emperor stopped again at the same place, and on leaving he said to his friend, the Christian minister, "Now, is there anything I can do for you, any place in the church I can give you, any way that I can make you happier?" "No, your Majesty," was the answer, "I want nothing. I am content with my position." The monarch was astonished. An humble minister of the Gospel, and wanting no preferment? He could not understand it. "What," he cried, "contented?" "Yes, your Majesty." "Is it possible that you want nothing that I can give you?" "It is possible, your Majesty. I am happy and contented." "Then," replied the astonished monarch, "over your door must be written, 'My kingdom is not of this world.'"

The emperor had written "without care," over his own door, but the cares had come thick and fast in spite of it. There is only One who can give abiding peace and rest, and it is he who appeals to you to-night, saying: "Come unto me all ye that labor, and are heavy laden, and I will give you rest."

Peter's experience shows us that a Christian life is one full of thrilling interest and one that is constantly enriched as it goes on. Every life that depends upon the world for its sustenance grows less and less interesting, and finally loses all; but he who puts his trust in Jesus Christ finds that the interest of life deepens and its treasures increase in value as the years multiply.

Sad illustrations are constantly coming to our notice which prove that those who trust in sensual delights and worldly pleasures are ever and anon coming upon fearful bankruptcy and disaster. The New York papers last June related the story of a young man who had once possessed a comfortable property and lost it by unfortunate investments, thus finding himself at the age of thirty-four without money or employment. He woke his wife in the early morning with a kiss, then shot at her, but fortunately failed to kill her. Supposing, however, that he had, he put his pistol to his own head and destroyed his life. He left this letter as an explanation of his course:

"NEW YORK, June 12, 1895.
"TO THE CORONER: Being unable to bear life's miseries any longer, so determined to end my life. Take my dear beloved companion with me. Colonel Ingersoll is right in his views and lectures, and as to my opinion, the most sensible man of the century." Etc., etc.

How different the future of this young man and his wife might have been if he had taken Jesus Christ for his counselor instead of the infidel.

One of the most pathetic incidents related in all literature is Comte de Brienne's account of the last days of the great statesman, Mazarin. He was a great lover of art and had expended a fortune in gathering together the most beautiful works of the great masters. But he had neglected to come into such fellowship with the King in his beauty as to make the approach of eternity a source of joyous anticipation to him. The poor old man clung to his beautiful pictures with a bitter grief that was full of pathos. The historian says that he was walking one day in the great man's palace, when he recognized the approach of Mazarin by the sound of his slippered feet, which he dragged, one after another, as a man enfeebled by a mortal malady. The young man hid himself behind a piece of tapestry, and heard him say, "I must leave all that!" He stopped at every step, for he was very feeble, and, casting his eyes on each object that attracted him, he sighed forth as from the bottom of his heart: "I must leave all that!" Could there be a more thrilling and terrible illustration of the awful folly of setting one's heart upon the things of the earth, even tho they be the most beautiful and refined that the world can afford, than the ghastly spectacle of this solitary, withered, gray-haired, slippered old statesman, tottering along, soliloquizing (unaware of the ears behind the tapestry), pausing now before a Caracci, and now before a Correggio, and again before a Titian, and muttering, unconscious that any one heard him: "I must leave all that! I must leave all that!"

Thank God! there is something better than that for humanity. How different is the picture of Peter which is suggested to us in this chapter! He comes to the end of life growing constantly in knowledge of the purposes of God, rich in memory of the past, happy in appreciation of the present, and pressing on with courageous heart toward glories yet to be revealed.

A gentleman who spent last summer up north of Lake Superior, saw an old Norway pine blown down in a great storm. He made an examination of it and found it to be two hundred and fifty years old. Stripping up a bit of the bark, he discovered that the old tree was, the day it fell, still growing. A Christian life is like that. It grows on and on and on. Death stopped the growth of the old Norway pine, but even death itself can not stop the growth of the child of God.

What a splendid source of courage are these words of Peter in the face of the encroachments of age and the drawing near of the time of our own departure from earth. "At evening time it shall be light" to the man who walks in fellowship with Jesus Christ. One of the most fascinating characters which "Ian Maclaren" sketches for us, in his annals of the Scotch saints, is the portrait of William MacClure, a Christian physician, whose life was one constant sacrifice offered up cheerfully and patiently for the good of his fellows. When the good doctor's time came to go, his old friend Drumsheugh held him by the hand. As the friend watched, a change came over the face on the pillow beside him. The lines of weariness disappeared, as if God's hand had passed over it; and peace began to gather round the closed eyes. The doctor's mind had been wandering, and a little before he had imagined himself out in the storm, struggling through the snowdrifts, to get to the bedside of his patient. But now he has forgotten the toil of later years, and has gone back to his boyhood;

"'The Lord's my shepherd, I'll not want.'"

he repeated, till he came to the last verse, and then he hesitated:

"'Goodness and mercy all my life,
Shall surely follow me.'

Follow me—and—and—what's next? Mother said I was to have it ready when she came. 'I'll come before you go to sleep, Willie, but ye'll no get your kiss unless ye can finish the Psalm.' 'And —in God's house—forevermore my'—how does it run? I can not mind the next word, 'my,'—

it's over-dark now to read it, and mother'll soon be coming."

Drumsheugh, in an agony, whispered in his ear: "'My dwelling-place,' William."

"That's it, that's it, I know; who said it?"—

"'And in God's house forevermore
My dwelling-place shall be.'"

The good old man whose work was done, and well done, then stretched himself with a sigh of relief, as he murmured:

"I'm ready now, and I'll get my kiss when mother comes. I wish she would come, for I am tired and wanting to sleep. Yon's her step, and she's carrying a light in her hand; I see it through the door. Mother, I knew ye would not forget your laddie, for ye promised to come, and I have finished my Psalm—

"'And in God's house forevermore
My dwelling-place shall be.'

Give me the kiss, mother, for I've been waiting for ye, and I'll soon be asleep."

The gray morning light fell on Drumsheugh still holding his friend's cold hand and staring at a hearth where the fire had died down into white ashes; but the peace on the doctor's face was of one who rested from his labors.

That's the way a Christian can die. I call you to this sublime faith in Jesus Christ, which brightens youth, adorns middle life, glorifies old age, and takes the sting out of death. He who trusts Christ may sing with the poet, in all confidence:

> "Homeward the swift-winged sea-gull takes its flight;
>   The ebbing tide breaks softly on the sand;
> The sunlit boats draw shoreward for the night;
>   The shadows deepen over sea and land;
> Be still, my soul, thine hour shall also come;
> Behold, one evening God shall lead thee home."

THE END.

Books by ❦ ❦

DR. LOUIS ALBERT BANKS.

Christ and His Friends.

A Collection of Revival Sermons, Simple and Direct, and Wholly Devoid of Oratorical Artifice, but Rich in Natural Eloquence, and Burning with Spiritual Fervor. The author has strengthened and enlivened them with many illustrations and anecdotes. 12mo, Cloth, Gilt Top, Rough Edges. Price, $1.50; post-free.

National Presbyterian, Indianapolis: "One of the most marked revivals attended their delivery, resulting in hundreds of conversions. Free from extravagance and fantasticism, in good taste, dwelling upon the essentials of religious faith, their power has not been lost in transference to the printed page."

New York Observer: "These sermons are mainly hortatory . . . always aiming at conviction or conversion. They abound in fresh and forcible illustrations. . . . They furnish a fine specimen of the best way to reach the popular ear, and may be commended as putting the claims of the Gospel upon men's attention in a very direct and striking manner. No time is wasted in rhetorical ornament, but every stroke tells upon the main point."

The Fisherman and His Friends.

A Companion Volume to "Christ and His Friends," consisting of Thirty-one Stirring Revival Discourses, full of Stimulus and Suggestion for Ministers, Bible class Teachers, and all Christian Workers and Others who Desire to become Proficient in the Supreme Capacity of Winning Souls to Christ. They furnish a rich store of fresh spiritual inspiration, their subjects being strong, stimulating, and novel in treatment, without being sensational or elaborate. They were originally preached by the author in a successful series of revival meetings, which resulted in many conversions. 12mo, Cloth, Gilt Top. Price, $1.50; post-free.

Bishop John F. Hurst: "It is a most valuable addition to our devotional literature."

New York Independent: "There is no more distinguished example of the modern people's preacher in the American pulpit to-day than Dr. Banks. *This volume fairly thrills and rocks with the force injected into its utterance.*"

BOOKS BY DR. LOUIS ALBERT BANKS — Continued.

Paul and His Friends.

A companion volume to "Christ and His Friends," "The Fisherman and His Friends," and "John and His Friends," being similarly bound and arranged. The book contains thirty-one stirring revival sermons delivered in a special series of revival services at the First M. E. Church, Cleveland. 12mo, Cloth, Gilt Top, Rough Edges. Price, $1.50.

Inter Ocean, Chicago: "The addresses are markedly practical, eloquent, earnest, and persuasive. Dr. Banks will especially interest the young. His illustrations are apt and pointed, and he gathers his facts from the wide range of literature past and present."

John and His Friends.

Thirty-three clear, straight, and forceful revival sermons, texts from the Gospel of John. They are of the same general character and excellence as the sermons contained in the three preceding volumes of this series. A companion volume to "Paul and His Friends," "The Fisherman and His Friends," and "Christ and His Friends." 12mo, Cloth, Gilt Top, Rough Edges, 297 pages. Cover Design in Gold, Bronze, and Black. Price, $1.50.

The Burlington Hawk-Eye, Burlington, Iowa: "A very gracious revival of religion was awakened by their delivery."

The Bookseller Newsdealer, and Stationer, New York: "Those who have read Dr. Banks's previous books need not be told that these sermons are original and practical and full of interesting illustrations and anecdotes."

Philadelphia Evening Item: "Revival literature has seldom if ever received so large a contribution from one man."

David and His Friends.

Thirty-one forceful revival sermons similar in general character to those in the preceding volumes of the "Friends" series. Texts from Samuel and the Psalms. A companion volume to "Christ and His Friends," etc. 12mo, Cloth, 320 pages, Gilt Top, Rough Edges. Price $1.50.

The Christian Guide, Louisville: "Will be sure of a hearty welcome from a multitude of preachers and religious workers who have found the preceding volumes so helpful and inspiring."

The Outlook, New York: "Evangelical, ethical, pointed with apt personal interest and narrative, every one of these sermons is a well-aimed arrow."

Chicago Times-Herald: "The sermons are not in the least orations, nor is their power in formal argument. It is rather in the power there is in statement and in pertinent illustration."

Hartford Courant: "These are the sort of sermons to be read at home, or even by a lay reader in the absence of the clergyman, for they are sufficiently graphic to dispense with a personal exponent."

The Christian Advocate, Detroit: "They are practical and are illustrated with everyday incidents. The author finds very striking subjects for his discourses."

BOOKS BY DR. LOUIS ALBERT BANKS—Continued.

The Christian Gentleman.

A volume of original and practical addresses to young men. The addresses were originally delivered to large and enthusiastic audiences of men, in Cleveland, at the Young Men's Christian Association Hall. 12mo, Buckram. Price, 75 cents.

My Young Man.

Practical and straightforward talks to young men. They are devoted to the consideration of the young man in his relationships as a son, a brother, a member of society, a lover, a husband, a citizen, a young man and his money, and the young man as himself. 12mo, Cloth, Cover Design. Price, 75 cents.

Central Christian Advocate, St. Louis, Mo.: "There are ten of them — brief, pointed, practical, luminous with illustrations and with poetical citations."

Hero Tales from Sacred Story.

The romantic stories of bible characters retold in graphic style, with modern parallels and striking applications. Richly illustrated with 19 full-page illustrations from famous paintings. 12mo, Cloth, Gilt Top, Cover Design. Price, $1.50.

Christian Work, New York: "One can not imagine a better book to put into the hands of a young man or young woman than this."

The Saloon-Keeper's Ledger.

The business and financial side of the drink question. 12mo, Cloth. Price, 75 cents.

The Christian Herald, Detroit: "The discourses are the masterpieces of an expert, abounding in apt illustrations and invincible logic, sparkling with anecdote, and scintillating with unanswerable facts."

Sermon Stories for Boys and Girls.

Short Stories of great interest, with which are interwoven lessons of practical helpfulness for young minds. 12mo, Cloth, Artistic Cover Design, Illustrated. Price, $1.00.

Christian Advocate, New York: "They are expressed in the freshness and simplicity of child language."

The Burlington Hawk-Eye: "He catches the eyes and ears of his hearers by bright little stories about animals, events in current life, and interesting features of nature, and then with rare skill, makes each of these stories carry a helpful message."

Globe, Toronto, Canada: "There are quickening tales told of Lincoln's humanity, and one of General Lee, who imperilled his life under fire by pausing to replace a nest of young birds dislodged by a shell."

Religious Herald, Hartford, Conn.: "The book is a character guide-book which must prove of inestimable assistance to mothers, teachers, and pastors."

BOOKS BY DR. LOUIS ALBERT BANKS—Continued.

Seven Times Around Jericho.

Seven Strong and Stirring Temperance Discourses, in which Deep Enthusiasm is Combined with Rational Reasoning—A Refreshing Change from the Conventional Temperance Arguments. Pathetic incidents and stories are made to carry most convincingly their vital significance to the subjects discussed. They treat in broad manner various features of the question. 12mo, Handsomely Bound in Polished Buckram. Price, 75 cents.

Herald and Presbyter, Cincinnati: "The book is sure to be a power for good. The discourses have the true ring."

Jersey City News: "Such able discourses as these of Dr. Banks will wonderfully help the great work of educating and arousing the people to their duty."

Revival Quiver.

A Pastor's Record of Four Revival Campaigns. 12mo, Cloth, $1.50.

This book is, in some sense, a record of personal experiences in revival work. It begins with "Planning for a Revival," followed by "Methods in Revival Work." This is followed by brief outlines of some hundred or more sermons. They have points to them, and one can readily see that they were adapted to the purpose designed. The volume closes with "A Scheme of City Evangelization." It seems to us a valuable book, adapted to the wants of many a preacher and pastor.

White Slaves; or, The Oppression of the Worthy Poor.

Fifty Illustrations. 12mo, Cloth, $1.50.

The Rev. Dr. Banks has made a personal and searching investigation into the homes of the poorer classes, and in the "White Slaves" the results are given. The work is illustrated from photographs taken by the author; and the story told by pen and camera is startling. It should be borne in mind that the author's visits were made to the homes of the worthy poor, who are willing to work hard for subsistence, and not to the homes of the criminal and vicious.

The Christ Dream.

12mo, Cloth, $1.20.

A series of twenty-four sermons in which illustrations of the Christ ideal are thrown upon the canvas, showing here and there individuals who have risen above the selfish, and measure up to the Christ dream. In tone it is optimistic, and sees the bright side of life.

Common Folks' Religion.

A Volume of Sermons. 12mo, Cloth, $1.50.

Boston Journal: "Dr. Banks presents Christ to the 'common people,' and preaches to every-day folk the glorious every-day truths of the Scripture. The sermons are original, terse, and timely, full of reference to current topics, and have that earnest quality which is particularly needed to move the people for whom they were spoken."

BOOKS BY DR. LOUIS ALBERT BANKS—Continued.

The People's Christ.

A Volume of Sermons and Other Addresses and Papers. 12mo, Cloth, $1.25.

New York Observer: "These sermons are excellent specimens of discourses adapted to reach the masses. Their manner of presenting Christian truth is striking. They abound in all kinds of illustration, and are distinguished by a bright, cheerful tone and style, which admirably fit them for making permanent impression."

Heavenly Trade-Winds.

A Volume of Sermons. 12mo, Cloth, $1.25.

From author's preface: "The sermons included in this volume have all been delivered in the regular course of my ministry in the Hanson-Place Methodist Episcopal Church, Brooklyn. They have been blessed of God in confronting the weary, giving courage to the faint, arousing the indifferent, and awakening the sinful."

The Honeycombs of Life.

A Volume of Sermons. 12mo, Cloth, $1.50.

Most of the discourses are spiritual honeycombs, means of refreshment and illumination by the way. "The Soul's Resources," "Cure for Anxiety," "At the Beautiful Gate," "The Pilgrimage of Faith," and "Wells in the Valley of Baca," are among his themes. The volume is well laden with evangelical truth, and breathes a holy inspiration. This volume also includes Dr. Banks's Memorial tribute to Lucy Stone and his powerful sermon in regard to the Chinese in America, entitled "Our Brother in Yellow."

Immortal Hymns and Their Story.

The Narrative of the Conception and Striking Experiences of Blessing Attending the Use of some of the World's Greatest Hymns. With 21 Portraits and 25 full-page half-tone illustrations by NORVAL JORDAN. 8vo, Cloth, Gilt Top, $3.00.

An Oregon Boyhood.

The story of Dr. Banks's boyhood in Oregon in the pioneer days, including innumerable dramatic, romantic, and exciting experiences of frontier life. 12mo, Cloth. Tastefully bound and printed. Illustrated. Price $1.25.

FUNK & WAGNALLS CO., Publishers, 30 Lafayette Pl., NEW YORK.

BOOKS BY DR. LOUIS ALBERT BANKS—Continued.

Anecdotes and Morals.

Five hundred and fifty-nine attractive and forceful lessons which may be profitably utilized by the public speaker to freshly illustrate divine truth. They are almost entirely composed of incidents, happening throughout the world within the past few months. 12mo, Buckram, Gilt Top, Uncut Edges, 463 pages. Price, $1.50.

Boston Journal: "More than half a thousand anecdotes, some witty, all pointed and instructive, make up this unusual book. His anecdotes all have a purpose, and are prettily expressed."

The Globe-Democrat, St. Louis: "The index to the contents and the system of cross-references make the stories immediately available to whomever wishes to use them in illustration."

The Lutheran Observer, Lancaster, Pa.: "They are aptly related and always enforce the truths intended."

Herald and Presbyter, Cincinnati: "Altho there are so many selections, each new page contains some original lessons and a constant variety is maintained throughout."

The Christian Observer, Louisville, Ky.: "In this collection are found many anecdotes that are striking, well put, and in good taste."

Poetry and Morals.

Clear, straight, and forceful lessons emphasized by familiar passages of prose and poetry. The author has arranged several hundred simple truths in paragraphs appropriately headed in full-face type. The truths are explained in a few terse sentences, and then a verse, entire poem, or prose selection having direct bearing on the truth is added, forming a perfect storehouse of suggestive material for the preacher and writer. A companion volume to "Anecdotes and Morals." 12mo, Cloth, 399 Pages, $1.50.

A Year's Prayer-Meeting Talks.

Fifty-two suggestive and inspiring talks for prayer-meetings. Helpful material is provided for a whole year's weekly meetings. The talks have been already used by Dr. Banks in a most successful series of services. The author's well-known skill in presenting the old truths in bright and striking ways is evidenced in these interesting talks. The book is designed to be a right-hand aid for preachers and religious workers. 12mo, Cloth. Price $1.00.

Christian Work, New York: "The reader will be sure to be attracted and helped by such talks as these."

Baptist Outlook, Indianapolis: "Anecdotes, stories, bright similes, and poetical quotations enliven the talks."

Boston Times: "The subjects are treated in original ways, but never in a sensational or unwholesome manner."